AF184149

Confused Perceptions, Illuminating Analyses

Albert Hirschman's Legacy
Works and Discussions

Luca Meldolesi
Series Editor

Vol. 8

Luca Meldolesi

Confused Perceptions, Illuminating Analyses

Theoretical Essays on Albert Hirschman's Work

Volume 1

PETER LANG

New York · Berlin · Bruxelles · Chennai · Lausanne · Oxford

Library of Congress Cataloging-in-Publication Control Number: 2025008228

Bibliographic information published by the Deutsche Nationalbibliothek.
The German National Library lists this publication in the German National Bibliography; detailed bibliographic data is available on the Internet at http://dnb.d-nb.de.

Cover design by Peter Lang Group AG

ISSN 2576-9723 (print)
ISBN 978-3-0343-5604-6 (Print)
ISBN 978-3-0343-5605-3 (E-PDF)
ISBN 978-3-0343-5606-0 (E-PUB)
DOI 10.3726/b22613

© 2025 Peter Lang Group AG, Lausanne
Published by Peter Lang Publishing Inc., New York, USA
info@peterlang.com - www.peterlang.com

All rights reserved.
All parts of this publication are protected by copyright. Any utilisation outside the strict limits of the copyright law, without the permission of the publisher, is forbidden and liable to prosecution. This applies in particular to reproductions, translations, microfilming, and storage and processing in electronic retrieval systems.

This publication has been peer reviewed.

CONTENTS

"Confused perceptions make it possible [for Leibniz] to explain, as in the case of art, the fact of instinct [...] without having to resort to some autonomous practical faculty other than reason. It is still knowledge, but not distinct knowledge, and only through its development can it reach the level of proof and definition.

Confused perceptions also explain the state of "restlessness" which is the springboard of the "aiguillon du desir," and in general they offer Leibniz a way of probing all the intermediate states of pre-rationality and the preconscious will."

Eugenio Colorni 1943a; now 2023 p. 310–11

"Asked in a questionnaire of which achievements in his life he was most proud, Hirschman listed his work with the Italian anti-Fascists and with Varian Fry first, before his academic work on development in Latin America Latina and his books and articles."

Lewis Coser 1984 p. 163

"You must read *La trahison des clercs* di Julinen Benda[1] – Albert Hirschman wrote to his wife Sarah in a letter (May 1941) – [...] a contemporary document of utmost importance (and *adorable* for its partiality). [...] I have an idea (a little one, to be sure) [...] I am struck at the moment by certain parallelisms in modern thought in different disciplines.[...] The complete separation of the disciplines from the *ends* implied by different human activities. [...] Political economy, has no longer any purpose as the *utility* or Material Welfare but is solely concerned with applying the most rational means for ends that are imagined outside it [*désignés du déhors*]. [...] We ask *politics*, the science of *means* par excellence to formulate the ends by which political economy, ethics, etc. will render themselves accordingly as the *serviteurs affaires*. Here you have the abdication, the treason of the intellectuals in a new sense, I think, and we can explain it partially by the development of this hybrid position of intellectuals in the modern world: neither masters, nor prosecuted, but technicians. [...They don't ask basic questions about] the thirst for power and domination. Fascism is *politicaillerie* on a giant scale. [...] Why dominate? Fascism will not survive the moment in which we have found the leisure [*loisir*] to pose this question."

(Cit. in Jeremy Adelman 2013, p. 198–99)

"In 1944, I heard about Eugenio's death. I was then in Algiers and learned the news from the group of Italian antifascists I had met. For me it was a terrible blow. I realized that he was the person who had counted most in my life."

Albert O. Hirschman 1998, p. 76

---

1 Brenda 1927. A radical critique of French and German intellectuals who, according to the author, had rejected a classical legacy of dispassionate research and had instead become apologists for nationalism, jingoism and war.

INTRODUCTION

I hope that, from a (primarily) Southern, Mediterranean, humanistic-social perspective, the essays included here succeed in showing off their possibilist inspiration in the dazzling light of the extraordinary analytical and proactive virtuosity of Eugenio Colorni and Albert Hirschman.[1]

In fact, it is worth pointing out that my own contribution is inevitably "situated"—as all of us are (Albert Camus). We must always remember this, and always be ready to welcome with open arms many more contributions. For as a stateless person, Albert Hirschman belonged to the whole world before he too became (from time to time) "situated." For this reason his general dimension is approachable (by the reader as well as by the critics) only gradually, by taking up the discussion from his different "locations" (the United States, France, Italy, Germany, Colombia, Brazil, etc.).

Of course, as much as I have tried to objectify these essays, their inspiration has to be seen as interactive—in the sense that even when I was in the United States, I inevitably analyzed Hirschman's writings from an Italian

1 Written at different times for specific occasions as the offspring of the Italian editions of some of Albert's texts and the *post factum* reconsideration of study and dialogue with friends and collaborators etc.—the essays that follow have been revised and (in parts) corrected and enriched.

perspective (from Rome and the Mezzogiorno), at the same time highlighting Albert's interest in our country, also in relation to his experience as a whole.

This study concerns the young Hirschman's experiences in Europe, focusing mainly on his two "Triestine" years (and the basic lesson they offer), and concludes with *National Power*, written in California in 1941–42,[2] and some consequences involving economic theory.

In their intentions at least, the essays assembled here together represent a distinctive way of looking at the extraordinary intellectual revolution wrought over time by Albert Hirschman—a hard-won perspective acquired, in successive theoretical-practical bursts, starting from Italy, the Mediterranean and beyond.

As such, my essays would suggest to other scholars and professionals the use of a variety of points of view. It was indeed Hirschman's intention (and remains part of his legacy) that the change of optics for observing reality (to nudge it onto a favorable path) should be the business of "everyone," no one excluded. And it is also because, to grasp such a general approach and be in a position to put it into practice, each individual needs to relive it, to own it from his or her point of view—spatial, temporal, environmental, generational, etc.

My hope, then, is that the somewhat unusual matter referred to will succeed in engaging many others, and will thus, on balance, prove useful.

"*Nel mezzo del cammin di nostra vita…*" [Midway through the journey of our life…] says the poet. Today we live a little longer (I was forty at the time)—in any case, with a hint of self-mockery, I too can start my own argument in this way—not of course to compare it with the original.

I took note of my (disappointing) "theoretical cluelessness"[3] and set out to do remedial research. I visited Paris because I had read (and "modeled")

2 On the other hand there is as we know a second "Italian" period in Albert's life, the one that began in the American army (from Algiers to Rome, Siena and Florence) and moved on to "Follow Events in France and Italy" for the U.S. Federal Reserve Board and his participation in the Marshall Plan. Finally, after a long phase (dedicated to development economics and then to "everybody") during which Hirschman's interest in Italy was only intermittent, he began once more to turn his attention to Europe (France, Germany and Italy), a period in which my own involvement began, in 1983. Each of these phases—for both its merits and its limitations—is in my opinion of great interest.

3 Meldolesi 1982.

Fernand Braudel's *Afterthoughts on Material Civilization and Capitalism*.[4] Later, leaving the University of Calabria and at the invitation of Giovanni Arrighi, Nicoletta Stame opened (to me, as well) the way to America. This was how, sometime later, she and I met Albert Hirschman at the Institute for Advanced Study in Princeton, NJ.[5]

Albert needs no introduction. His well-known brilliance, creativity and scientific industriousness were incalculable, inimitable. Innovative, sharp, daring and cautious at the same time, he often said that one must seek "the good and the new"—in the sense that there is unfortunately good that is not new, and new that is not good.

Understanding his work calls (*sua sponte*) for a probing of its origins along with its possible consequences. Thus it happened that with the passage of time, the essays that follow got started spontaneously—during the long periods Nicoletta Stame and I spent with the "distinguish couple" (as, with typical self-irony, Albert and Sarah Hirschman introduced themselves), and proceeded in memories and insights—through "Long is the Journey" (A Colorni-Hirschman International Institute's online *Review*), and through the internal debate at the Institute and several Conferences.[6] Amid the chaos and turbulence of the world around us, I hope that these essays may prove helpful in keeping one of the few 'threads' that might cast an enlightening, encouraging ray of sunshine on our lives from slipping through our fingers.

We shall speak of this further along. Here I would like to preview some of the reasons why I suddenly sought to venture down Albert Hirschman's path, with the intention, first and foremost, to understand the logic of it.

Briefly put, it was theoretical-practical dissatisfaction with economics (in general) and with critical economics (in particular)—especially because, even in their most elaborate forms, neither the one nor the other had stood up in the face of the tumultuous and rebellious experience of the 1960s–1970s.

Upstream of this was my interest in the political aspect of reality, which the various schools of economics generally consider a mere consequence, with

4 Braudel 1977; Meldolesi 1984.

5 While Nicoletta did Terry Hopkins and Immanuel Wallerstein's Master's course in sociology at SUNY Binghamton, I read *The Passions and the Interests* by Albert Hirschman, wrote a comment (Meldolesi 1985 and 1991–92) and sent it to him. Marcello de Cecco, an old friend who was at that time at the Institute at Princeton, invited us to visit and introduced Albert.

6 Meldolesi and Stame, eds. 2017, 2018, 2020.

no autonomous sphere of its own—so taught, in ancient times, [*docebat, temporibus illis!*] Lucio Colletti, from a prestigious chair of philosophy.[7]

And I also needed to understand why, unlike the great economists I had known close-up,[8] Albert Hirschman—I sensed—had been able to move beyond their typical cogent and abstract way of seeing things.[9]

I was curious about the composite nature of Hirschman's education as an economist, and also about the theoretical-methodological pointers that he later occasionally (partially) supplied.

And finally, there was the importance, but also the limits of what I had been able to understand up to that time—a realization that prompted me later to question the role played indirectly by Eugenio Colorni in Albert's work.

In this way, step by step, the development of this latter aspect, resulting in the publication—in Italian and English—of Colorni's complete work, which I have just finished editing, forced me to start from scratch with what I had concocted in the 1980s–1990s regarding Hirschman's work. This is the reason for the 'return journey' that follows.[10]

---

7 In fact, following a tradition that goes as far back as Saint-Simon, his course in the literature department at Rome's La Sapienza University in the 1960s invariably ended with an invitation to the students to take up economics…

8 I am mainly referring to the "Cambridge school" (UK) that formed around John Maynard Keynes (Joan Robinson, Richard Kahn, Piero Sraffa, Dennis Nicolas Kaldor, James Meade, Maurice Dobb etc.).

9 This is the conclusion that, undoubtedly the introductory chapter of the present collection leads to. Evidently, up until that moment I had been unable to grasp *political economy as a moral and social science* (this [*Economia politica come scienza morale e sociale*] is the title of the first book of Albert's essays that I edited: 1987b). It is undoubtedly one of the pivotal reasons why I have taken such a prolonged interest in Hirschman's work; and then Eugenio Colorni's.

10 In a certain sense this is true. Because I did in fact go back after a long time to writing about Albert Hirschman's life and work. But the essays collected here were sketched out along the way and have only now reached a conclusion. They did not spring from the surprise of my meeting this author forty years ago (which is what actually happened in the case of my *Discovering the Possible* – 1995) and do not represent a group of "self-subversive" theoretical exercises (like those in *Late Hirschman* – 2023). They are instead interpretive, reflective essays—not least on my experience as an heretic economist in (and for) the Italian South. By and large, they retrace Hirschman's trajectory with the aim of showing young social scientists how much can still be learned from a significant part of Albert's work—of course from one's own point of view and spatio-temporal location—almost suggesting an ideal passing of the baton…

Indeed, this set of interests and cultural concerns is reflected in the progress of the present work, which brings together essays that are sometimes one-offs, but have been collected with the idea of trying to unwind a logical thread, albeit implicit.

Albert Hirschman (a bit like Piero Sraffa) had no didactic-pedagogic inspiration. He did not like teaching—even though on occasion, in a low voice, he would offer observations and advice that then became engraved in the mind of whoever he had been talking to. On the contrary, what interested him was receiving stimulus from others. Working for the Marshall Plan he had battled his colleagues' doctrinaire attitudes. He later worked in Colombia before establishing himself as a full-fledged pioneer in development economics. But after Yale, Columbia, and Harvard universities and the decline of development economics as a sub-discipline, he stopped teaching and moved to the Institute for Advanced Study (initially founded by Albert Einstein) to build an "interpretive social science" with Clifford Geertz.

Moreover, beginning in the 1970s, the dominance of ultra-liberal economic-political thinking, which had become suffocating in U.S. culture, led Hirschman to look increasingly to Western European intellectuals—English (Skinner), German (Lepenies, Offe), French (Furet, Manin), and Italian (Ginsburg, de Cecco, Ferraresi).

Knowing something of this "interest," it looks to me like these latter colleagues were put to the test—one after the other. Andrea Ginzburg's rapid downgrading (after publishing the first book of Hirschman's essays in Italian) is probably explained by his attempt to box the author into "Sraffism."[11] (Though the fact remains that Andrea was the only one of us who tried to evaluate in depth the theoretical-economic part of Albert's work—an aspect that I would like to take up in a later volume.)

The encounter with Franco Ferraresi (who had come to the Institute at the suggestion of Michael Walzer) came to a halt, if I am not mistaken, with the Turin Honoris Causa degree in 1987. Instead, Hirschman's dialogue on economic history with Marcello de Cecco from the 1980s continues to be, in my opinion, interesting and illuminating. Not least, because—as we shall see further along—Asso and de Cecco's (in some ways problematic) "brainwave" on the question of the caesura, the methodological rupture which, between *National Power* and Albert's later writings, helped him focus on his militant

11 I refer here to the introduction to Hirschman 1983, Andrea Ginzburg, ed.

choice to "take sides"—a key point that would otherwise have remained under the radar.[12]

As for myself, I was lucky.[13] Nicoletta's and my long collateral attendance (with respect to the mainstream trend) at the Institute probably stemmed from the topic I had chosen. In fact, "this Italian economist," as Hirschman remarked with a chuckle to all and sundry, "is interested in the most interesting subject ever—me!" That is to say—Albert, stringing me along a day at a time, wanted to see how far I would get…

At first he was enthusiastic that I was trying to reconstruct his trajectory—so much so that he had my 1987 essay on the origins of possibilism republished in French, in the *Revue Française de Science Politique*—perhaps in the hope of finding an opening in Paris, which in the end…didn't open.

Later, however, as I laboriously progressed with the writing of *Discovering the Possible*, his attitude began to change. In the case of *The Strategy*, he told me that I had compensated for my limited knowledge on the subject with some insights from bibliographic research on reviews of the book. Then, checking carefully page by page what I was writing, he realized that, on the whole, the endeavor was in fact "worth the effort." It was the first instance (which then, admittedly, remained the only one) of a punctilious, extensive (though partial) theoretical reconstruction of his thought.

The Ford Foundation helped me tour five Latin American countries (with a grant that, frugal as we are, was enough for Nicoletta as well). The book was published by Il Mulino (the family publishing house, as Hirschman called it), then by Notre Dame University Press in the United States and the Fondo de Cultura Econòmica in Mexico City. Albert even had it submitted for an award (which of course was not awarded to me). Overall, I think his judgment was

12 And also because (in contradiction) Marcello, as we shall see, later wrote an interesting "Preface" to the posthumous publication of Hirschman's dissertation (2004).

13 In the sense that my "constellation of circumstances," as Hirschman liked to put it, was favorable—both objectively and subjectively. In fact, I realized later that Albert's attitude toward me had been prompted (mainly) by two factors. One was objective, cultural (my availability, which had no counterpart on the American scene, was welcome), while the other was subjective—I had met Hirschman at a particularly favorable time. The fact was that after so long, he was now willing to talk about his past, however gradually. [Only compare in this regard my initial essay "Alle origini del possibilismo" ["At the Origin of Possibilism"] (1987), my monograph *Discovering the Possible* (1995), Hirschman's *Passaggi di frontiera* (1994; English trans. 1998b), "On Self," the second part of *A Propensity to Self-Subversion* (1995), and finally the papers and interviews in his *Odyssey* (Adelman 2013), to see that on Albert's part there was a gradual "unbuttoning"].

positive, but also a bit "so-so" (he had a hand gesture)—except for the last chapter, which he liked, he said, because it is pervaded by a future-oriented political-psychological tension (an aspect that undoubtedly reconnected him to Colorni).

For me, the commitment was immense. Probably Albert expected me to know things that I could not have known at that time. He probably wished that, in general, I had gone deeper into a horizon that was difficult to master—from the prewar period onward, with many languages, many disciplines, many experiences, etc.

And all this happened in spite of the fact that—as one reviewer wrote—the book as it was unfolded on two levels, that of the historical-theoretical exposition and that of the notes.[14] Probably, in Albert's opinion, even with the book already in press, I should have gone further… perhaps adding a third level to an edifice eternally under construction.

The upshot was that my subsequent pursuits—at the university, in public institutions, on the ground—got a lukewarm reception from Hirschman (and especially from his wife Sarah).[15] Yet an important "European project" of Albert's was beginning to take shape,[16] with the participation of Nicoletta and myself, and for this we managed to hold ourselves together in a sort of (unstable) equilibrium, until… the irreparable happened—Hirschman's fall in the French Alps in July 1995, resulting in his very long illness.

I suspect that Albert, committed as he was to developing his own ideas, felt the (all too human) need to focus on aspects that at any given time he considered as priorities, as essential, while avoiding those that lacked such

14 Hultman 2001 p. 389.

15 Despite *Spendere meglio è possible* [Spending Better is Possible] (Meldolesi 1992), the "clean hands" movement (world renowned), the local resourcefulness of numerous Neapolitan students, my own presence in the national government—factors that even carried me (with Nicoletta) to Brazil, as the guests of Ruth and Fernando Henrique Cardoso (long-time friends of the Hirschman's)… This attitude of Albert's toward us reminds me, not surprisingly, of his position towards his daughter Katia and Alain Salomon during the student rebellions of the 60s–70s. As if to say—yes, I experienced these things in the past, but today they do not excite me… In particular, it was specifically movement work that Albert then perceived as foreign to his busy life—although, in retrospect, he had come to recognize its importance (especially in *Shifting Involvements*—1982).

16 I am referring in particular to the painstaking organization in Berlin of a "Colloque" on Hirschman's work (reserved for a small group of intellectuals from a few carefully selected European countries), which unfortunately never quite managed to come together.

characteristics—and thus turning a deaf ear (alas!) to classical culture, to Italian culture, to the Mezzogiorno...[17]

Perhaps Hirschman wished I had continued pursuing my involvement with him, retracing his German-French-Italian-American-Latin American technical-academic trajectory. Even assuming (and not conceding) that I had been able to do so, I had no opportunity. Still, I think that in the event I would not have accepted it because... it was simply not part of my intentions.

I thus resisted his occasional invitations to approach the technicians at the Bank of Italy and the Treasury,[18] to reduce my commitment (in research, teaching, and advocacy) to the South and to Italian culture, and I sought instead a homegrown, theoretical-practical path toward "re-comprehending" the whole affair, "fishing" as it were for my new path in that final chapter of my 1995 book that had so interested him, and thus concerning myself with Colorni.

For this reason, even while grappling with a hundred obligations, this is where I have stood for some time now—aiming, perhaps intermittently, to dig deeper (and also trying to fill in, every now and then, some of the compartments in my typical "cultivated ignorance of the economist," as Veblen put it). Perhaps, in doing so, I have finally reached the last act of the whole affair (vol. 1). This is the task I hand over to these essays, written—as I have already noted—at different times, but always pointing towards the same end.

17 In this, if I am not mistaken, he resembled those who fall in love with one part and decide to do without the rest. And perhaps, with not very democratic reasoning, they would also like it if others stopped caring—about everything else!

18 That is to say, I avoided embarking on an extra-university *cursus honorum* which, although entitled to it (as a Stringher Fellowship winner), I had long since discarded in favor of teaching. What I now wanted, on the contrary, was to invent (on the edge of possibilism) the opposite relationship. Namely, that it was precisely this kind of teaching of economic policy at the Federico II University of Naples that could influence the Bank of Italy and other public institutions—which, at a certain point, actually happened *pro tempore*...

· 1 ·

TOWARD A NEW INTERPRETIVE HYPOTHESIS ON THE HISTORY OF MODERN ECONOMIC THOUGHT*

In economics, as in other disciplines, interpretive hypotheses on the state of the discipline are often linked to certain intellectual propositions. Anyone who believes they represent a continuation of a particular tradition of thought cannot help but emphasize the links that exist between their own and the traditional point of view, while those who present themselves as advocates of change generally feel the need to explain their reasoning in relation to the ideas previously in vogue. Thus Keynes called his best-known book *The General Theory of Employment, Interest and Money* in order to point out that his opponents' theory was particular (limited to the case of full employment), and Sraffa wrote *Production of Commodities by Means of Commodities: Prelude to a Critique of Economic Theory* (marginalist). In both these cases the interpretive hypothesis (and critique) is an integral part of the new theorizing. This is not, however—it should be said right away—the route that will be taken in the pages that follow. Rather than addressing such completed theoretical trajectories, we shall pursue a more limited objective here. Given the recurring

* *Rivista di storia del pensiero economico*, n. 1–2, 1987a. This essay is republished for introductory purposes, as a partial anticipation of the theoretical-economic framework within which the story I intend to narrate took place.

relationship that exists between a critical hypothesis and an intellectual proposition, perhaps new interpretive ideas on the history of modern economic thought—this is my starting point—might help us understand the intellectual difficulties we find ourselves in.

The reasoning thus stems from a certain dissatisfaction (or is it disappointment?) with the state of economic theory, both mainstream and opposition. As is well known, mainstream theory has increasingly moved toward general economic equilibrium; it has abandoned less robust sectors of its original proposal and has proceeded with a reframing of its own—mainly by way of the rational expectations hypothesis. Hence the image of a theory going through a renewed youth—a theory capable of dominating the different fields of the discipline and building (or invading) new ones such as public choices, the family, crime, history.

This may be too strong a statement not to hold some surprises for us in the future. It is clear, however, that it has been a game-changer in the American social sciences. The ingenuity deployed in recent decades by a group of economists in applying the traditional postulate of *homo oeconomicus* to a range of extra-economic phenomena has activated the mechanism of outrageous paradox that typifies much of the research. "Servants of the state," voters, lovers, parents, and criminals who have always been regarded as prey to complex passions are presented by these economists as laboriously pursuing a "constrained maximization" of their own material interests. This has once again caused a moral trauma that has made the fortune of these analyses. Thus marginalism, for a century or more the delight (or bane) of economists, has now become "a problem" for the vast majority of American social scientists—political scientists, sociologists, psychologists, historians.

Nevertheless, with regard to "critical economics," which by definition ought to be the area of social science most qualified to resolve such a problem, my impression is that the *émiettement* of recent years has not led to the desired results. Those who have constructed (or reconstructed) a Ricardian economics, or taken the rehabilitation of the classics back to the point of supporting the relevance of Adam Smith's *Wealth of Nations*, or tried to extend the rehabilitation of classical thought to Marx (not least to expand the boundaries of the discipline by this route), or attempted a reunion between some of these achievements and the teachings of Schumpeter and Keynes—to name just a few cases close to me—may be pleased with the results of some of the battles, but may also wonder whether this is then sufficient with respect to their commitment to a real reform of the discipline.

If this is the case, there may exist in some of my readers the conditions for a (partial) change of viewpoint. Critical economics, one might reason, has had up to now a theoretical charter of its own—the very existence of marginalist theory has imposed on it, as one of its primary tasks, a critique of traditional thinking. But this should also have pushed it to clarify why neoclassical theory is dominant—or rather, *how and why* it became dominant. If we could manage—in a broader intellectual sphere—to bring this "epochal" event into better focus, we might perhaps see more clearly into the difficult work that has been built up so far and what its prospects are.

As is well known, the vast literature on the subject contains some recurring claims. One of the first, even in a chronological sense, is the contention of continuity between marginalist economics and earlier economic thought. A second idea—more "continental" in origin—views the establishment of marginalist economics as a "revolution" facilitated by advances in the physical-mathematical sciences. Finally, a third notes the connection of the "new economics" with positivist thought (regarding economic equilibrium, harmony of interests, efficiency, etc.) and, as a contrast, sets it in relation to the development of conflict in society. The affirmation of marginalist theory would primarily represent deepening social contradiction as reflected in the field of ideas.

It is in my view undeniable that all three of these propositions have something to teach us. Yet even if we try to combine them, they still don't quite "do the job." Indeed, marginalist economics is in the first place an intellectual construction that was not created entirely from scratch. Its analytical continuity, however, is not with classical thought—as a long tradition from Marshall to Samuelson has claimed. Rather, it co-exists (within determined limits) with the "appearance" economics of the Say, Senior, and Bailey variety. In addition, the thesis of the emergence of marginalist economics as an intellectual revolution linked to the development of mathematics undoubtedly has a specific historical basis. But in itself it cannot explain to us how this theorizing later became dominant and ousted other conceptions, including the classical one that had previously long prevailed. Finally, the thesis of connection, through opposition, with social conflict can also undoubtedly play a role within an overall explanation. And yet, taken on its own, it can stray into mechanicism.[1] [On the other hand, if we embark on a more minute reconstruction of these ideas, taking them separately, it is easy to see that several pieces do not fall

1 As sometimes happens to Henry Denis 1967; cf., e.g., vol. II p. 152.

into place. For example, the claim of marginalist economics to be a revolution spreading internationally is not reflected in the long exile of Léon Walras and his disciples, while the Jevonsian turn in England, as Maurice Dobb[2] honestly explains, cannot be considered a response to the publication of the first book of *Das Kapital*...].

So, in conclusion, all we know is the following: modern marginalist theory, in its various components, represents a theoretical development, in many ways surprising and "cascading," that can be traced back to some of the theses of appearance economics. It originated in the 1870s by borrowing some techniques of analysis from the physical-mathematical sciences and was affected, more generally, by the positivist culture of the time. It established itself gradually, progressively, even in relation to evolving social conflict.

On the other hand, these interpretive elements, whose importance I certainly do not mean to underestimate, have been available to scholars for a long time, and for this reason as well I think it useful to alter our angle of observation. Rather than immersing ourselves in the history of economic thought, as per tradition, and then taking external influences into account almost as if they were factual data, we can try to understand the evolution of political economy from the outside, so to speak—as part of the overall progression of ideas and culture. This approach (which some might improperly consider idealist) turns out to be very useful in practice because it adds new knowledge to what we already have.

The economist can thus appreciate that the positivist culture of the time, which gives extraordinary impetus to the natural sciences, finds expression not only in the physical-mathematical sciences through the logical-deductive method, but also in the medical-biological sciences through a method that is inductive and experimental. The influence of this ethos on the social sciences leads not only to mathematical economics, it also fosters the emergence of a number of new sciences—such as psychology, sociology, anthropology—along with the reformulation of old ones—such as geography, philosophy, politics and history. (And it has a considerable influence on art—consider the Impressionists).

Now if we keep before us this vast moving picture of culture at the end of the 19th century, the evolution of political economy, which generally absorbs the attention of insiders, begins almost to look as if it is going against the grain with respect to the general flow of the social sciences. This brings us to the

2 Dobb 1973 p. 166.

main point—why then does the discipline of economics, like statistics later on, end up embracing the deductive-mathematical method rather than the inductive-experimental method prevailing in other social sciences? Or rather, and perhaps more appropriately, why does it fail to find any *reasonable mediation* between these different cognitive approaches?

We may note at this point that the three propositions recalled above have little to suggest on this point. (Why was this continuity established? Why this "revolution"? Why this reaction to social conflict and not some other[s]?) This way, while still holding onto what we already know about the intellectual tradition of the discipline and about social pressures, we can try to embark on a new reconnaissance of the "two stages" which, according to Joseph Schumpeter,[3] shaped the rise of marginalist economics.

The first of these was the process of the dissolution of the classical school which, despite the theoretical accommodation proposed by John Stuart Mill, gained ground in the mid-nineteenth century, opening the field to a multiplicity of possible outcomes. What is generally presented as the glorious birth of the marginalist school—Jevons, Walras and Menger's work in the 1870s—in reality represents the formation of a minority current within the discipline that initially faced cultural conditions that were anything but propitious (as illustrated by the affair of Auguste and Léon Walras).[4] This school then coexisted with traditional currents in the discipline and other new currents as well, such as the "Socialists of the Chair" and the Historical School, which based themselves on a methodology quite different from the mathematical school. The question was at the time anything but resolved—one need only recall the famous "battle of the methods" (beginning in the 1880s) and its American counterpart, the institutionalist controversy.

So let us get back to our question. What was it that prompted political economy at the turn of the century to in the end embrace the solution we know so well? "It may be conjectured," answered Albert Hirschman,[5] "that the development of the self-interest concept and of economic analysis in general in the direction of positivism and formalism was related to the discovery, toward the end of the nineteenth century, of the instinctual-intuitive, the habitual, the unconscious, the ideologically and neurotically driven—in short, to the extraordinary vogue for the non-rational that characterized virtually

3 Schumpeter 1954 vol. 3 ch. 5.

4 Cf. Dumez 1985.

5 Hirschman 1986 p. 51.

all of the influential philosophical, psychological, and sociological thinking of the age."

Therefore—this hypothesis suggests—it is not only Karl Marx and the socialist movement that need to be taken into account. There is another history within the culture (in its interactive relationship with ongoing reality), one that concerns such leading personalities as Sigmund Freud, Henry Bergson and Georges Sorel. And then Le Bon and Tarde with their psychology of the masses, Durkheim, Spencer, Weber, Simmel—the founding fathers of sociology—and many others.

In the face of this explosion of intellectual vitality surrounding it on every side, what could political economy do? Being entirely based on the paradigm of the rational pursuit of self-interest, the discipline could not incorporate the new discoveries into its analytical apparatus. It reacted by distancing itself as much as possible from psychology and ridding its fundamental concepts of their psychological origins.

In evaluating this thesis, it can be noted that it appears *prima facie* more plausible for countries such as Austria, Germany, Switzerland or Italy than for France and England. Nevertheless, this has not prevented the process from eventually becoming established in these latter nations as well.

Initially, it could be argued, the very lively presence of the new cultural currents in Paris probably played an important role in slowing the spread of Walrasian economics in France, while in England, the muted resonance of the new ideas perhaps had a negative influence in the failure to recognize the "Jevonsian revolution" (and in the protracted prevalence of Alfred Marshall's economics).[6]

But French and English culture are traditionally the most widely studied on the continent, and their lesser initial conformity (for better or worse) with the relationship proposed by Hirschman may have hindered perception of it up to now. Not by chance, it was brought to light as a general hypothesis by a Euro-American scholar (born in Berlin) at the end of an unusual intellectual journey. Hirschman in fact reconstructed a sequence of changes and ideological transitions over four centuries in the history of ideas in the West, a

6 Marshallian theory, long considered an authoritative current in the new economics, can be seen (perhaps more aptly) as a construction intended to mediate between "the spirit of the times," a specific perception of reality and the English cultural tradition. In other words, its success was also linked to the intellectual consensus it was able to create around itself. Moreover, its long decline probably arrived in port only after World War II, across the Atlantic.

sequence that follows the evolution of the concept of self-interest from the initial euphemism to the tautology of modern times. While self-interest has long been used as a euphemism for usury, cruelty and avarice, it has finally reached the point that every action of an individual—from the most self-centered to the most compassionate, from the most prudent to the most reckless—is generally regarded as being in his or her best interest.

The reconstruction of this long journey, initially undertaken to clarify the links between economic development and political systems, allows, finally, an explanation of the progressive dilution of key concepts in traditional economics such as self-interest, utility, and value. The move away from Benthamite psychological assumptions, Hirschman argued, enabled marginalist economics to usher in a "survival strategy" that would prove remarkably successful. It is an objectifying process that is particularly evident in the development of consumer theory—that is, in the well-known sequence of cardinalism-ordinalism-revealed preference that finally arrived at "choice value." (And those who, at every step in this elaboration, have rightly tried to point out that the theory remains indebted to the initial psychological assumptions have failed to realize—and this is the irony of history—that they are unwittingly going along with the current trend.)

Here then, according to this hypothesis, is the origin of the tradition of proud separateness, the "ivory tower" of the discipline (which then triggered the "invasion" of other fields that we have witnessed). Even critical economics, which in the 20th century always ran parallel to "official" economics, was unable to overcome its theoretical isolation—in method and in content—with respect to the other social sciences, and thus ended up operating from within this "original sin" of modern economics.[7]

There have been, however, two attempts—very elaborate and different—to get to the bottom of the whole issue. The first came from a French sociologist, François Simiand, who was concerned with economics and statistics. The second from an Italian economist, Vilfredo Pareto, who was in frequent epistolary and intellectual contact with Georges Sorel and envisioned his *The Mind and Society* (Italian: *Trattato di Sociologia Generale*, lit. "Treatise on General

7 This is also ultimately true of the heated discussion that has developed around Piero Sraffa's *Production of Commodities by Means of Commodities* (1960; 1975). While at first, as we know, the emphasis was placed on the "rehabilitation" of classical thought and Marx, with some even proposing to expand the analysis to aspects not strictly economic, what emerged later was the opposite hypothesis. That is to say, despite the author's intentions, Piero Sraffa's main work actually led to an emptying of content vis-à-vis Smith, Ricardo and Marx.

Sociology") as an "indispensable complement" to pure political economy. In both cases, papers were presented on the relationship between sociology and economics that were quite different from the traditional "carelessness" that prevailed among economists.

For Simiand, as in general for the school of Emile Durkheim, there is no reason for the separation between sociology and economics to exist. Political economy, like sociology, geography, history, etc., should be based on an inductive-experimental method (and on statistical series), becoming by this route an economic sociology, or positive economics. For this reason, at the beginning of the twentieth century, through a vast campaign of reviews, Simiand undertook an intense barrage against marginalist works (which, partly for this reason, did not have an easy time in Paris). Then, between the two wars, he developed his own experimental conception of economics, which exerted considerable influence on the economic history of the *Annales* (but much less on political economy).

For Pareto, on the other hand, the separation between economics and sociology was necessary, indeed indispensable. The one concerned logical human ideas—that is, ideas linked to the means-ends relation, while the other was about non-logical ideas. This is the route by which the Italian patrician became one of the leading theorists of pure economics and participated prominently in the stripping away of basic psychological assumptions by means of concepts such as preference and indifference, ophelimity and Pareto efficiency. At the same time, he established himself as an inexhaustible (and for many sociologists insufferable) analyst of a sociology of the non-rational.

After World War II, some Italian economists, such as Siro Lombardini and Paolo Sylos Labini, felt they should not follow the path of strict separation between economics and sociology indicated by Pareto and proposed an initial opening of the economic discipline to political and social considerations. This point of view sometimes found itself in tune with the "rediscovery" of classical thought and Marx in the 1960s–70s, but after some time it must unfortunately be admitted that the underlying theoretical-practical issue was not addressed judiciously (and wholeheartedly).

· 2 ·

EUGENIO COLORNI AND ALBERT HIRSCHMAN IN TRIESTE (1937–38)*

I

Ab initio, Eugenio

1 – Throughout our long association (in the United States and elsewhere), Albert Hirschman and I often spoke of Eugenio Colorni.[1] Hirschman spoke of

* Meldolesi 2013 ch. 2. Written originally for a study conference in Rome 29 May 2009 on the occasion of the national celebrations of the centenary of the birth of Eugenio Colorni, the first part of this essay was published in *Eugenio Colorni dall'antifascismo all'europeismo socialista e federalista*, Maurizio Degl' Innocenti, ed. 2010. By courtesy of the editor and publisher it is republished here in an expanded edition, not least in recognition of other papers that appeared later. The second part of the essay was written instead as a follow-up to my "editing" of Colorni 2023.

1 At the beginning of my association with Albert Hirschman, "it immediately became clear to me that his greatest innovations in thinking concerning both less developed countries and, in his later work, developed countries as well, had roots that went far back. I therefore began to work on 1936–38 [...]. What particularly excited me, and still does [about that period] is that Colorni invented not only a series of ideas, but also a way of looking at reality which, transferred to the young Hirschman, was grafted, you might say, onto economics and social science and produced an intellectual flowering that was very different from traditional thought" (Meldolesi 1996 p. 82).

him almost as if he were a brilliant and respected friend he could talk to and learn from on a daily basis (even though, unfortunately, he had just stepped out)[2] – this is how alive and recognizable the imprint of his theoretical and practical work remained in Hirschman's reflections (and remains, inevitably, in mine).

"Eugenio," I wrote in 2004,[3] "was an intellectual who, in terms of his perspicacity and the influence he had on the work of Albert Hirschman and on an entire current of thought, is still among us. This is how Albert and I see him: we speak of him in the present. [...]. And certainly for Albert that period between 1936 and 1938 that he spent with Colorni in Trieste, when he learned to develop his 'small ideas,' was crucial for his work even many years later."

So when I picked up my pen to begin this work, it was only natural to me to take the path of visual immediacy—while (of course) respecting historical contingencies.

Eugenio Colorni was a strapping young man with a dark complexion, typically Mediterranean looking. He was full of life, and loved to talk and laugh with his friends. As a young Milanese philosopher, he belonged by birth (with his sister Silvia) to the small world of Jewish liberal professional families

2 The idea of talking about Colorni in the present is an ingenious device because, even taking into account the historical context in which Eugenio lived, it invites us to consider the *general theoretical sense* of his teaching. You could say that the point of it is to keep that crucial content constantly before us. But at the same time, it can be an invitation to observe today's reality from Colorni's visual perspective. We shall see some of the consequences further along. Just one example: on the occasion of the sixtieth anniversary of Colorni's death I sent Albert, by email, an invitation to a meeting (an initiative of Rome's Municipality III, the Euro-Sapienza Center, the European Training Center and the Federalist Movement) that we held in Rome on 18 May 2004 (Bumbaca, ed. 2004). Addressing my wife, Nicoletta Stame, and myself, Hirschman replied, "I am grateful to you for renewing our friendship with Eugenio Colorni." This seemed perfect. Indeed, it is always worthwhile to reactivate communication with an ironic, irreverent, constructive and inspiring spirit like Eugenio's. It is an injection of intellectual and practical vitality; it rekindles a crucial learning process. Rediscovering in this way a relationship of familiarity and friendship with 'the Eugenio' (as they say in Milan) is a more than secondary purpose of the present work (cf. Meldolesi 2004 p. 35).

3 Ibid.

that Giuseppe Mazzini had called "an Italian province without territory."[4] His father (who died when Eugenio was 11) was an entrepreneur (a dealer in agricultural equipment), while his mother came from a well-known Pisan business family (her name was Clara Pontecorvo).

To briefly (and somewhat imaginatively) introduce the story I would like to tell, I need a *tale e quale*[5] [a "spitting image"]—a brief portrait to serve as a starting point which, given the iconoclastic subject, needs to be as vivid, truthful (and anti-celebratory) as possible.

Ab initio, then—from the beginning—there was Eugenio. Having no intellectual likeness available, the best I can do is think about what might be required to track him down. According to the testimony of friends and family, Colorni "is remembered as a restless man, volcanic, irreverent, cheerful, tireless, rigorous, upright, deep, thoughtful, courageous, sincere, Socratic, original, generous, a reader (slow, but avid), patient, free spirited—almost as if his unique interpenetration of intellectual activities and personal and political experiences created an 'alloy' that was impossible to pigeonhole."[6]

2 – Yes, the picture is clear, the reader will be thinking. But before we are overwhelmed by his exuberance it would be at least worth recalling (briefly) how such a character came into the world.[7]

This requires proceeding in stages—a pen stroke at a time. We would want to access the lives of the educated and affluent Italian Jewish families—the Levis, the Serenis, the Pontecorvos, and of course the Colornis[8]—of the 1920s and 1930s, who brought their children up with "a strict, no-frills education."[9]

---

4 Coming from a well-to-do family, Eugenio maintained good relations with several of his uncles and cousins. "On the occasion of his customary visits in Milan," wrote Maurizio Degl' Innocenti (2010, p. 12) "the fact that they were Fascist Party members did not stand in the way of his meeting one or another of them; conformity was widespread in Jewish circles at least up to the time of the racial laws."

5 As they call a photograph in Neapolitan—imaginative but not inappropriate.

6 Meldolesi 1998 p. 10. Cf. Colorni 1998 pp. 163–198; 2021a pp. 61–9. He was, according to Leo Solari (2004 p. 23), "constantly […] concerned with remaining strictly faithful to the peace treaty he said he had established with his 'categorical imperative'—that is, with his conscience. A very demanding conscience!"

7 A more extensive description, accompanied by some additional discussion, can be found in my introductions to the volumes of Colorni's complete works (2019–23).

8 As well as the Milano, Amendola, Marpurgo Tagliabue, Tagliacozzo, and Sraffa families… and their circles of friends.

9 Sereni C. 1993 p. 192.

Eugenio, born in 1909, recounts in his writings some of the formative aspects of his personality—he was often at odds with his Sereni cousins, especially Emilio (Mimmo), who was unshakable in his convictions (according to his daughter, Clara).[10] Colorni recalls how, during his long summer holidays with his cousins in Versilia, he often felt distressed—these times were a small thorn in his side that, paradoxically, eventually came in handy because they provoked him to react.[11]

The background was the family life of a commercial and professional bourgeoisie which, while extraneous to the declining landed aristocracy, nevertheless resented its privileges and lifestyle; this in a country—Italy between the wars—that was still overwhelmingly agricultural. Undoubtedly this family life was part of a rising modern "upper-middle class" which, resting on this solid private foundation, could allow itself a certain conformist (and somewhat hypocritical) detachment from the public sphere, at the time the preserve of a vulgar and triumphant fascism.

This is the social environment in Milan where Eugenio's story begins—in opposition as always. He lives with his mother, administrator of the substantial inheritance left by his father. Showered with attention (and wrestling with the delicate problems of adolescence), he nevertheless begins to find the strength to rebel inwardly against the current state of affairs. At university he is already starting to become an anti-fascist reference point. With his friends, his ethical and political leadership comes spontaneously.[12] He is patient, introspective, Socratic. This sense of security also allows him to push himself (intellectually and personally) ahead of the others, but without taking unnecessary risks.

All of a sudden, apparently, he discovers the theoretical and practical calling that would stay with him for life. At the Regia University of Milan, after various ups and downs, he enrolls in philosophy, where his aim is to

10 Ibid., passim.

11 Colorni 2021a ch. 4.

12 Thanks to his mother's hospitality, Eugenio's university classmates often met at his house to discuss politics. "His ideas," wrote Guido Piovene (1975 pp. 267–268), "came to life when he spoke. He possessed the ability to guide others in expressing complex ideas, free of inconsistencies and defenses, and exposing their plain and inevitable extreme logical consequences. But perhaps this would not have been possible without a more fluid element that served as a carrier—an intimacy [...], a confidence before which everyone was brought to accept painful conclusions and demolitions. The emotion flowed fervidly, without limit or mercy, toward courageous thinking and clarity of mutual understanding. The meetings were not sad, nor even too serious. Tension was often dispelled in laughter."

"understand in order to act." He finds inspiration in the aesthetics of Borgese and the philosophical idealism of Martinetti with the idea of using both as the starting point of his intellectual (and political) adventure. He gets into fights with the fascists and sets out on a personal journey in search of freedom and justice.[13] He indeed chooses the profession of philosophy, following the precepts of the discipline, but he does not settle into the wake of his teachers, for example undertaking some interpretive study for its own sake. On the contrary, he uses their teachings and explanations to free his own thinking and open an intellectual gateway toward the future. Essentially, he makes use of his own personal position, complex maturation process and spontaneous brilliance, and achieves, even at this young age, extraordinary cognitive and political results.

3 – Consider, for example, his aesthetic critique of Benedetto Croce,[14] a well-written book which is both accurate and imaginative (Gennaro Sasso). To borrow one of his own favorite metaphors, of a building with many rooms, corridors, lofts, balconies, cupboards, cellars, etc., it may be said that Eugenio, barely 23 at the time, is seeking in this volume to "liberate" the building from the mental structure that has been superimposed on it (the utterly binding Hegelian logic to which, as we all know, "everything must return")—this in order to instead give credit (whose purpose Croce did not understand) to his extensive and diligent construction, in its various aspects.

Colorni's work is rapidly directed toward the reform of current thinking, as a basic need. "He maintains that the culture of the time is misleading and outdated, and that the possibility of change, political change included, emerges from a kind of cultural re-foundation. This is what he has in mind when he abandons Croce."[15] But the road to truly mastering the kind of philosophy

13 "Eugenio," Solari recalls (2004 pp. 18–19), "had a connection with the group 'Scholars for Freedom,' an anti-fascist student group founded after the murder of Matteotti, whose activities were cultural—mainly pitting a cosmopolitan vision against the intellectual provincialism of the regime. One of the most interesting expressions of this dissent was the magazine *Pietre*, inspired by Gobetti and founded in Genoa in early 1928 and then transferred to Milan." Colorni took part, contributing the article "Roberto Ardigò" (Cf. Colorni 1928, 2022 pp. 76–80; Marcenaro, ed. 1973). Later, Eugenio joined the group "Freedom and Justice." Finally, as we shall see below, he joined the "Internal Socialist Center" on his return from Germany in 1933.

14 Colorni 1932a; 2022 pp. 135–211.

15 Meldolesi 1996 p. 83.

that he intends to pursue[16] is long and contorted. On the advice of Martinetti, Eugenio engages intensively with Leibniz, graduating with a thesis entitled "The Development and Meaning of Leibnizian Individualism." He studies numerous texts by Leibniz, in Germany as well as in Italy. He writes, as an advanced thesis, "The Early Philosophy of Leibniz." He edits Leibniz's *Monadology*.[17] He thus contents himself for many years with "the Leibniz compromise"—as he later writes from Ventotene to his wife Ursula Hirschmann.[18]

Contemporaneously, however, Colorni makes "the conscious decision to get rid of the *Weltanschauung*, or conception of the world, a viewpoint which at the time carried great weight in idealist (and Marxist) thought. He is a highly determined individual—when he is sure of the road he is on, he covers ground with impressive speed… Colorni advances an argument which even today continues to have great importance in the culture, especially in the social sciences. He says that any conception of the world, any preconceived overall belief structure, any single general paradigm around which reasoning revolves, ought to be abandoned."[19]

In this way Eugenio performs a *general epistemological inversion* that frees thought from systemic perspectives (and all their modern imitations) and thus opens the way to a new research methodology.

Simultaneously, Colorni discovers his flair for novelty, for invention, innovation, stratagem and forethought, as well as for conversing with himself and examining his subconscious. His protracted research on Leibniz (a multifaceted and ingenious philosopher, of whom Colorni becomes one of Italy's leading specialists[20]) indirectly facilitates this inspiration. It is a journey into the

16 Cf. Colorni 2021a pp. 75–90.

17 Colorni 1935; 2023 ch. 4.

18 Colorni 1939, 21 February.

19 Meldolesi 1996 p. 83.

20 Colorni 1935; 2023 ch. 4. Almost as if to recover from the past a significant key to the intellectual tangles of the present, Eugenio treats Leibniz as the main road to a more open way of thinking, intending to bring under the cloak of reason the greatest possible number of phenomena (in opposition to deductive logic as delimited and imposed by Descartes, still prevalent today in economics and other social sciences). Finally, Colorni proposes to retrieve "from Kant" the construction of an innovative way of thinking that fits with the times; to renew interest in discovery itself—in the individual cognitive act that requires freedom from anthropomorphic illusions and thus affects the mind of the discoverer. Along with intense insights from different fields of knowledge (especially in mathematics and the natural sciences, and in psychology, which he considered particularly useful in the pursuit of his project), the effort to follow this path also led him to the daily comfort of reading Nietzsche (cf., below, n. 22)

past as an *emendatio intellectus* (Bobbio[21]), an improvement with respect to the narrow and repetitive idealist, actualist, futurist philosophy of the time. But it also allows him to observe this from a distance, both in preparation for his own radical critique of contemporary philosophy, and as a way of approaching psychology, the natural sciences, physics, and mathematics. In essence, his "interminable" Leibniz research (as he sometimes called it) also helped Eugenio build his own original point of view, capable of offering new perspectives at once general and specific.

4 – The young Colorni does not let the fleeting moment escape. Pointing to the "philosophical illness" he needs to recover from,[22] he moves freely in every direction. He wants to alternate cultural work with political, to break away from any sort of artificial division of intellectual labor and master broad areas of learning, engaging with whatever aspect of human knowledge he deems most useful at any precise moment for promoting his vision of an intellectual revolution and building the house of the future—(like the yearning "fourth son" in his Kantian parable).[23]

All this, on the other hand, draws nourishment from his practical activities (and affects them in return). As bearer of an original way of thinking, Eugenio usually works with friends and activists whose ideas are different from his. He doesn't hold back from expressing his point of view, but at the same time he must deal with the problem of understanding others, their mental processes and potentialities, and supporting them in their learning efforts (autonomous and independent).

---

21 Bobbio 1975 p. xii.

22 Recalling "Pierino's" (his own) first clumsy attempts to try his hand in university philosophical discussions, Colorni wrote (2021a pp. 107–08): "Pierino reads *The Critique of Pure Reason* with a commitment, scrupulously maintained, not to move forward without fully absorbing every single paragraph. But there are authors he is absolutely unable to digest—Nietzsche, for example. He has picked him up several times, but has always had to leave off after the first few pages. Nietzsche has no beginning and no end; there are no 'transitions.' So disconnected and inconsistent! An uninhabitable world. The beginning of each fragment reads as if you were starting a new book—you see no connection with what came before. You have to pay constant close attention; you can never surrender to mechanical reasoning or predict a conclusion; you never feel that you are being helped along or supported by the harmony of the structure. You can't give an opinion on the book—you have to give a hundred thousand, it contains so many ideas. Pierino hates aphorisms. Kant is so much easier. (If I think of everything that separates me today from my friend Pierino, the most symptomatic is this—the only philosopher I am now able to read is Nietzsche)."

23 Colorni 2021a ch. 6.

He discovers in this way a largely new style of political leadership, one of involvement and collective management dictated by the needs of the anti-fascist struggle and his intellectual role as mentor to his co-workers and to the public—a sort of fraternal attention which, according to the testimony of Leo Solari,[24] would later make him extraordinarily different from other leaders of the Resistance.[25]

In conclusion, the creative and enterprising ingenuity of a capable and determined person like Eugenio Colorni without doubt plays a key role in the events I would like to evoke. "It makes clear how it was possible—in certain historical conditions—to convey this feverish impulse little by little to someone else [whom he meets along the way]. It is precisely this aspect of the question that has remained *indelible* in the memory of those who knew him."[26]

But even someone like myself who never had this opportunity can still seek to open communication with Eugenio. "Personally," I argued, for example, in a June 1994 debate, "I am [...] quite critical of economic policy [...] built on a base of theoretical models put together a priori and then imposed on reality. The tradition of economics is largely this, and the high and somewhat ecclesiastical prestige accorded to [...] economics professors, be they macro- or micro-economists, liberals or interventionists, is linked to the use of such armchair constructions. Of course it is important to know them [these constructions]—this much is obvious—and perhaps to use them as simple working hypotheses. But the formulation needs to be modified to achieve a better fit with reality, to find concrete solutions that start with surveys and studies (and not only statistics), and with the exploration of unusual but possible routes to development and democracy. Certainly Hirschman and Colorni talked about this in their 1936–38 discussions. There is an essay of Colorni's on economics[27] which is very important—not least because fifty years later it is evident that the things he predicted have actually happened [...]. The central paradigm of

24 Solari 2004 pp. 24–25.

25 Take anthropomorphism, for example (cf. Colorni and Spinelli 2020 ch. 6). Eugenio was convinced that the standard human condition is that of a "desiring being." This motivates us unconsciously to color everything with our longings, to attribute to things characteristics that typify our own thinking, as Kant explained with reference to space, time, substance, causality, number—a point of view that Eugenio intends to generalize. As a result, talking to his friends and colleagues, he enjoys pointing out this unconscious propensity when it shows itself in their thinking, and going on to explain that only by curbing our anthropomorphism will we be able to understand the world around us—and possibly decipher some of its characteristics, a possibility thus far denied us... by our own desire (and behavior).

26 Meldolesi 1998 p. 27.

27 "On Psychologism in Economics" (cf. Colorni and Spinelli 2020 ch. 7).

economics—the famous "homo economicus" who pursues only his/her own material interest – has fallen to pieces."[28]

Incredible, but True

5 – We arrive at 1936–38. Albert Hirschman we will introduce more fully later. Here, for introductory purposes, it is enough to recall that he, like his sisters Ursula and Eva,[29] belonged to a wealthy Jewish family, and was the child of Edvig Marcuse, a woman connected with Berlin's (financial) high society, and Carl, a well-known surgeon who had come from the East. Concerning his experience as a student, young Albert quickly learned how to make a virtue of necessity. After attending the Französiche Gimnasium, he had enrolled in law at the University of Berlin for the a.y. 1932–33, with the intention of becoming an economist[30]—even though (compared to careers like that of a doctor or lawyer) that profession was then considered a "breadless art" (*brot-lose Kunst*). Evidently, the social atmosphere of the time had led him to think that economics could be the key to politics.[31]

Shortly before the arrival of Nazism, Ursula and Albert had met Eugenio Colorni in Berlin, where he had gone to study Leibniz's original texts

---

28 Meldolesi 1996 pp. 83–4. "Colorni," I continued, "fought dogmatic thinking in philosophy with a view of freeing political and social thought in general."

29 For simplicity's sake, we will call him Albert O. Hirschman from now on (and not by his original name: Otto Albert Hirschmann). Because, having enlisted at the beginning of the World War in the French army (and in the resistance), he was already calling himself Albert instead of Otto (to the point that, upon demobilization, he took the name Albert Hermant, born in Philadelphia to French parents—see Tesnière 2020 on this subject). And when he landed in the United States in late 1940, he officially became Albert Otto. Finally, his surname lost a final n in 1942, when he enlisted in the U.S. Army (and later obtained U.S. citizenship).

30 This decision was certainly a political one, influenced by the economic and social consequences of the great crisis of 1929 (which ended up even "affecting" the savings of his family: see Adelman 2013 p. 47–8). "At that time," recalled Hirschman (1998 p. 54), "I was still looking; I studied something between law and economics." But this was for only one semester at the School of Law and Political Science at the Institute of Political Science and Statistics at the University of Berlin. His papers on the subject were entitled, "The Critique of Smith's Doctrine of Money and Capital through Marx" and "The Limits and Purpose of Ricardo's Labor Theory of Value" (Adelman 2013 p. 76). [In our countries, in order to study economics, the choice of law rather than economics and business was long considered preferable: I can personally testify to this ... thirty years later].

31 "The reason I went into economics," Hirschman declared (1990 p. 153), "I believe was the experience of mass unemployment and the political upheavals of the 1930s."

(meanwhile working as lecturer in Italian at Marburg University).[32] Colorni and the two Hirschmanns were at the time attracted to the Labor Movement. Ursula and Albert had joined the young social democrats, and Colorni, already an expert in the antifascist struggle, gave them a hand.[33]

But then things changed. The political situation took a turn for the worse. And it was just then that Albert and Ursula's father, following a cancer operation, suddenly died. In April 1933, perhaps partly because of Colorni's indirect influence,[34] Albert and then Ursula decided to leave the country and move to Paris (where they were later followed by their mother and sister Eva). Albert enrolled at the "École des Hautes Etudes Commerciales" (HEC), a *grand école* of French business.[35] He got his diploma, and thanks to a providential study grant, he spent a year at the London School of Economics.

---

32 Following the "custom" of philosophy students of the time who could afford it (and who wanted access to the original texts in classic German philosophy), "the twenty-two year old Colorni also went to Berlin and then to Marburg as Italian lecturer. At Marburg he was able to spend time with Erich Auerbach [...], his direct superior, who was working on writing *Mimesis* (1946). Upon giving up his position, Colorni indicated to Auerbach his successor, first Nicola Chiaromonte, who refused, and then Franco Lombardi." But "Colorni maintained his connection to the department of romance philology at the University of Marburg, remaining 'closely linked' through Auerbach's successor, Klaus Werner" (Degl'Innocenti 2010 pp. 49–50).

33 "Ursula and Otto Albert plucked up the courage to ask Colorni to keep a printing machine in his room in a hostel in Charlottenburg. There they could compose their broadsheet; since he was a foreigner, the Nazi would not suspect his involvement. Thus began," Adelman writes (2013 p. 80), "a formative influence."

34 The current opinion in polite Berlin society at the time was that Hitler's rise to power would not last long. Colorni, on the other hand, who came from Italy's well-established fascist experience, was of a very different opinion. And in fact Albert, first-born male in a family of Jewish origin, was already in grave danger. As so often happened subsequently, his "sixth sense," helped him make the difficult decision to emigrate to Paris.

35 In terms of study and then in application, the HEC pushed Albert down a technical-professional path (something, as we shall see, that he disliked, but considered to have been necessary for a young man like himself with the problem of making ends meet and thinking about his future). This attitude was strengthened in confrontation to Eugenio. The latter, in fact, went from being an intellectual to becoming *more* militant, while Albert in a sense followed the opposite course—from being a militant he had to become *more* technical. On the other hand, Hirschman had never had the mind of an "organic intellectual"—able to convince others so as to develop a political hegemony of some kind. In fact, in retrospect (see the second epigraph before the introduction, above), Albert later evaluated very positively what he had managed to "accomplish" with the anti-fascists and with Fry—not least because later on, as we shall see in the second volume of these essays, he embarked on a different path, moving away from the old one.

Eugenio, on the other hand, before Fascism imposed the notorious, painful "oath" on university teachers (and then secondary school teachers), had won a competition for a tenured middle school position in philosophy and pedagogy. He started at Voghera, and was then transferred to the Giosué Carducci Magisterium in Trieste where, after a short time, he was joined by Ursula Hirschmann (blonde, fascinating, a bit like Ingrid Bergman). The two got married. So Albert (after taking part briefly and painfully in the Spanish Civil War[36]) decided to follow them to Trieste where, to complete his studies, he enrolled in the economics department of the local university for the academic year 1936–37.

Thus, having overcome these numerous vicissitudes (personal, professional and political), the Berlin "trio" (Eugenio, Ursula and Albert) miraculously found themselves back in Trieste—an especially lively city from the standpoint of culture, its placement at the border, and the political sensitivity of its workers and the liberal bourgeoisie of the period. They found themselves in a state of (unexpected) tranquility—additionally protected by their bourgeois appearance (with a lot of theater, tennis, trips to the mountains, etc.).[37] And it was here, in almost daily contact with Ursula and (especially) with his brother-in-law Eugenio, that the extraordinary creativity of Albert Hirschman flourished for the first time.

6 – As a student, he was concerned with making rapid progress—that is, with quickly achieving a degree of confidence in his own strengths that would meet his (present and future) needs. This had to happen on several fronts: learning statistics and economics well, writing, on a trial basis, a few reports on the Italian economy for a Parisian magazine, learning Italian, getting his degree… and (above all) improving, while in contact with Eugenio, his cultural and political orientation.

36 Where at the end of August 1936 he probably took part in the battle of Monte Pelato and was slightly wounded. (Adelman 2013 pp. 133–34).

37 With the benefit of hindsight (for some time Colorni had been under surveillance and he was arrested on 8 September 1938), we know that this was the calm before the storm. Nevertheless, this unanticipated calm was experienced by our protagonists as a breathing space, as true serenity—pleasant, creative, inspiring, undreamed of—and remembered in this way even after the passage of many, many years. The truth is that in this frontier city, once irredentist (and then rebellious against the regime), and marginal to the mainstream of Italian events, the police moved with caution—they followed every move of Eugenio the socialist leader and of his group, but did not think it yet worthwhile to intervene.…

What happened, in fact, was that Hirschman was won over by the spontaneous and cheerful working and living style of his brother-in-law, his sister and their friends. Indeed, in his numerous activities, Colorni then effortlessly represented a point of reference: "He nurtured and stimulated people's ideas even before they were fully formed; he offered approaches, expedients, indications for developing the widest variety of intellectual activity; his psychological insights were outstanding. At the same time, he was bursting with his own sagacious ideas, such as the rejection of systemic logic and the search for new discoveries."[38]

The two brothers-in-law lived in the center of town, near the sea front, a few blocks from each other, and met almost every day. They understood one another very well, in spite of their differences. Eugenio was exuberant, magnetic, a cultural and political leader (he had just become head of the Internal Socialist Center). Albert was thoughtful and quiet, with his own implicit, peculiar charm (shortly thereafter, in Marseilles, he would acquire the nickname Beamish—cheerful, radiant, capable of getting up to all sorts beneath the surface, but lightly and with a smile).

Because of these differences in temperament, pedagogical inclination and age (they met again in Trieste at ages 28 and 22),[39] Eugenio began to act as Albert's "mentor." He taught him the "deeds and misdeeds" of philosophical thought, and showed him how people often (unknowingly) shut themselves off from the possibility of seeing things as they actually are. He began to show him the alternate path of discovery and creative innovation, discussing with him the research that he himself was conducting in political science, in psychology, in mathematics, in physics, in philosophy of science, in epistemology.[40]

Albert gradually absorbed the lesson and tried at the same time to transfer what he had been learning into still other disciplines. For starters, in fact, he

38 Meldolesi 1995 p. 213.

39 Of course, it was Hirschman who needed Colorni and had the problem of staying close to him (rather than vice versa), to the point of harboring a certain jealousy of anyone who (mostly for reasons connected with political activity) had greater access than himself to Eugenio's inner circle, (Adelman 2013 p. 148).

40 Cf. above, secs. 3 and 4, and notes 20 and 25. "The truth," Colorni had written, for example, in 1932 (now in 2023, pp. 58–9), "(our truth, powerfully inherent in our very conformation and constituting our purest mode of consciousness) is also our truest way of being [...]. It is in this way that intelligence (real intelligence, which frees more and more snippets of truth from their shell [...], real intelligence, that is, a sharp, scrupulous, tireless investigator—is a form of morality; indeed it is morality itself."

planned to improve his grasp of the basics of statistics and economics and their multiple applications.

A sort of interdisciplinary "spillover" between disciplines (*mutatis mutandis*) thus began to show up in the dialogue between the two brothers-in-law—a transfer (at the time potential more than effective) of knowledge initially gained in a predominantly philosophical context into economics and the social sciences in general. This was the process the adult Hirschman became a master of, with his ideas of "trespassing" and "crossing boundaries."[41]

The Logic of Effervescence

7 – At this point, the two brothers-in-law were carried away by what can only be called *effervescence*. While still respecting their own disciplinary (and interdisciplinary) fields, they began competing with each other in intellectual inventiveness, for pure enjoyment (and passion for knowledge).[42]

Obviously, Albert the young economics student didn't want simply to memorize this or that argument to pass an exam. He was aiming much higher. He experimented with curious and unusual logical pathways. For example, in learning statistics, not known in any case as the easiest of the human sciences, he would set out a problem and then close the book and try to imagine the solution. And not only that—while writing his first scientific articles on demographic statistics,[43] he set out at some point to "discover" some aspect of the discipline, *ex abrupto*. Working in this way, having chosen the argument, he would try to prove it before studying it, so that he could then check whether he had approached it correctly, or had perhaps even come close to the actual solution. "Putting the cart before the horse," you might say, *ante litteram*.[44]

41 Undoubtedly, Albert was infected by Eugenio's extraordinary drive toward free research, his clever and entertaining way of setting up problems, political included. At the time he probably knew the conclusions, more than the logical train of thought, of this volcano of ideas. And since he was also just at the beginning of his intellectual journey, the gradual acquisition of Eugenio's way of thinking could not be transformed, *sic et simpliciter*, into actual assimilation. Later, however, during his long intellectual life, Albert returned repeatedly to examine Eugenio's contributions. For example, he expressly recognized Eugenio's influence in shaping the process of "surprise – discovery – theorizing – generalizing – gradual recognition of results," which is typical of Hirschman's work.

42 In the disciplines they were passionate about, of course. Not in the others…

43 Hirschman 1937 and 1938.

44 It will be recalled that "putting the cart before the horse" is a stratagem he theorized about in 1958 (*The Strategy*, ch. 5).

In one case—he later told me—he believed he had come up with a new theorem. But then, checking in his book, he found that the theorem had in fact already been invented. Yet, contrary to what you might expect, he was happy about it because he had proved to himself that he had progressed enough to undertake (and successfully complete) a specific intellectual enterprise. He still felt he was Eugenio's pupil, but he was climbing rapidly.[45]

8 – It is clear that what Albert Hirschman was then seeking was (above all) to "learn to learn"—to be able discover things (first and foremost) for himself. He felt a need to learn in order to innovate. For this, in the unexpected peace of Trieste, he turned to his brother-in-law for a kind of almost daily technical-scientific assistance.

In fact, contrary to what many economists (and many more students of economics)[46] continue to believe, Eugenio taught Albert that our own certainties must be continually *questioned*—passed through the sieve of experience, obviously including the direct and indirect signals we receive daily from reality. He taught him that our senses must be deployed receptively—in such a way as to adequately accommodate and process the messages that come from our life and studies, especially those that are unexpected and ought to make us question what we think. And that we need to fight our psychological resistance, to battle with ourselves for a glimpse of the truth (with a small t, because the one with a capital T trumpeted by the philosophers does not exist)—an authentic truth, *a little more* than what we already know. Along with this, we need to accept being caught off guard, being surprised by facts and ideas that prove us wrong (the methodological theory of surprise), and even that we should be embarrassed (without shame, of course) by what we believed before (because,

45 This was the attitude that Hirschman later called (1971 p. 13) "a certain turn of mind, the desire to speculate and to search in a certain direction, rather than the application of any infallible and objective technique."

46 Here I am alluding in particular to the fact that the modeling obsession—which overwhelms so many economists—ultimately results in the notion that reality must be adapted to the model, and not the model to reality. As we shall see below, Hirschman developed his point of view on economics (which many consider idiosyncratic) by gradually freeing himself from a (non-critical and supine) acceptance of inherited economic theory—respecting analytical results by all means, but gradually making sense of them from an epistemological point of view, in order to reuse and modify them *pro domo sua*.

Eugenio explains, the deepest knowledge is the kind that passes through us, that gets us moving, and that we will not so easily forget…).[47]

These are conclusions that Eugenio had reached by turning the traditional approach to the world (or system) on its head. In the place of a "holistic" vision (which has something superhuman about it and oppresses even its creator), he instead advises the wise researcher to move freely, always alert, but with ease, taking into account some small perceptions that accompany his day, focusing on the object of study one step at a time, often "cutting up" the analysis into unusual shapes, relying on the power of introspection (well worth strengthening; and on their own subconscious)—not least to ensure a certain degree of *post facto* compatibility and consistency among the different building blocks of the intellectual project under construction; almost like the tiles of a mosaic that we gradually begin to discover, but which never ends.[48]

9 – Colorni's teaching focuses on the relation between subject and experience. He suggests that the former should make every effort to accommodate reality's

---

47 So it is by no means a coincidence that twenty years later, the preface to *The Strategy* opens with the following statement from Whitehead (which, Albert says, encouraged him greatly during the initial planning of the book). "The elucidation of immediate experience is the only justification for any thought; and the starting point of thought is the analytical observation of the components of this experience" (Hirschman 1958 p. v; Whitehead 1930 p. 6). This is a thesis that obviously presupposes the breakdown of experience into its components. That is to say—a typical lesson of Leibniz and Colorni, which we shall discuss (cf. below, sec. 16).

48 But on the subject of what to do regarding one's own subconscious the ideas of the two brothers-in-law did not coincide. I offer just one example. Albert argued, as we know, that personal development can be additionally strengthened by the tensions it creates. "Perhaps it is the penetrating influence of psychoanalysis", he wrote in *The Strategy* (1958 p. 209 n. 5), that has kept us in the dark about this. "For Freud, difficulties, conflicts and anxieties were mainly pathogenic; their constructive and educational functions in individual development have been discovered only recently." Had he come across a distant echo here? It is of course true that very early, in his high school years, Albert encountered the three great demystifiers of German-speaking culture: Marx, Nietzsche and Freud. While acknowledging the importance of the unconscious (and Freud's talent in leading mankind to take account of it), he did not see any need (either then or thereafter) to venture into the complex tangle that comprises it – a point of view which, as he told me in 1987, he had defended and strengthened in discussions with Eugenio Colorni. While Colorni was willing to "turn the lens on himself" by thoroughly investigating his own mind and others' as well, Hirschman preferred an inverse approach (of Leibnizian origin). That is, attributing individual and collective actions and tensions to reason—as far as possible—so that their energy and constructive force could be made use of. This is a proposition that, as may be gathered from the passage from *The Strategy* cited above, he later applied in development economics.

messages, to think about them and integrate them with previous knowledge. The subject should actively analyze (and develop) these messages, not least through the use of imagination, hypothesis, conjecture, speculation and reflection, so as to grasp the whole of what they contain, *in actu et in potentia*. It should then be possible to extract from them a range of alternatives useful in human decision-making that is wider than would otherwise be relied on. (In his "attempt to delineate common themes and to discover an underlying methodology and perhaps philosophy" for his work, Albert would later explain that the possible generally encompasses more than the probable).[49]

Research and discovery are therefore a miracle of applied intelligence. Colorni calls for the thorough development of this human faculty, and for a rejection of the easy, lazy life, so common in every latitude, that shuns contemplation and mainly uses the brain as a sort of autopilot—not to rest and refresh its cognitive functions, but often and willingly as an indolent *substitute* for it.

Eugenio explains tirelessly that true intellectuals are hardworking, honest with themselves, vigilant, and always ready to correct the way they think. Eager to do so, in fact, so as to continually improve their work—in reciprocal communication both with the times they live in and with good books which, as it happens, have often been written by the best minds of past generations…

Doubt and Action

10 – In this way, influencing each other (asymmetrically) in their Triestine "laboratory," the two young men found a way to release their intellectual creativity in many different directions and to make rapid progress. This "condition" inspired them; while, at the same time, allowed research into ingenious proposals and routes of escape from the current situation—it pushed Eugenio and Albert, that is, toward unprecedented *audacity*, both intellectual and practical.

Starting from a position of doubtfulness,[50] "we can draw specific elements of knowledge from our intimate perplexities about reality, which in their turn

49 Hirschman 1971 p. ix.

50 Colorni later wrote to his wife Ursula (21 September 1938; now 2019 p. 53): "My Dearest, I'm reading *Faust*, one page per day […]. What strikes me about Goethe is his—how can I put it?—his doubtfulness before he gives an opinion or makes a value judgment. Take the "Prologue in the Theater." Are you really sure he agrees with the poet rather than the theater director or the actor? OK, he agrees. But he seems to want to say: I am capable of understanding the others' points of view as well. The way the others see things also 'exists.'"

induce us to act with greater awareness of the issues at stake. The two brothers-in-law shared the intellectual and political passion for sharpening their skills in perception and analysis in order to cast doubt on ideas that do not correspond to reality, and then to discover new, more solid, alternatives. The admirable example of intellectual openness and commitment to public life probably led Albert to wonder just *how* Eugenio was able to develop his unusual talents and put them into practice" in an era regrettably guided by quite another sort of logic.[51]

This is a crucial aspect of the argument that we must not let slip away.[52] "If I had time," Albert declared concluding his speech in acceptance of the *honoris causa* degree in political science awarded him by the University of Turin on 12 November 1987,[53] "I would argue that we all can still learn from this example [of Colorni and his friends]. For this a sort of combination of participation in public affairs with intellectual openness seems to me the ideal micro-foundation of a securely democratic society."

Of course, Hirschman did not have time that afternoon to fully clarify his conclusion. But it isn't hard to imagine what he had in mind. He was just then, in fact, in the midst of a new elaboration on democracy[54] that would appear in one of his most important books, *The Rhetoric of Reaction* (1991) which, significantly, would be translated into Italian (as well as Spanish and Portuguese) with the title *Retoriche dell'intransigenza*.[55] And this, in my opinion, is the

---

51 Meldolesi 1995 p. 213–14.

52 Some time ago (cf. ibid., ch. 8) I used this key as the end point of a review of Albert's texts on democracy.

53 Hirschman 1990a p. xxxi.

54 This is a line of reasoning that started from below (in Latin America) and, through successive generalizations, was at the point of taking on a general meaning—both positive (tolerance and openness in the political process; patience; uncertainty or doubt about outcomes and the way forward; open deliberative processes, fully laid out, involving key groups, political and representative bodies) and negative: cf. Hirschman 1986b, 1988, 1989, 1989a.

55 "My publisher [Harvard University Press]," as Albert later explained (1995 p. 60), "objected to having 'intransigence' in the title. That term was said to be largely unknown to (and, if known, likely to be mispronounced by) the average American." So he went back to his original title. But by then the die was cast, as shown by the Italian, Spanish and Portuguese editions of the book. In our author's oveall œuvre it is possible to speak, in this regard, of a "Wagnerian crescendo"—from the "todero" mentality, criticized before its time (in *Journeys* – 1963 ch. 4), to his polemics against "stubbornly professed opinions" (1989, 1989a) and against the *rhetoric* of intransigence (evidently involving the prophets of the cathedral of Bamberg, who appear on the cover of *The Rhetoric* – 1991), to the *destructive nature* of intransigence. Cf. also Hirschman 1995 ch. 2.

central point of the argument—even today, as an alternative to the cultural and political intransigence that is so harmful to the effective functioning of democracy, the admirable example of Eugenio and his friends indeed continues to *educate* us all.

II

The Leibniz Compromise

11 – Let us now return *ab ovo*, with open-pit mining as our method. Having discussed the (dominant) political side, we now move to a (more) theoretical-philosophical plane, bringing to bear some suggestions drawn from my long work on Eugenio Colorni's *opera omnia* (inspired, among other things, by the need to trace the root of the important intellectual innovation that later took the name of 'possibilism').

For Colorni, in the mid-1930s, the 'Leibniz labyrinth' had already served its function as 'primordial soup'—a sort of welcoming gymnasium for a long (and sweat-soaked) training session that had finally yielded important results (and pointed toward others). Let me try and clarify this point schematically, relying as much as possible on Eugenio's own observations.

To understand the *Monadology*, otherwise incomprehensible, Colorni had written a "Bio-bibliographical note" and an important "Anthological Exposition of the Leibnizian System." The second of these is a vigilant and precise reconstruction that in the end produces a masterful 'quilt' featuring bright, carefully chosen colors. To be in a position to draft such a reconstruction, Eugenio had had to carve out a long (painstaking) trail through extensive and fragmentary material.[56]

The result of this strenuous circumnavigation (filo-Grotius and filo-Thomist), as Colorni later wrote to his wife Ursula,[57] was that "I could untangle

56 "With a clarity and simplicity that can only come with long familiarity with an author," wrote Norberto Bobbio (1975 p vi), Leibniz's fragmentary and wide-ranging thought is separated [in Colorni's "Anthological Exposition"] into its basic parts, and then reconstructed and boiled down to brief summaries of the main themes, accompanied and illustrated by aptly selected passages from Leibniz's works and letters, a true 'Leibnizian system in compendium.'"

57 Colorni 1939 p. 65, 21 February; now 2023 epigraph.

the knots" and "search for what lies beneath the words." Presumably from both a political and theoretical standpoint.

Eugenio had freed himself from the concept of a system, in this way breaking a scientific taboo which is even today slow to release its grip. Leibniz, in his view, had been a spontaneous (not imposed) systemizer. And in all likelihood he really believed, without effort, in theological-systematic harmony (or so it would seem). And perhaps it was for this reason that he chose to couch his scientific discoveries in the language of the time, which nowadays strikes us as more or less indigestible. This was what gave Colorni the idea of "translating" Descartes and Leibniz to make them available to modern readers. He completed a first attempt at this in 1937,[58] presenting two opposing worlds: that of Descartes, of the will; and that of Leibniz, of intellectualism—that is, of knowledge requiring concrete research, among other things. But that was as far as it went.

For these "translations"—if I'm not mistaken—he wouldn't have had to commit himself to patiently taking apart the constructions of Descartes and Leibniz (the way he had done with the aesthetics of Croce), since that of Leibniz seemed to be "untangled" already. Probably it would have been enough to reread it in its specifics, *in medias res*—in such a way that ideas and elaborations that seem on the surface to be senseless games instead take on important meanings.[59] Colorni's discovery was here as well—in reuse!

In fact, many of Eugenio's achievements from that period come from this work.[60] It marked the birth of the *possible*. At the same time, Colorni began to want to get out of the Leibnizian labyrinth. Retrospectively, "the Leibniz

58 Colorni 'Eternal truths in Descartes and Leibniz,' March 1937a (now in Colorni 2023 ch. 5). Cf. also Colorni 2019 p. 71–2.

59 Cf. ibid.

60 As noted, Eugenio also worked on a book of essays on Leibniz (which never saw the light of day). In addition, beginning in 1935, several extraordinary political texts emerged indirectly from his philosophical-political pursuits. I can't tell whether or not Colorni applied one particular stratagem or the other in these articles. Perhaps it is not necessary to know. Perhaps, for someone sufficiently 'trained,' it is more useful simply to change the script, and even (pro tempore) forget about the previous one. Perhaps it is better to concentrate on the new problem. To solve it he would be helped even unconsciously by his previous training. In a certain sense, it can be said that the freshness and spontaneous brilliance of Colorni's political writings from this period represent, even visually, a kind of pleasing counterbalance to the laborious and patient collection of Leibniz's quotations. In any case, the way of thinking that gradually took shape during his long years of Leibnizian studies was already *possibilist*...

compromise" was very useful to him. It made him calmer—contemplative, refreshed, amiable. He became more aware of his strengths. He got married. He gained the ability to choose the right moment to gradually emerge from his shell by drawing energy from Ursula.[61] This emergence was what he began to design with his new studies in psychology, mathematics, and physics that would lead him to his analytical formulation—those of Ventotene, Melfi, and Rome.

12 – In late 1936, as this new approach was by now taking hold, Albert Hirschman turned up in Trieste. By this time, Colorni's breakthrough had already occurred and he was undoubtedly speaking a language that was surprising to his new brother-in-law.

Albert came from another world (Franco-German more than English). His education was different, but it allowed him to converse with Eugenio, who took the young Hirschman under his wing, helped him get his bearings, and urged him on, at full speed, in his independent research. Hence demographic statistics, Italian economics, the Poincaré franc, the vicissitudes of the lira, etc. (see below, ch. 3). Looking closely at these papers, it is clear that the author is already him, Albert Hirschman.[62]

Hirschman quickly takes on board Colorni's theoretical and political lessons, which then tend little by little to re-emerge in his work, starting as early as his writings from the 1930s.[63] The push from Eugenio 'made its mark,' which we will return to more than once. It is for this as well that Colorni 'is always present.' To conclude, what remains in the field is a certain way of thinking and of setting up research, along with the relevant Leibnizian and Colornian stratagems which can be drawn on, without limit.

Of course, we shall see later, in Hirschman's treatments this 'ancestry' is intertwined with other motives that still remain valid in the evolution of the discourse. Yet, perhaps it is true that without the *small perceptions*,[64] these intimate motives of our author could not have been effectively fulfilled. So it

61 Colorni 1939 p. 65, 21 February; now 2023 epigraph.

62 It is enough to compare the two 'reports' that Albert wrote before the war— *Il franco Poincaré e la sua svalutazione* [The Poincaré Franc and its Devaluation] (his bachelor's thesis 1938b, now 2004; 2025) and *Le contrôle des changes en Italie* [Exchange Controls in Italy] (1939a, 1987; 2025).

63 Cf. the experience "of a more fundamental nature." Hirschman 1990a p. xxx–xxxi; 1995 p. 118.

64 Cf. Hirschman 1971 Introduction; Adelman 2013 pp. 115–16.

is especially important to know how to 'fish' for this piece of the puzzle, *in corpore vili.*

But how? It would require a fishing pole or perhaps a net like the ones that used to exist at the mouths of our rivers that the fisher sitting in his little box would lower into the water only when he saw that the fish was about to pass through...

Let us see, then, what this net or network would consist of. It has already been hinted at—Leibniz's texts are fragmentary, uneven, scattered. This characteristic is usually seen as negative, but from our perspective it is much less so. This is because (in contrast to the need for unification, conciliation and harmony that Leibniz himself was also after)[65] it facilitates the 'reuse' of the methodological stratagems their author actually employed.

Leibniz penetrated every science, each in its peculiar and irreproducible aspects, Colorni explains,[66] and he knew how to take possession of the specific features of each method that suited his purpose. He thus created a vast collection of particular positions (where we obviously need to shine our lantern).

This much is clear, but how? Trying is believing. We have to dip the net into Albert's river at the right moment....

13 – What I said to myself at this point was that these are the general terms of the dialogue between Eugenio and Albert in 1936–38 that interest me. Unfortunately, though, they are still insufficient for getting into specifics, especially when we look at the issue from the position of the youthful Hirschman. In fact, as we shall see better in the next chapter, he was at the time fully engaged in finishing his university studies and simultaneously 'probing' some professional possibilities.

In the midst of all this, the many insights he received from Eugenio represented from the outset a daily stimulus and an important point of reference—in

65 By this I do not mean to argue, of course, that each investigation must be separated from the others; but only that it is convenient for us to start out with its delimitation and its specific (expected future) outcome, and then leave the study of its possible connections for a later stage. This is because, Colorni seems to mean to say (1938a, now in 2023 p. 348), Leibniz's spontaneous tendency in this case (and in many others) is the reverse, and we thus run the risk typical of so much of philosophy of forcing reality into the way of thinking, instead of working the other way around (adjusting thought to reality). This is why Albert accepts the linkage procedure only *post factum* (1971, 1981) and perhaps tends in this regard to trust the sub-conscious more than the conscious.

66 Colorni1935 p. xxii ; 2023 p. 102–03.

the sense that Albert intended to develop his work (which in part emanated from Paris and London) in a way that was at least 'compatible' with (and perhaps complementary to) Colorni's approach.

And moreover, while he was acquiring it, this way of thinking began to influence his own research, sometimes explicitly, sometimes behind the scenes.[67] In addition to some typical Colornian stratagems for setting up his work (listed above), there were undoubtedly others which manifested themselves more clearly in Hirschman's later development, but of which we do not (unfortunately) possess precise textual indications.

There is little, then, that we know with absolute certainty. We cannot even say whether the famous 'overflow,' the potential (before actual)[68] transfer of knowledge happened live, perhaps *in medias res*. Whether Albert had in his hands the *Monadology* edited by Colorni, which had been recently published. Or even whether Eugenio's inputs (verbally or in writing) needed discussion, reflection, rethinking, oscillation, summarizing, adjusting, etc. Or perhaps recovery or even *ex novo* discovery—as in daily life when you are looking for something and end up stumbling across… something else.

About all this we know nothing. Because Albert limited himself to occasionally clarifying (and this was an event in itself) his way of working. But he rarely spoke about the process by which he came to 'think the way he did' (much less, of course, about its distant origins). In some ways he was like a Renaissance master who never revealed the secrets of his workshop.[69] The consequence was that between his oft-stated acknowledgment of Colorni's influence on his work (on the one hand) and his books (on the other), a gap opens

67 Unfortunately, we do not know the details of this important process of "transfusion" from Eugenio to Albert. It is likely that it happened little by little, in a way that was anything but systematic—not in writing or in dedicated lessons, or even through ad hoc meetings. Probably, it originated sporadically, face-to-face and verbally, but repeatedly. Because Eugenio had a tendency to return to cognitive aspects that he considered crucial. As a result, those who knew him also enjoyed the (implicit) privilege of keeping some aspects of the actual meaning of his teaching alive in their minds, even after a long time; whereas, on the other hand, ordinary mortals (such as the writer) who seek to penetrate such "arcana" are forced to rack their brains, lest they give up in the face of the well-known *verba volant*.

68 Cf. above, the conclusion of sec. 7.

69 As previously mentioned, he was a person of few words, although these were carefully chosen. He also used silence for his own purposes. He said only what he thought was necessary—a tactic that proved useful in the short term on more than one occasion, but had no lasting power. He fought his battles alone.

in the mind of the observer, a wound that no one, to my knowledge, has even attempted to truly heal.

A Conjecture

14 – But in spite of all this, in my view, *some progress is still possible.* Basically, I began to think this way as I moved forward with the publication of Eugenio Colorni's complete works at Soveria Mannelli and in New York, as an unexpected but welcome consequence of interminably reading and rereading the texts to prepare them for publication (including numerous drafts, of course).

This impression was reinforced by a change in the order of the different items. That is, starting with the early writings of Hirschman in Trieste, rather than those of Colorni. In fact, reading in succession Albert's essays from 1937–39 (cf. the next chapter), I became aware of how the interpretations of the different issues dealt with were gradually shaped. Furthermore, when Hirschman refers to the same topic (or similar topics observed from different angles), looking through the texts in both directions (i.e. from first to last, but also in reverse), can reveal some main points where his judgment changed somewhat—and then it is possible to question why this is so.

Undoubtedly, Colornian stratagems are important in understanding our author's formative process.[70] So in order to get an idea (and at least partly overcome the gap in our knowledge) it seems to me necessary to proceed *hypothetically.*

During the period 1936–38 Colorni was in the last stage of his lengthy research on the works of Leibniz.[71] In addition, in 1935—as mentioned—for an educational series directed by Giovanni Gentile, he had edited Leibniz's *Monadology*, supplementing it with a rich "Anthological Exposition of the Leibnizian System."

From here, at some point, a specific hypothesis popped into my mind—especially when I read (or re-read) Albert's answer to the question, "Did you also study philosophy [in Trieste], in addition to economics, statistics and similar fields?" "No," Hirschman replied.[72] "I certainly read some philosophy, under the influence of my brother-in-law, but this was hardly my main interest."

70 And also the great turning point in his later research interests. I allude, of course, to the Hirschman of 1970 and 1971.

71 That marked, as well, the beginning of his extraordinary philosophical reflections, which he would later develop during his confinement in Ventotene.

72 Hirschman 1998 p. 67.

All right, I said to myself. But how many of the conclusions he had now reached from his studies on Leibniz had Eugenio simultaneously transferred to Albert, even verbally? Perhaps some (at least) of the ones he later mentioned in letters to Ursula from his internment. Might it not be reasonable to suppose this? Isn't it worth retracing our steps to reread his letters to his wife?

And also, in Trieste might Albert Hirschman (among the many things he was doing) have had occasion to read Leibniz's *Monadology* edited by Colorni, of course including the "Anthological Exposition"?

To me it seems plausible. Eugenio could have lent Albert that precious booklet (or perhaps, as is often the case with editors, he could have had an extra copy to give to him). Letting him read that text could have been an easy, handy way to introduce Hirschman to some of Leibniz's stratagems.[73] And also because the pages of philosophy that Albert read under Colorni's influence might have interested him not only for their meaning, but also from a professional, methodological standpoint, for the suggestions they might offer for his own work.

15 – It was from this dual hypothesis that I worked out a small program.

My idea was to ruminate first of all (and perhaps fantasize a bit) over some of the passages in Eugenio's correspondence with Ursula, thinking about what effect they might have had if spoken aloud as part of the intense Triestine dialogue between the two brothers-in-law. Here are a few of them.

"*Leibniz*: The one thing that impresses him most of all is the causal connection of all things with each other. From any occurrence, through a chain of cause-and-effect links, you can go back to any other occurrence. This means that from anything that happens you can go back into the past and come back into the future, so you can start from any occurrence and describe the world!"[74] Mightn't this proposition have interested a budding intellectual who, as it happens, later went on to theorize about sequences and linkages?

---

73 His "Anthological Exposition," which would later prove to be too long for Ursula to use for a philosophy exam (cf. Colorni 1939, June 1st; now 2019 p. 71), might instead have been within the reach of the young Albert—considering that "the *Monadology* that Leibniz wrote at the end of his life to bring together in an overall vision all his philosophical concepts can be understood only by someone with a certain familiarity with his thought" (Colorni 1935; now 2023 p. 77).

74 Colorni 1939, June 5th; now 2019a p. 122.

In another letter to Ursula, one I cited earlier,[75] Eugenio also wrote: "For years I settled for the Leibniz compromise. With Leibniz I could untangle the knots, I could search for what lies beneath the words without abandoning philosophy, dear old solid soothing philosophy. And I had become more confident, calmer, a good counselor, a valuable friend, a clarifier of problems, a supporter of the uncertain—a good teacher."

Yes, fine, Albert might have replied if his brother-in-law had told him something like this verbally. But my dear Eugenio, how did you do it? How can I in turn learn from Leibniz and from you those stratagems for improving (first and foremost) my mathematical-statistical and economic work, as well as (of course) my personal and political orientation?

Leibniz and Descartes, Colorni wrote, "really did have something to say both in the field of science (one invented infinitesimal calculus, the other analytical geometry) and in scientific methodology. Only they preferred, for reasons of convenience, to express these things in the language then in use, a theological-systematic language. Therefore, to understand them it is necessary to "translate" from that systematic language to ours. Once this is done, the theses and demonstrations that appear to be senseless games take on an important meaning, one that is in no way systematic."[76]

---

75 Cf. above notes 57 and 61 – Colorni 1939 p. 64, 21 February; now 2023 epigraph.

76 Colorni 1939, June 1st; now 2019a p. 71. Read carefully, this letter seems to suggest by analogy (mutatis mutandis) the hypothetical direction we are about to take. Indeed, immediately after the passage just quoted, Eugenio writes to Ursula, in preparation for her philosophy examination at the University of Venice: For Leibniz "what you need is the first (anthological) part of the book, but it's a little too long." And yet it may not have been "a little too long" for other people (like—as mentioned—Albert Hirschman) and for other purposes—such as the study of the meaning of the thesis and demonstrations just evoked. It is true, however, that after "The Eternal Truths of Descartes and Leibniz" (1937; now 2023 ch. 5)—Colorni's submission to the IX Congrès International de Philosophie (Paris, 6 août 1937), which in this letter he calls "an attempt at that 'translation' I was talking about," Colorni—beginning with "Leibniz and Mysticism" (1938; now 2023 p. 239 n.)—preferred to work, as is well known, on "a book [never completed] on the formation of the Leibnizian system." Perhaps because he considered such 'translation' activity less interesting or even obvious, pleonastic. This in the sense that he had already seen through personal experience that by stepping outside the theological-systematic framework it was possible to make use of Leibniz from time to time in order to achieve one's own specific purposes (as is indeed evident from the letter to Ursula dated 21 February 1939, quoted above: sec. 11 n. 57, and sec. 14 n. 75),

But one might object at this point that Eugenio's "editorship" of Leibniz's *Monadology* does not represent the necessary "translation" at all. It only contains an exposition—or rather, to be precise, an "Anthological Exposition of the Leibnizian System"—aimed at middle school students. Is this not the case?

16 – So what we need to do is change register again and go hunting for specific cues—perhaps as an extreme measure, an intellectual experiment (tentative and by no means exhaustive). What I mean is, I found it useful to go through the many pages Colorni dedicated to Leibniz's life and work (and which luckily have come down to us) *with this problem in mind*—beginning precisely with that extraordinary edition of the *Monadology*.

Without difficulty, in fact, we come across several passages from Leibniz (and Colorni) that might be useful in this regard (freeing them, of course, from the typical Leibnizian pretense of steering them *sin embargo* toward his system—that of the well-known pre-established harmony[77]).

In my view, therefore, it is worth our while to explore this hypothesis close up, explicitly inquiring as to *which* methodological features would have interested the young Hirschman.

To get an idea of this, we need to take up one of the possible readings of the text (of course far removed from those generally favored by scholars of philosophy).

We can begin with the "Bio-bibliographical note." For Leibniz, Colorni wrote,[78] "philosophy proper was only one aspect of a larger whole—almost a fragment in the big picture. For us, this fragment has become the center. We draw from it concepts and ideas that are still very much alive, methods which, translated into the terms of current problems, may yield new and very interesting results."

The temptation is to take Eugenio at his word and ask: how? How could we draw concepts, ideas and methods from such a fragment that are also useful for today? The answer (unfortunately) is missing—a real pity....

And yet several pages later,[79] Colorni doubles down, writing that "Leibniz was essentially a man who was curious about all problems and interested in all arguments. Whatever question arose or came under his eye, he attempted to

77 A spontaneous claim (I have already mentioned it) from which, generalizing, Eugenio probably saw confirmation of the tendency of philosophers to build systems—as he explained in a nutshell to Ursula Hirschmann in his first letter: 10 December 1936; now 2019a p. 103.

78 Colorni 1935 p. vi; 2023 p. 79.

79 Ibid. 1935 p. xxii; 2023 p. 102.

solve it, and most of the time he succeeded brilliantly. Whatever environment he found himself in, he tried to adapt to it quickly. He acquired the tools and techniques of virtually every science with astonishing rapidity, and in this he was often guided by chance or circumstance."

What might a young aspiring economist like Albert Hirschman infer from this? Probably that he, too, would want to learn to delve quickly into every humanistic and scientific discipline, to take on board their methodological peculiarities, etc.—perhaps starting with those he then kept a stone's throw away.[80] And he might also be struck by the necessity of concentrating his efforts on one thing at a time, on the problem at hand, and only later turn to the question of how the solutions thus devised could be connected to those already acquired. Finally, he would perhaps be surprised by Leibniz's tendency to gradually generalize his reasoning—*cum judicio.* That is to say, to gradually and skillfully broaden the spectrum of concepts, concrete facts, and observations. He would come to appreciate Leibniz's very special way of reasoning through subtleties, distinctions, reversals of discourse—so as to hold alternations and continuities together. These elements, as we know, would find fresh vitality in Hirschman's work.

17 – Furthermore, reading the second chapter of the "Anthological Exposition" Albert might have come across a "*topos*" that would have been immediately appealing to him.

Leibniz is known, in fact, to have intended to reduce all reasoning to calculations, with the aim of creating a single writing system, a common human language, for the purpose of facilitating understanding and especially verifying the correctness of reasoning. It was a noble, idealistic goal, but of course illusory (which may have intrigued Hirschman and brought a smile to his lips, but without winning him over—given his strenuous battle against all illusions).

And yet there is an advantage to such a way of proceeding. Indeed, pursuing this "*General Science, Characteristic, Ars inveniendi*" (an art of invention in general, that is), Leibniz wrote: "And since I have had the good fortune to perfect considerably the mathematicians' art of invention or analysis, I have begun to have certain fresh conceptions that aim to reduce all human reasoning to a

80 The surprise, of course, is certainly not that a young scholar kept such a desire "deep in his heart," but that he gradually succeeded in satisfying it, slowly creating his own approach and with it his own trans-disciplinary intellectual horizon within social science. This is therefore not a rhetorical or idle question. For Albert has shown that it is possible to learn the scientific craft.

kind of calculation that could be used to discover the truth, within the limits of what is possible *ex datis*, i.e., what is given or known to us. And when given knowledge is not enough to answer the posed question, this method, as in mathematics, would bring us as close as possible to a solution and allow us to determine exactly what is most probable."[81]

"The project," Colorni commented at this point, "was never realized. But what is interesting is the development in Leibniz's thinking that resulted from the studies he undertook for it. The method of arriving at these simple elements or "characters" from whose composition all the objects of human knowledge derive, is a method that involves *breaking down the ideas we find before us already composed*, starting from their definitions."[82] Are we not looking here at a way of proceeding (by "breaking down," and therefore, in reverse, by "building up") which, as we shall see, would preside over the solutions proposed by Hirschman regarding, for example, development economics in 1958,[83] and the debate on "*dependencia*" in 1978, the European Community in 1979?

The earliest (and perhaps most ingenious) formulation of this method is contained in the *Ars Combinatoria*, which Colorni recalls in footnotes via a lengthy excerpt.[84] "Any given term," Leibniz wrote, in this youthful work, "is resolved into its formal parts, that is, a definition of it is laid down; these parts are again resolved into parts, that is, a definition of the definition of the terms is laid down, and so on, right down to simple parts, or undefinable terms. For, 'one does not always look for a definition,' and these last terms are now better understood not by means of a definition, but by means of an analogy. As soon as one has found all the primitive terms they should be placed in one class and designated by certain symbols, It will be most convenient if they are numbers. Among the primitive terms should be placed not only things, but also modes or relations. Since the composite terms vary in their distance from the primitive terms according to the number of primitive terms they are composed of — that is, according to the exponent of the complexion [combination] — one must create as many classes as there are exponents, and terms that are composed of the same number of primitive terms should be included in the same class" etc.

81 Leibniz 1935 p. 31; Colorni 2023 p. 142. The passage is from "Letter to the Duke of Hanover," 1685.

82 Leibniz 1935 p. 33; Colorni 2023 p. 144. (Emphasis added).

83 Cf. above n. 47.

84 Leibniz 1935 pp. 33–4; Colorni 2023 p. 144. The passage is from *Ars Combinatoria* 1666.

18 – Moving on. In the other sections of this chapter (The Predicate Contained in the Subject, Freedom and Causality, Prediction and Predetermination) Albert would have encountered interesting ideas like learning experimentally or probabilistically as a consequence of cognitive imperfection, like contingent truths that "nudge" subjects without necessitating their behavior, or like freedoms and their limits.

But perhaps only at the beginning of the third chapter "Force and Motion," dedicated to natural philosophy, would Albert have again come across a problem that he could get excited about. "The problems analyzed here," Colorni explained,[85] "have a particular affinity with those of the physical sciences: the composition of matter, the existence or non-existence of atoms and of the vacuum, the origin and function of motion, energy, etc. For Leibniz the solutions to these problems do not derive from general principles of metaphysical philosophy. He deals with them as themselves, following techniques specific to them, maintaining his practice of getting to the heart of every inquiry while appropriating the particular characteristics of each science for his own use. Then later, having arrived at certain solutions and definitive positions, he relates them to the solutions obtained in the other fields, thus achieving ever richer and more comprehensive syntheses."

Could this be an opportunity—the young Hirschman might have wondered—to catch "in the act" Leibniz's way of proceeding? Unfortunately, this is an expectation that in Colorni's (albeit very thorough) exposition would not be fulfilled.

Take the concepts and their development. Leibniz abandons the atom as the basic element of matter because it is contrary to his principle of divisibility and continuity. He develops his theory of movement which arises from a starting point (*conatus*). Its extension in space forms matter, and its extension in time creates mind in the form of memory. But then he replaces the concept of movement with that of impetus or life force and finally links this approach of his to results obtained in other fields…

A young economist like Albert would have needed the patience of Job (or help from his mentor) to follow such reasoning step by step. But delving into

85 Leibniz 1935 p. 51; Colorni 2023 pp. 161–62.

the exposition of the monad (in the fourth chapter)[86] would have put a smile back on his face. A bit further on, in fact,[87] Eugenio wrote: "Just as in the art of combinations the goal was to find, by means of the decomposition of concepts, the simple terms of which human thought consists, and then, through various combinations of them, to form again every possible concept, so now an analytical investigation in the logical, physical, metaphysical field led to the notion of the monad as a simple substance, constituting the world. Now the task was to show concretely how the world consisted of monads, how every aspect, every phenomenon of it could be explained through combinations, modifications, and different aspects of monads."

19 – On the other hand, reading further, Albert would have discovered a concept that was soon to play a leading role in his own work (so much so that it would even become part of the 'familiar lexicon'[88])—the notion of small ideas linked to small perceptions.

"One monad by itself and at a single moment," Leibniz states, "cannot be distinguished from another except by its internal qualities and actions, and these can only be its *perceptions* (that is to say, the representations of the compound, or of that which is without, in the simple), and its *appetitions* (that is

86 "Two fundamental principles of Leibnizian philosophy," Eugenio wrote by way of presentation (Leibniz 1935 p. 74; Colorni 2023 pp. 183–84), "were examined in the previous chapters: the universality of individual substance, and the incorporeal principle of force in the material world. The first was derived from the elaboration of logical concepts, and the second from the rigorous consideration of physical theorems. The union and fusion of these two principles gives rise to the *monad*. What they have in common is the fact of enclosing within themselves, in a potential state, an infinite possibility of development. Individual substance is the starting point in a chain of causes and effects that encompasses within its links the past and the future of the entire universe, and the animated unity of the corporeal world is a force capable of developing motion and, despite its incorporeal character, of giving rise to the formation of materiality. Of these two elements, one is universal but abstract, while the other is concrete, real, incorporeal, but still without universality. In their fusion, one of them supplies what the other lacks, and the monad will be a principle that is immaterial and universal at the same time, but nevertheless concrete, such that it is what the existing world actually consists of."

87 Leibniz 1935 p. 76; Colorni 2023 p. 186.

88 Cf, Adelman 2013 p. 115.

to say, its tending from one perception to another) which are the principles of change."[89]

To make his reasoning coherent, Colorni explains,[90] "Leibniz appeals in this regard to *petites perceptions* or unfelt perceptions, which continue to influence the soul, even if they do not reach its consciousness. They belong to the soul's representation, but the soul is not aware of them. In this way, the absolute innatism of all truth, whether necessary or contingent, whether of reason or fact, is brought into agreement with the current limitation of our knowledge. Petites perceptions allow Leibniz to conceive of the monad as both limited and universal."

"At the same time, there are hundreds of pointers," Leibniz wrote,[91] "to the conclusion that at every moment there is in us an infinity of *perceptions*, alterations in the soul itself—however devoid of apperception[92] and reflection. We aren't aware of them because these impressions are too tiny and too numerous, or too unvarying, so that they don't stand out enough to be noticed. But when combined with others they do have their effect and make themselves felt, at least confusedly, within the whole. This is how we become so used to the motion of a mill or a waterfall, after living beside it for a while, that we don't attend to it. Its motion does still affect our sense organs, and something corresponding to that occurs in the soul…, but these impressions in the soul and the body, lacking the appeal of novelty, aren't forceful enough to attract our attention and our memory, which are occupied with more interesting things. Many of our own present perceptions slip by unconsidered and even unnoticed, but if someone alerts us to them right after they have occurred, e.g. making us take note of some noise that we've just heard, then we remember it and are aware of having had some sense of it."

---

89 Leibniz 1935 p. 82; Colorni 2023 p. 192. "For the simplicity of a substance," the passage continues (from *Principes de la nature et de la grace*, 1713–14), "does not prevent the plurality of modifications which must necessarily be found together in the same simple substance; and these modifications must consist of the variety of relations of correspondence which the substance has with things outside. In the same way there may be found, in one *center* or point, though it is perfectly simple, an infinity of angles formed by the lines which meet in it."

90 Leibniz 1935 p. 85; Colorni 2023 p. 194.

91 Leibniz 1935 p. 87; Colorni 2023 p. 196–97. The passage is from *New Essays*, 1701 ff., Preface.

92 "Apperception" refers to conscious perception (*Apercevoir:* notice) cfr. *Monadology* § 14.

Small perceptions, *decomposition*, *sequences* and more—these are methodological suggestions that would come back to Albert's mind and prove very useful. Time after time, like a small Atlas, Hirschman would lean on one or more of these stratagems to build a critical perspective on current thinking, and to propose alternative solutions, perhaps using such a starting point to build one of his "castelluzzi"—as he would later say in the manner of Machiavelli.[93] As we will see, his distinctiveness did not simply lied in his having identified an original observation, a small idea as such, perhaps through the mechanism of doubt and surprise; but rather in his having been able to develop on top of it its theoretical-practical consequences to the fullest, incorporating them and enriching them as he went along.

93 In a letter to Ursula Hirschmann, March 23rd 1966 (cit. in Adelman 2013, p. 146).

· 3 ·

EARLY WRITINGS*

A Few Cultural, Political and Professional Horizons

1 – Beyond his antifascist, federalist and socialist political activity, Albert above all admired Colorni's ability to be "a constant critic, questioner, stimulator."[1] "By 1937, at age twenty-two," Hirschman later recalled, "I had myself lost some of my earlier certainties, but, with my German upbringing, I still sensed it as a real defect not to have a full-fledged *Weltanschauung*. Colorni [...] seemed on the contrary to cultivate and relish an intellectual style that took

* A partial version of this essay appeared in English as the introduction to Albert O. Hirschman *Early Writings* 2024, Bern-New York, Peter Lang.

1 As he later wrote in a letter to Ursula in the early 1970s (cit. in Adelman 2013, p. 114). Colorni thus became Albert Hirschman's second mentor (the first, Heinrich Ehrmann, had initiated him at the age of fourteen into reading Karl Marx, Austro-Marxism, Lenin, etc. Fortunately, our author never became a doctrinaire Marxist: cf. Hirschman 1998 p. 48 and pp. 67–8).

nothing for granted [...].[2] At the same time, he and his friends held fast to one certainty: they were firmly committed to opposing the Fascist regime. What was fascinating to me was that there was an intimate connection between the intellectual posture emphasizing the lack of firm ideological commitment and the commitment to perilous political action."[3]

There was, therefore, a close relationship between great freedom of thought and risky political action experienced as "the natural, spontaneous, almost joyful counterpart" of such intellectual openness, without boundaries. Under the Fascist regime this meant learning to discipline one's own life, rigorously separating its official and clandestine aspects.[4] That this was no simple matter is shown, among other things, by Albert's first paper "Fertility of Italian Women by Age and Number of Children Borne" (mimeo, March 1937), which implicitly

2 Behind the scenes in this whole affair there was Eugenio's corrosive irony concerning systems in general, there were Leibniz's specific achievements, liberated from his claims of preset harmony, and there was the daily stimulating push from Colorni. Probably, young Albert had not fully mastered the whole "score" Eugenio had put in front of him, but he could sense ... that he was right. While maintaining his intellectual independence, he relied on his brother-in-law, and thus became in turn (methodologically) a kind of pioneer in "uncharted territory" in economics and the social sciences in general.

3 Hirschman 1990a pp. xxx–xxxi, 1995 pp. 118–19. The passage continues: "It was precisely the questioning and exploratory style with which Colorni and his friends were approaching philosophical, psychological and social issues that impelled them to action in situations where freedom of thought was suppressed, or where they felt that injustice was obvious and stupidity intolerable." Undoubtedly, outgoing as he was, Eugenio spoke with Albert about his studies in philosophy, psychology, physics, mathematics, etc. And in all likelihood he also explained how in the 17th century Leibniz, by focusing on a specific topic each time (small perceptions included), had managed to achieve amazing cultural discoveries. It was probably this philosophical "rib" that gave rise to what Hirschman later wrote in the famous dedication to Colorni that opens *Exit, Voice, and Loyalty*: "To Eugenio Colorni (1909–1944), who taught me about small ideas and how they may grow" (Hirschman 1970, Colorni 2023, Meldolesi 2023).

4 Paradoxically, it is this factor that Norberto Bobbio (1975 p. xxxix), referring to Eugenio Colorni, did not in my view sufficiently take into account.

criticized the policy of the regime[5] and was for this reason not published by the *Giornale degli Economisti*.[6]

In any case, we must not lose sight of the fact that the Trieste papers were written while Albert was doing "his work with the Italian anti-Fascists."[7] He had not taken a position favoring any particular antifascist current. He had simply "made himself available" as a friend of the movement against the regime. He was accordingly entrusted with the delicate (and risky) task of serving as liaison[8] with certain Italian antifascist exiles in Paris, which included importing to Trieste some of the underground antifascist literature. This was then channeled into working-class circles according to a novel logic, elucidated simply and persuasively by Eugenio Colorni in a now-famous essay.[9]

5 Cf. below; Hirschman 1998 p. 66; and Finzi 2004 p. 129. The first photocopied page of the article, delivered to me personally by Albert, contains an annotation in the margin advising greater caution (perhaps written by Pierpaolo Luzzatto Fegiz, director of the Institute of Statistics of the University of Trieste, or by Giorgio Mortara, editor of the *Giornale degli Economisti*) referring to *A Mathematical Theory of Population*, 1917, by George H. Knibbs. It reads: "Knibbs knew his subject well; which means he saw some difficulties that you do not see!" In any case, following this, in the summer of 1937, Mortara did warn Albert (Hirschman 1998 p. 68) that the situation in Italy was bound to get much worse: "much time will be needed before this obsession, this cholera, will be spent." "Mortara recommended that Hirschman not publish any more essays that questioned fascist data and policies so long as he remained in Italy – and indeed urged him to consider returning to Paris and offered to put him in contact with several of his colleagues there" (Adelman 2013, p. 150).

6 But Albert learned quickly. Indeed, in January 1938 he published (now in Hirschman 2025 ch. 2) a "Note on two recent tables of marriage rates in the Italian population" in the *Giornale degli Economisti* which came to the more modest (and not at all dangerous) conclusion concerning "a fine point of demographic statistics" (Hirschman 1995 pp. 117–18), according to which "two different tables of marriage and mortality rates for bachelors should be constructed and consulted according to the type of investigation to be undertaken."

7 Coser 1984 p. 163.

8 Mainly serving as a shuttle between Eugenio Colorni and Angelo Tasca (Hirschman 1998 p. 64). Indirectly, one can get an idea of this from Eugenio Colorni's 1937 correspondence with Joseph (Giuseppe Faravelli). Cf. Colorni 2019a.

9 Colorni 1937, 2019 ch. 2. It is a surprising and innovative article, contrary, at the time, to the prevailing doctrines inside the Workers Movement.

For Hirschman it amounted to a continuous back-and-forth[10] that made use of his pristine German passport.[11] In addition, instead of double-bottomed suitcases, which Italian inspectors sometimes checked, he made use—as he told me personally—of double lids that had been specially crafted for the purpose. It was the first instance of the ingenuity in clandestine activity that would become proverbial in Marseille.[12]

2 – In enrolling at the University of Trieste, Hirschman had of course presented ample documentation of his previous studies—attendance at a number of courses (halfway between economics and law) at the University of Berlin, his diploma from the École des Hautes Études Commerciales (HEC), and the courses he had taken at the London School of Economics (LSE).[13] He was thus permitted to enrol in the fourth year in the department of economics and business, but with the stipulation that in order to graduate he had to take five

10 Enabled by his ability to blend in (an attribute difficult to classify), along with his cool head, his premonition for what was about to happen, and his having quickly become something of a polyglot (with his native German, his perfect French, his English, and now his Italian); and also—it must be added—by the timidity (sense of inferiority, refuge in bureaucracy, etc.) with which Fascist officials of the time treated good-looking Germans…

11 "The strange thing was," Hirschman explained later (1998 p. 63) "that I had a German passport in good order, issued two years before, without any stamp indicating that I had entered in Spain or that I had left it!"

12 His main tasks within the Emergency Rescue Committee directed by Varian Fry were "obtaining passports, identity cards and other emigration documents for the refugees, devising escape routes they could use to get out of the country, and founding mechanisms for transferring money from the United States to support the Committee's activities," Franco Ferraresi "Laudatio," cit., November 13th 1987; Albert O. Hirschman 1990a p. xxvii, 2022 p. 23.

13 Cf. Finzi 2004 pp. 124–25. Courses in Elements of German Private and Public Law, History of Roman Law, General Political Economy, and Economic Policy at the University of Berlin; courses in Principles of Currency, International Trade and Foreign Exchanges, Banking, Banking in the United States, and Financing of Industry at the London School of Economics.

law exams[14] (as well as a "recommended" complementary exam—corporate law, of course).[15]

At the same time, Hirschman was thinking of his future profession.[16] In Paris he had attended, among others, the Institute de Statistique of the Université de Paris, which had issued him a "Certificat d'Aptitude." With this background, he was introduced in Trieste by Colorni to Pierpaolo Luzzatto Fegiz, director of the Institute of Statistics at the local university, and began to do some volunteer work of a sort[17] at that Institute as an internal student.

This experience—as already mentioned—soon gave rise to a genuine contribution in statistics concerning Italian demography[18]; and with it Hirschman glimpsed a first, possible, professional horizon. "My work at the time," he later maintained, "was mostly centered on demography, one of my real passions." And he added: "Because the Fascist regime, to promote its natalist policy, helped to publish many statistical data and studies in this field which

14 Ibid. p. 126. These were: Public Law Institutions, Business Law II and III, International Law, Financial Law and Finance Science.

15 For Albert, this "intensive treatment" in law turned out to be more or less indigestible. Despite this, by June 1937 he had passed four of the six exams that stood between him and graduation. But on October 25, 1937, he failed (with a ten even written on the booklet) the Commercial Law II/III exam. In addition, his request to be allowed to retake the exam in the second round of the fall session was not granted. ("It was as if they had flunked me all over again" – he told me). Thus Hirschman had to re-sit this exam on June 12, 1938, still scoring a meager 24/30 (ibid. pp. 127–28), which—inter alia—prevented him, as we shall see, from obtaining honors in the following graduation session.

16 Or rather—we shall see this better later—a kind of *multiple interrelated professions*—a kind of reasoning (also, in a sense, of Leibnizian-Colornian inspiration) which he later called "How One Thing Leads (or Does not Lead) to Another" (Hirschman 1958, 1995 ch. 3; Meldolesi 1995 ch. 3); and which he eventually placed alongside his theses on "trespassing" and "crossing boundaries" (Hirschman 1981, 1998).

17 Perhaps, the fact that Albert later considered this to be an assistant's position (Hirschman 1998 p. 63 and 66) is perhaps the first of his famous "half-truths" (which I will mention later: see n. 74).

18 "La fecondità della donna italiana secondo l'età e il numero di figli avuti. Osservazioni critiche" [Fertility of Italian Women by Age and Number of Children Borne. Some Observations.] (mimeo, March 1937; 2024 ch. 1). Some ingenious considerations, technically well argued, perhaps a bit impulsive, of no less than eleven full pages of criticism of a paper by Mario de Vergottini – "Tavole di fecondità della donna italiana secondo l'età e il numero di figli avuti" [Fertility Tables for Italian Women According to Age and Number of Children Borne] – which had appeared in the February 1937 issue of the *Giornale degli Economisti*.

have never been published before: for examples, on the fecundity of the Italian woman according to the number of children that have been conceived or have survived, and so on [...]. I based an article on it in which I demonstrated that the official policy could have counterproductive results: for example, when you had six children there would be four survivors, but when you had seven children there might be only three survivors. Therefore I asserted in the article that even from the point of view of a natalist policy it was absurd to give prizes to women who give birth to all these children! I thought it was a good argument and still think it is, but I still did not succeed in getting it published. Perhaps I shall publish it posthumously."[19] This is, indeed, a significant aspect of our "Hirschman's Legacy"—in fact, publisher Peter Lang and I are finally able to publish the essay—more than 8 decades after it was written![20]

3 – This brings us to a second horizon. In that period, Hirschman maintained retrospectively,[21] "I acquired a nicely limited area of competence: the Italian economy. I had come to Italy from France and had been asked by a Paris publication to send in, on a trial basis, some reports on the Italian economic situation.[22] At the time, the Mussolini regime began increasingly to restrict the publication of official economic statistics, so that it took some attentive reading of what did get published and of the daily financial press (*Il Sole, Ventiquattro Ore*)

19 Hirschman 1998 pp. 66–7. Of course, in the text this inspiration (admittedly amplified by memory) requires reading between the lines.

20 Note how the essay arose from the observation of some demographic statistics that potentially contradicted the conventional thinking on the subject. So that already in this first youthful work there is a "small idea" against the grain that is made to grow (cf. above n. 3). As we shall see below, even Albert's first book – *National Power and the Structure of Foreign Trade* (1945) – took off from some statistics (concerning Germany's foreign trade with some small and poor Balkan countries) that were at first glance of little importance, but instead were of decisive significance...

21 Hirschman 1990a p. xxx, 1995 p. 118.

22 Is it possible, Roberto Finzi wondered (2004 pp. 118–22), that Hirschman was given this assignment even before he had gained any expertise, however limited, in the Italian economy? Finzi looked for some clues in this regard (which, incidentally, did not concur) in various documents of the regime (which obviously were not to be taken retrospectively as gospel). I would answer his misgivings with the observation that in order to be able to claim that the commission (received "on probation" from Paris) must have materialized "*toward the end* of his stay in Trieste," my friend Roberto must not have had in his hands the essay in question—the one that Albert Hirschman gave me personally; and on whose photocopied facsimile he wrote in his own hand: "Ecrit en Italie et envoyé a Paris. Fin de mars 1938."

to figure out what was going on [...] I enjoyed the detective work involved, and whatever success I could claim in outwitting the Fascist authorities."[23]

The outcome of this experience was encouraging. Albert fired off "an accurate reconstruction of public finance (the budget, deficit financing, capital taxation of corporations), monetary policy, consumption, production and foreign trade. The "picture" or "pattern" that emerged [to be read in France of course, not in Fascist Italy] showed that in spite of its capable management at a technical level, the autarkic and war production policies of fascism actually produced hypertrophic growth in the public sector and were at the root of numerous signs of impoverishment of the population and suffocation of the productive and financial apparatus."[24]

Hirschman's intention was that "Les finances et l'économie italienne. Situation actuelle et perspectives," published anonymously in Paris on 1 June 1938 by the *Supplément au bulletin quotidien* of the "Société d'études et d'informations économiques,"[25] would be the start of a possible profession as an economic journalist specializing in the Italian economy—a prospect that was instead brutally interrupted by the enactment of the Fascist racial laws and then by the outbreak of the war.

Moreover, "Les finances et l'économie italienne" is a quite different kind of paper, much more lively and instructive, than what might *ex ante* have been expected—not only for its intelligent and careful reconstruction of such a "Situation actuelle et perspectives," but also because it clearly shows the extraordinary continuity of the author's multidisciplinary inspiration (first and foremost psychological and social, but also statistical, economic and financial)—in its developmental process.[26]

---

23 Hirschman 1938a, 2025 ch. 3. "Les finances et l'économie italiennes," he wrote, "sont de plus en plus difficilement pénétrables. [...]. Pour avoir an idée approximative de ce que peut être la situation financière du Royaume, on en est réduit à une méticuleuse compilation de quelque communiqués officiels du Conseil des Ministres et du Grand Conseil du Fascisme, des exposés fort peu explicites du Ministre des Finances à la Chambre et au Senat, des études toujours très discrètes paru dans les journeaux et les revues de la Peninsule."

24 Meldolesi 1995 p. 8.

25 Hirschman 1938a. The essay demonstrates without a shadow of a doubt that the "trial period" under which Hirschman had been commissioned by the "Société" had been passed brilliantly.

26 Such that, at an interpretive level, it already suggests (as we shall see better below) a point of view partly *alternative* to that expressed by our friends Pierfrancesco Asso and Marcello de Cecco (1987 p. 35).

It is as if, by focusing each time on a different aspect of his work, Hirschman was implicitly drawing together (or perhaps allowing to emerge spontaneously from deep in his mind) the many acquisitions—at first glance disparate, but in reality highly relevant to his specific purpose—which he had "stored up," perhaps even unconsciously, during the course of his intellectual and political wanderings through some of the major European countries.

In this essay, in fact, Hirschman lists in rapid succession the three essential factors that had permeated Italian economic life in recent years (the war in Abyssinia, rearmament, and repeated efforts favoring autarky), along with their economic and financial consequences (which increased government spending from one-third to one-half of national income). Furthermore, he identifies the main types of measures that were used to cover the deficit these factors caused in the national budget (long-term loans, short-term loans, inflation, and miscellaneous means)—going on to address in detail the tax on the capital of joint stock companies.[27]

This last element in particular shows (unexpectedly) a distinctive technical virtuosity that leads Hirschman to the following conclusion: "The operation, it has to be said, is masterly. The shareholders actually pay the tax for the company, but not only do they hardly notice it, since they each receive a share in exchange, they even believe they are making a profit, since they receive two free shares for each share subscribed. And, in fact, they can sell their subscription rights for an immediate gain, unaware of the reduction in capital value their shares have suffered or will suffer as a result of the tax." Thus, scrolling through the text, one undoubtedly senses that the technical prowess (not just economic in the strict sense!) of Italian officials at the time exerted a considerable attraction on the young scholar—almost revealing *ante litteram* an attitude that would characterize him in the future.

"In general," Hirschman on the other hand concluded "remaining faithful to a long and famous tradition, Italian finance makes technology give everything it is capable of giving. This does not preclude the fact that the current amount of military and investment spending should be considered exceptional, and that the indefinite continuation of this strain would create an

27 That is, the institution of a 10% levy on the capital of joint stock companies: "*by far the most important measure of the dual financial and economic point of view.*" (Emphasis added)

impoverishment and disintegration of the economic and monetary system that no financial science, no matter how skillful, would be able to avert."[28]

Some Early Writings on France and Italy

4 – To conclude his studies, Hirschman had to attend his graduation session, presenting (and discussing with the college of professors) a thesis and two additional papers.[29] The first of these latter, in economic geography[30] (under Prof. Giorgio Roletto), was entitled "Whether and in What way the Economic Element was a Determining Factor in the Philippine Islands' Independence." The second, in statistical science (under Prof. Pierpaolo Luzzatto Fegiz), had the title "Two Methods for Constructing Marriage-Rate Tables," and clearly echoed the "Note" that Hirschman had published six months earlier in the *Giornale degli Economisti*.[31] The "centerpiece" of Albert's degree, however, was of course his thesis, *The Poincaré Franc and its Devaluation*,[32] supervised by Jewish-born Prof. Renzo Fubini (later tragically killed at Auschwitz).

28 The exploration that followed, contained in "Histoire de la Lire de la revalorisation au contrôle des changes" [History of the Lira from Revaluation to Exchange Control] (1938e, 2025 ch. 5: cf., below notes 49 and 61), inevitably leads to a more elaborate and interesting picture of the situation and its prospects, which become progressively bleaker. "The history of Italian currency," the paper concludes, "has been very uneven since Fascism took over its fortunes. Interventionism, contrary to the early economic program, but so in keeping with the very essence of Fascism, had already revealed itself through the experience of revaluation. At that time it still had to hedge itself with orthodox buzzwords, such as abandoning forced circulation, and returning to the gold system. During the crisis, the Fascist state gained control of the banking system and key industries out of necessity rather than its own initiative. In the third period, Fascism, having become fully aware of its power over the national economy, isolated the Lira from freely negotiable currencies and made it a cog in the direction of the entire economy toward essentially extra-economic ends. Gradually, often reluctantly, the Lira had changed fields, just as Italy had."

29 Finzi 2004 p. 129.

30 Economic geography "a la française," a friendly subject for Albert ever since he had attended Albert Demangeon's classes at the HEC in Paris. (See Hirschman 1995 p. 116).

31 Cf. above, n. 6.

32 Hirschman graduated with a score of 110 (although, much to the dismay of some commissioners, it was not deemed worthy of honors). "At this point," the author stated retrospectively (1998 p. 68), "Ursula, Eugenio and I went for a brief vacation to Selva di Val Gardena in the Dolomites. It was July and immediately afterward I left for Paris. Eugenio was arrested with a great deal of fanfare as soon as he returned to Trieste. This would certainly have happened to me too, as I was denounced in the Fascist press as a collaborator with Eugenio and as a German Jew."

Through this challenging text, I would like to touch briefly on another, more important professional horizon that seemed to open up for Albert during his stay in Trieste. For this purpose, however, it is necessary to take a step back—almost to pick up the argument from the beginning.

It is first of all necessary to take into account—as I have already mentioned—the fact that Hirschman's early cultural and political development had taken place within a German cultural context (including, of course, the influence of a Labor Movement which, in its various components, claimed to be the beating heart of a great process of social emancipation on an international scale).[33] It is true, moreover, that contemporary political events had pushed our author, along with his sister Ursula, onto a path of rapid politicization.[34]

On the other hand, Albert had from a very early age shown a notable attraction for French culture, and, comparing it to German culture, had even in a sense experienced a premonitory 'friction' between the two. In 1931–32, in fact, while attending the Fronzösische Gymnasyum in Berlin, he took part in a group working on Hegel's *Phenomenology of the Spirit* and wrote a short dissertation on a passage that "today appears incomprehensible to its own author. 'Perhaps,' he observed, 'the torment of having to make sense of Hegel had an unintended side effect later in France: to make me fall in love with the French moralists of the 17th century, such as Pascal and La Rochefoucauld; they seemed to me just as deep, but in a marvelously easygoing manner.'"[35]

In Paris,[36] this early philosophical attraction for French culture began to "expand" to literature, poetry and the arts, and especially to statistics and

33 In this regard, I would say that Christian Fleck (2020 pp. 383–94) is right to maintain that biographical reconstructions of the beginnings of Albert's life and work (including my own) do not sufficiently take account of his youthful politicization and the two-way relationship it had with his early way of thinking. Cf. Adelman 2013 ch. 2 and 3 passim.

34 Clearly linked to his interest in Marxism, classical economics and economic crisis theory. Among many activities, he and his sister Ursula participated in a conference held by Otto Bauer on the "long Kondratieff cycle" (Adelman 2013 p. 66)—a theme that not coincidentally would reappear later in Hirschman's work (but in a self-deprecating vein) at the beginning of *Shifting Involvements* (1982).

35 Hirschman 1984a p. 2–3, Meldolesi 1995 p. 4. "This 'falling in love' which extended to Montaigne and Diderot and 'the whole eighteenth century' [Hirschman 1990 p. 155] is perceptible in the first chapter of the *National Power and the Structure of Foreign Trade* (1945), and is further manifested in *The Passions and the Interests*." Meldolesi 1995, p. 217, n. 2.

36 Paris soon became his city of choice, the starting and ending point of his many European forays.

economics. In addition, in his travels he had again encountered the effects of the Great Depression (less severe in France than in Germany, but getting worse). It is therefore likely that Hirschman's wish (understandably) was to become a public economist, engaged in government activities, and his first choice for training would therefore have been the "École libre des sciences politiques" (SciencesPo).

Instead, he was authoritatively dissuaded from this decision,[37] and ended up enrolling at the "École des Hautes Études Commerciales" (HEC), a sort of *ante litteram* business school devoted mainly to accounting and the rudiments of engineering.[38] His disappointment was very great.[39] And yet, viewed retrospectively, this two-year experience had the double advantage of opening Albert's eyes to the world of private business (which would later stand him in good stead, above all in the second part of his postwar adventure in Colombia), and at the same time not preventing him from pursuing his goal of becoming an economist dealing with public policy.[40]

---

37 Hirschman 1995 ch. 8.

38 "I did enroll at HEC," Hirschman later recalled (ibid. pp. 115–16), "and spent two exhausting years there. I had a lot of courses in accounting and something called technology, which was about various sequences of industrial operations invariably starting, I seem to recall, with *concassage* (crushing)." He nevertheless made actual progress just the same in some subjects, mainly in banking and monetary economics, international trade (up to a point) and economic geography—three fields, each of which left an important mark on his work. In the preparation, that is, of his thesis, (*The Poincaré Franc and its Devaluation* – 1938b, 2004, 2025 ch. 4), in the genesis of his first monograph (*National Power and the Structure of Foreign Trade* – 1945), and of *The Strategy of Economic Development* (1958): cf., on this, Hirschman 1995 p. 116.

39 Mainly because Albert had no intention of going into business or even one of the many business-type professions (although, at one point, he did have to consider a job in a bank, which, however, did not pan out).

40 Although the child of several continental European cultures, Albert Hirschman (1990 p. 153) considered himself an autodidact from a professional standpoint. In fact, after his first semester of economics and law at the University of Berlin, he didn't learn much economics in the strict sense in Paris, mainly because the discipline was still largely marginal to French mainstream culture. For this reason his year in London turned out to be particularly important in his education as an economist. "Actually," Hirschman later wrote (1995 p. 118), "this experience fitted well with another of a more fundamental nature, which came to me through the example of my brother-in-law and friend, Eugenio Colorni." Paradoxically, it might be argued, it was thanks to this uneven type of economic training that he was so ready to learn the even more fundamental lesson imparted to him by Eugenio and his intellectual circle, and to begin, by that route, a journey as a *sui generis* economist who proved over time to be original and creative.

5 – Actually, it was during his years at HEC that Hirschman developed an interest in statistics and applied economics – "a certain kind of inductive applied economics (intelligently presented factual reconstruction) that was nurtured by the Parisian ambiance. It is important to remember,"[41] I observed on this point, "that there were several features which, for a series of reasons generally left aside, were peculiar to French economics at the time. These include an inclination toward practical descriptions of economic facts, a fair degree of tolerance for various schools of thought (liberal, historical, social, mathematical, sociological etc.), and a marked interest in the political aspects of economics [...]. This, together with HEC courses on money and banking taught [...], probably made up the breeding ground of Hirschman's research projects on French monetary policy from the 1920s to the 1930s."

"I had had some excellent teachers in economic geography, and in money and banking, such as Albert Demangeon and Henry Pomméry" – Albert Hirschman stated on the occasion of his honorary degree in economics at Nanterre (Paris) 1993a. Moreover, he added later on, "from the point of view of my intellectual formation, it was very important to understand what was then happening in modern economics. For me this [1935–36] was a decisive year,[42] even though the London School was not at all Keynesian. It was rather anti-Keynesian—in fact Lionel Robbins and Friedrich von Hayek were among

41 Meldolesi 1995 pp. 6–7. Cf. also Dumez 1985 and Meldolesi 1991. At that time, political economy was taught very differently in different European countries, from the German historical school in Berlin and the applied-statistical approach in Paris, to London's economics. When viewed from a different angle (cf. previous note), this unevenness, which undoubtedly made life difficult for a young student exile, contributed quite by accident to an unusual process of education – the intellectual harbinger of interesting, unpredictable (and thus actually ... unforeseen!) developments. That is both (as we shall see below) in terms of the subject's central role, which was inevitably elicited by the unfolding of dramatic events, and from the point of view of the multiplicity of environments and themes encountered along the way (perhaps at the expense of systematicity), which our author soon learned to turn gradually to his own advantage (fending for himself, getting by, and adapting to reality while remaining vigilant and active) with respect to his own theoretical and practical goals, pursued with extraordinary constancy and ingenuity.

42 Of course, it is one thing to understand what it is all about, another to be ensnared by it (like a passing gnat attacked by a carnivorous plant), yet another to be able to protect oneself from the "dictatorship" of Economics, and another finally to know how to use it for one's own ends (and within what limits). Albert certainly learned Economics in London and later used it for some specific parts of his work (think of *National Power, Exit, Shifting*). But at the same time he did the things he already knew how to do—the use of statistical data, applied research, curiosity regarding the actual workings of state monetary management, etc.

its principal teachers. I took some of their courses. [...] There were also [...] some excellent teachers of international trade."[43]

6 – One can sense from this passage the attitude that Hirschman was beginning to develop towards economics. His idea was to learn the various theories and thoroughly weigh their utility for his own purposes (as witness his adopting a Keynesian position on various occasions)—but without 'taking sides,' without fully embracing the veracity of such theses, nor pushing himself to theorize further by perhaps joining one of the various currents that advocated them, claiming that they were 'self-contained' (and bomb-proof!),[44] without (even implicitly) asserting their validity *at the expense* of different knowledge from other disciplines or experiences (but rather, on the contrary, seeking to appraise by degrees the eventual combination of one with the other).

From then on, as Marcello de Cecco rightly observed,[45] from the time he negatively evaluated some of the English criticism of the French economic-financial policies of the 1920s and 1930s, "Hirschman seems to have resisted the tendency to turn economic theory and practice into orthodoxy and was apparently conscious of the legitimacy of those who appealed to both theoretical and practical pluralism. There are many roads that the financial organization that accompanies the development of capitalism can take and just as many that those who study it can tread."

43 Hirschman 1998 p. 59. In June 1919, as Giorgio La Malfa (2023) has recently recalled, Keynes, who had worked at the British Treasury during the First World War and had "participated in the Paris peace conference as a representative of the ministry, resigned in disagreement with the stance that the U.S., Britain and France intended to take toward the peace treaty. Following this he published *The Economic Consequences of the Peace*, his indictment against reparations—that they were senseless and would create such resentments that a new war would ensue 'before which the horrors of the late German war will fade into nothing.'" In addition, in 1923 he published *A Tract on Monetary Reform*, translated into Italian by Piero Sraffa in 1925, in which he wrote that "fortunately for the Italian taxpayer and Italian business, the Lira does not listen even to a dictator and cannot be given castor oil." Finally, as is well known, Keynesian polemic towards the traditional recessionary policies of neoclassical economics had taken the path of high theory.

44 "It was a great relief," Hirschman declared in retrospect (1990a p. xxx, 1995 p. 118), "to realize that one could do tolerably competent work in economics without having to resolve whether Keynes, whose *General Theory* I had bought in London in the year of its publication (1936) and then taken along to Italy for study, had all the right answers." Probably, this consideration already suggests a more general idea. Namely, that it was not necessary to bind oneself hand and foot to a specific economic theory (whatever it was) in order to be able to do the job of an economist decently—an issue to which I will return later.

45 de Cecco 2004 p. xii.

On the other hand, as Hirschman pointed out,[46] "I didn't follow a regular plan of studies [at the London School of Economics] [...]. I decided to study for my own account [...] the economic reform of 1925–26 and the history of the "franc Poincaré."[47] At the time, this was an important topic for the French, and since I had lived in France and was convinced I would return there, I decided to study some problems of recent French economic history. I started a research project in this field under the supervision of Professor Barrett Whale,[48] a fine teacher in international economics at the London School. This was in effect the project I developed later in my dissertation in Trieste."

It is important, I think, to emphasize this point. Albert had undertaken this work on recent monetary history *for the French intellectual market*, thinking that he could establish (and prove) himself in Paris as an expert on economics

46 Hirschman 1998 pp. 59–60.

47 Even choosing to take some courses that could help him in that endeavor. It is also likely that, in their opposition, the (not always accurate) criticism of French economic policies coming from the British government and financial circles played a significant role. Albert had become aware of this on arriving in London. And he probably began to realize that even in Anglo-Saxon countries, instead of an attempt to understand others, the claim prevailed (even among the educated) that others should exist "in their own image and likeness."

48 Whale was at the time Reader in Economics at the University of London. Judging from *International Trade* (1932), a booklet written for "The Home University Library of Modern Knowledge" that Albert included in his thesis bibliography, Whale's course at the London School of Economics was probably for 'beginners.' If so, Hirschman would have followed it as mental exercise to master the typical arguments of the traditional economic discipline relating to foreign trade (precisely those indicated by the chapter titles of that booklet: The Technique of International Payments, Foreign Exchange Rates and the Balance of Payments, The Theory of International Price Equilibrium, Disequilibrium in the Balance of Payments, The Theory of Comparative Costs and the International Division of Labour, Protection and the Regulation of International Trade, Commercial Treaties and Tariff Bargaining, The Prospects of International Trade). If this hypothesis has merit, then it is likely that Whale, despite his articles in *Economica* of 1936–37 ("International Trade in the Absence of an International Standard" and "The Working of the Pre-War Gold Standard"), was basically a supervisor at LSE focused on economic plausibility, rather than an economist participating in what Hirschman was then writing about the history of the Poincaré Franc. In other words, from what I can make out, I have come to the conclusion that in London Albert did indeed acquire some expertise on the subject, but that it was mainly the blending of this learning with his previous experience and with the many specific insights, from the point of view of analysis and policies, that he gradually unearthed about the Poincaré Franc that ultimately enabled him to give such a brilliant, clear and attractive theoretical-practical exposition of economic history.

and finance in a research center, or even as a theoretical-practical technician in the vast world that gravitated to (or was part of) the French public system. It was only after this that he thought to utilize the manuscript of "The Poincaré Franc" to get his degree in Italy.[49] The paper, in fact originally written in French, was translated by the author[50] into Italian ('making adjustments' here and there and probably developing a few points to fit with its new purpose), and in the end became Hirschman's graduation thesis.

In this regard, I think de Cecco was right to argue that it is an 'economic report' (in disguise)—almost as if it had been commissioned by a public authority, and not really a thesis in the usual sense of the term.[51] "It is a report of very high quality," he wrote, "firstly because it avoids any redundancy, dissecting the subject matter with elegant parsimony, but also because, from the very first page, it places the reader 'in medias res,' mixing facts and theories without any

49 This was a providential decision since, given the political situation, his graduation thesis obviously could not have been on the Italian economy. But the production line opened by *The Poincaré Franc and its Devaluation* continued (not surprisingly) with "L'histoire de la Lire de la revalorisation au contrôle des changes" [History of the Lira from Revaluation to Exchange Control], 1938e—a sort of *ante litteram* trespassing, in the sense that a certain way of setting up the work that had been tested on one country was then re-proposed (*mutatis mutandis*) for another. [On the other hand, it is true that, in his prewar analyses, Albert treated the economic policies of France and Italy separately, while —as Asso and de Cecco (1987 pp. 35–6) have argued—at the time of the Marshall Plan one was mirrored in the other. Yet this text on the history of the Lira in late 1938 (which de Cecco probably did not know of) shows that *a point of contact and transition from one to the other had existed previously*].

50 Translated by Hirschman himself, with a "Frenchifying" tone, sometimes inaccurate (e.g. referring to what in good Italian is the balance of payments as the "balance of accounts"). So that in Michael Gilmartin's English translation of 2024, account was taken both of the original text (which was given to me personally by Hirschman) and its inaccuracies, as well as of the 2004 "Trieste" publication of the thesis edited by Giorgio Gilbert.

51 In fact, Marcello continued (ibid. pp. vii-viii), "anyone reading Hirschman's thesis will immediately realize that it does not follow any of the canonical rules of Italian dissertations." That is to say, it does not adhere to "the tried-and-true template resulting from centuries of experience, in which the writer usually begins with a critical review of the literature" by which "he or she hedges against the possibility that the personal analysis of the thesis topic, which usually comes immediately after the review, is unoriginal. Normally, the main purpose of the thesis is academic—you want to show that you know the theories and can connect them to the facts, which are of interest only because they prove one or another alternative theoretical hypothesis." Obviously this was not Albert Hirschman's purpose!

rigidity in a relentless search for convincing explanations of French economic policies in the turbulent two decades between the World Wars."[52]

It is here, I would add, that our author's style gets its start—a style that is sober, free, professionally (and culturally) competent, pared down, sometimes ironic, and captivating. The layout of this thesis-report follows the temporal sequence of the issue as observed from different points of view: "Some Thoughts on French Monetary Policy after the de facto Stabilization of the Franc"; "French Monetary History from 1930 to the First Devaluation of the Franc"; "The Franc from an Economic Viewpoint (1931–1937)."

Having thus overcome the difficulty of 'immersion' in a subject that is anything but easy, the reader is (pleasantly!) surprised by the flow of pages dealing first of all with the Franc from a monetary point of view. The unexpected 'verve' of the text also lies, in my opinion, in a bold decision that had been made upstream. Namely, that of consciously leaving in the background (without losing sight of it) the solid theoretical framework of his supervisor,[53] while, at the same time, in his reconstruction, placing the history (essential, lively, full of unexpected reversals) of the Poincaré Franc and its devaluation ahead of the 'hard' economic-statistical facts—which are certainly very useful, but which, had they been used as an introduction, would certainly have veiled the reasoning.[54] That is to say, if Hirschman had followed the reverse path—the academic path that would privilege the exposition of theories and statistical data over historical reconstruction, the latter would have lost much of its appeal and effectiveness.

The socio-political environment "is sketched out in brief but effective hints and references. But the heart of the analysis deals with the economic policy problems of French governments, and the aim is to report on them as

52 Ibid. p. viii.

53 Cf. Whale 1932, 1935, 1936.

54 In the sense that it would have almost taken for granted an element that was undoubtedly crucial to Albert's reconstruction—the *ex ante* unpredictable nature of what was about to take place, not least because of the continually evolving constellation of internal and external circumstances conditioning the path of the currency. Opening "The Franc from an Economic Viewpoint," the third part of his thesis-report, Hirschman writes: "Up to now we have considered the Franc from a purely monetary standpoint—that is, we have mainly examined its surface phenomena. A chapter was dedicated to public finance since developments here were generally the immediate point of departure for monetary change. But it should not be forgotten that the situation of public finance and the decrease in revenue are themselves merely effects—whose causes are to be found in the economic crisis."

an economist—one who has at his disposal the most up-to-date panoply of analytical tools; including, of course, those that Keynes had just set forth in the *General Theory*, which Hirschman makes effective use of in his work."[55]

The reader's surprise (including de Cecco's[56]) lies precisely in the competent, but also passionate, sometimes irreverent style of the narrative. In fact, with a youthful impetuosity (tempered inevitably by the subject matter), the author presents here an elegant *pièce*, one might say, of French financial history punctuated by plot twists, more or less appropriate interventions by the monetary authorities and successive governments, strategic attacks and retreats, outside influences, fortuitous outcomes—sometimes lucky, sometimes not, and so on. It's one monetary skirmish after another—all solid harbingers of changing fortunes that at times pull the reader along, as if in a novel.[57]

To make my point, I will briefly offer a bird's eye view of certain aspects of Hirschman's reconstruction. The cause of the French monetary crisis, the author explains, is not to be sought in problems of private credit, as was the case in other developed countries, but in the trend of public debt. In 1932–33 the economic crisis did not seem serious, to the extent that the radical governments practiced an economic policy of waiting for better times. But in 1934 the situation worsened and the government decided on a policy of strict deflation of the public budget which, at least in its intentions, was meant to be "accompanied by general economic deflation—by a decrease in production costs: tax relief through fiscal reform, lower short- and long-term interest rates, and a reduction in the cost of living and consequent lower wages. But the only real achievement of the government was reducing the short-term interest rate."[58]

---

55 "Hirschman," de Cecco finally observed (2004 p. ix and xv), "is aware of the necessity, in his thesis, of having to remain on the high road of economic analysis in order to show his professionalism, without giving away too much to the other social sciences. Fortunately for the reader, this strict intent is sometimes betrayed by the young author." Because, I would add, what Albert writes shouldn't just be interesting for the reader (and defensible in the graduation session), it should also be convincing—first of all: for the author himself.

56 I can testify that in the 1980s Marcello de Cecco invited Hirschman several times (unsuccessfully) to theorize in his own way on monetary issues—both intellectual and historical.

57 And it also initiates, then and there, the theme of Hirschman's historical reconstructions, which after these events involving the Poincaré Franc, would cover (again according to the logic of trespassing) topics as diverse as the Latin American policy making in *Journeys* or the evolution of the economic-political culture of the seventeenth-eighteenth century in *The Passions*.

58 Hirschman 2004 p. 21.

The country's economic situation thus deteriorated further as the government, albeit with some second thoughts and wobbles, decided to increase its deflationary medicine with the July 1935 decrees—to the point where a change in economic policy was finally inevitable. Blum's Popular Front government thus embarked on a policy of "reflation" in 1936–37, subordinating budget balance to economic recovery. However, due to the overall context (international and domestic reasons—doctrinal-punitive on the one hand, political-social on the other) this eventually led to devaluation.

It will already be clear from these first hints how the fortunes of the currency and those of economic policy are interrelated, and how the history of the Poincaré Franc can be explored a little at a time by "juggling" with the trend of the public debt and the interest rate, the movements of capital in and out, the alternating trends of the crisis, etc. What emerges is an ever-evolving fresco of problems and solutions traced with surprising expertise and a sure hand, and then confirmed point by point, as mentioned, by the final part of this thesis-report.[59]

Obviously it was not only a question of professional interest. Hirschman was attracted by the complexity of the situation as observed from the monetary angle, and by the Parisian world. He wanted to dig into the financial workings of the crises that repeatedly occurred in those years, not least to get a handle on their developmental processes from a technical-historical standpoint.

But the reverse is also true. That is to say, as mentioned before, the dramatic nature of the situation that was taking shape had spurred Albert to make every effort to understand how things actually were. This, if I'm not mistaken, led to his decision (by no means a foregone conclusion) to become a sort of auditor at the LSE, and to work at the same time on his own (under Barrett Whale's supervision). Because Hirschman had judged these decisions to be

59 For example, the conclusion regarding devaluation undoubtedly had its limitations (in order of magnitude so as to agree in advance with the United States and England, in the partly unavoidable social adjustments it brought with it, in the harmful gold import-export legislation, etc.). Yet, I would add, after much deflation and prevarication, the public authorities found the courage to actually devalue the Franc, thus paving the way for a second realignment (still in progress at the time the text was written).

most in keeping with his own personal, intellectual and political needs (which inevitably interacted with one another).

7 – Back in Paris (and under the circumstances forced to remain there[60]) Albert put to use the *expertises* he had acquired in Italy.[61] "I was able," he later affirmed, "to establish myself as an expert on the Italian economy, writing quarterly reports on it for a newly founded Institute on Economics and Social Research directed by Charles Rist and Robert Marjolin."[62] In that role he came into contact with John Bell (Jack) Condliffe,[63] a New Zealand economist who had studied at Cambridge (UK) and was organizing a "Conference generale d'études sur les politiques economiques et la paix" a Bergen, in Norway, for the League of Nations.[64]

60 In fact, Albert had narrowly escaped the September 9, 1938 police raid that led to the capture, imprisonment and then internment of his brother-in-law. Cf. above, n. 32.

61 Among other things, in the wake of his thesis, he wrote (as mentioned in notes 28 and 49) "Histoire de la Lire de la revalorisation au contrôle des changes"—an essay that at the prudent behest of its author did not even appear in "Albert Hirschman's Works," the bibliography I (*temporibus illis*) had painstakingly reconstructed (Meldolesi 1995 p. 293).

62 Hirschman 1990a p. xxx, 1995 p. 118. "I met Marjolin first in Paris in 1938," Albert later wrote more explicitly (1998 p. 36 and pp. 36–7). "Marjolin gave me my first job as the Italian specialist in *L'Activité économique*, a quarterly review on recent economic trends in Europe, which he published for the new Rockefeller Foundation-financed 'Institut de Recherches Economiques et Sociales.' At twenty-eight years, he [Marjolin] did not show any traces of his unorthodox upbringing; rather, he seemed to me by then a true *patron* (or boss), perhaps a bit too cordial to a newcomer like myself. Only when I was allowed to meet the actual *patron de la maison*, who was none other than Charles Rist, the eminent economist and former governor of the Bank of France, did I realize that there were many shades of *patrons* in this world."

63 A noted French statistician, Henri Piatier, who had read Albert's pieces on Italy (and had met him) spoke of him to Condliffe (Adelman 2013 p. 162).

64 "Conference generale d'études sur les politiques economiques et la paix," Institut International de Coopération Intellectuelle, Société des Nations, Paris, June 1939. For obvious reasons the projected conference took place only in part. Condliffe's opening paper and Piatier's summary on exchange controls were published in 1940, while most of the other papers, including specific studies on 82 different countries, circulated in mimeograph form.

At Condliffe's request, Albert then wrote "Mémoire sur le contrôle des changes en Italie,"[65] a highly detailed and important report on various aspects of the question[66]: the origin of controls, their administrative organization, the mechanisms of payment, trade policies, currency, the economy, and economic trends.[67]

Another paper he wrote for Condliffe was "Étude statistique sur la tendence du commerce extérieur vers l'equilibre et le bilateralisme."[68]

65 In this report, as in the thesis on *Il Franco Poincaré*, as Marcello de Cecco later observed (2004, p. x and xiii), "Hirschman's analyses and judgments have stood the test of time. The self-assurance with which he offers his own viewpoint on the political, economic and social dilemmas of the 'Latin sisters' in the decades between the two wars is equaled only by their ability to endure at a distance." And again, "those familiar with Hirschman's output [...] cannot help but notice [...] his special attention to the interweaving of economics, psychology, sociology and politics—something that has consistently fascinated our author."

66 In which "there is not much space for theoretical reflection" (Asso and de Cecco 1987, p. 20). Even here, however, Hirschman follows his inspiration, which spontaneously crosses traditional disciplinary boundaries through psychological, political, institutional, military, social, etc. observations. Observe, for example, how much he wrote to explain how Italy managed to cope with the large trade deficit in 1937. While "L'histoire de la Lire" (cf. above, notes 28, 49 and 61) anticipates the conclusions, the "Mémoire sur le contrôle des changes" presents numerous analytical aspects of the question. Taken together, the two papers offer the reader a convincing picture. Much of Albert's work arises in this way—from his being struck by reality, including through statistics, and then puzzling over it and finally identifying the interpretation that he considers most appropriate.

67 This "essay on Italy," Asso and de Cecco wrote (1987 pp. 19–20), "is [...] one of the few papers concerned with this issue. It is worth presenting even if only for this reason." And the opportunity to do so is heightened by archival findings and subsequent studies that have confirmed the "information skills and remarkable gifts of insight and analysis" that the 23-year-old Hirschman displayed in this work. (cf. also Meldolesi 2013 p. 79 and n. 9). Going through this text it is easy to see that Albert's expertise on the Italian economy had reached a surprisingly advanced level—especially regarding the intricate state-controlled trade network which at the time, with its sub-imperialist nature in relation to Germany, characterized the economic structure of our country. (Together with the statistics on German trade, this detailed knowledge of exchange controls in Italy in all probability had a significant role in the genesis of *National Power*).

68 In "Étude statistique," Albert placed his youthful statistical expertise at the service of economic analysis and initiated a fourth professional horizon, the statistical-economic exploration of international trade. (With the author's consent, the "Indices of Bilateralism" that it contains would later be published in fine print by Jack Condliffe in 1940 p. 283).

"Using the formula of standard deviation to measure the extent to which imports and exports from and to particular countries are consistent with the relation between total imports and exports," Condliffe recalled, "Mr. Hirschmann has calculated indices of bilateralism" for five countries: Great Britain, Germany, The Netherlands, Belgium and Sweden. The result (1929–37) showed a strong trend toward bilateralism (and thus an exit from multilateralism) for all five of these countries…

Confirming previous studies made with different methods by the Economic Intelligence Service of the League of Nations, "Dr. Hirschmann's results," Condliffe added,[69] "offer striking evidence of the extent to which bilateral is replacing multilateral trade.[70] There are three main reasons why this trend to bilateralism has been economically disadvantageous in recent years. It destroys the effective international specialization that is based upon price comparisons in a world market, directs trade into politically rather than economically advantageous channels, and renders this trade more erratic since the bilateral bargains on which it depends may be abruptly terminated for political reasons."[71]

Small Perceptions

8 – All this happened *just before* Hirschman became absorbed by political-military involvement in the Second World War. An adventure that included enlistment in and then demobilization from the French army, and eventually led him to the Marseilles exploit as assistant to Varian Fry[72] and to emigration to the United States.

Having in the end enlisted in the U.S. Army, Hirschman learned in Algiers in 1944 of the murder of Eugenio Colorni by the Nazi-Fascists. It was

69 Condliffe 1940 pp. 283–84.

70 Later on Albert returned to this subject. Working in the international division of the U.S. Federal Reserve Board, he wrote (as his first contribution to that institute's foreign economics bulletin – *The Review of Foreign Developments*), "Bilateralism and 'Proportionalism' – Two Aspects of Trade Structure" – 1946. In this article, along with bilateralism, Hirschman considers "an additional aspect of trade structure; namely *the degree to which a country maintains the same ratio of imports to exports with all its trading partners*." Original emphasis.

71 As a side issue, I would add that this early statistical analysis of bilateralism (perhaps along with that cited in the preceding note) ought to be read in American middle schools, as a serious reminder for those who discover protectionist bilateralism casually and without historical memory—as if it were an 'egg of Columbus,' instead of "the ultimate tool of power politics."

72 Cf, above, the second epigraph to the book.

"a terrible blow."[73] He realized, at that point, the indelible role Eugenio had played in his intellectual and political formation. In his memory, his "Trieste period" then seemed to him a fruitful, if irreproducible, parenthesis within a tragic era.[74]

The conversations with Eugenio in Trieste, Albert later recalled,[75] focused his attention on "what we call the small ideas, small pieces of knowledge. They do not stand in connection with any ideologies or worldviews, they do not claim to provide total knowledge of the world, they probably undermine the claims of all previous ideologies."[76]

"These *petites idées*," it appears from the interviews collected by Jeremy Adelman,[77] "really stuck for Hirschman, who for the rest of his life would jot down observations on scraps of paper or notebooks hoping they might evolve from insights into ideas. 'They are like aphorisms,' he explained, 'very astonishing remarks, perhaps of a paradoxical nature, but which are perhaps true because of it.' Since these little ideas lay all around like leaves, the skill was in figuring out how to 'gather them up' and make them into 'a great idea.' It was not for an abstract system to define the significance of daily experiences and

73 Cf. above, the fourth epigraph.

74 Later, in the United States, to those who advised him to enroll in a PhD program in economics, he replied that he already had a doctorate from Trieste (and he continued to affirm this, along with the claim that he had held the position of an assistant in statistics—cf. above, n. 17). These, if I'm not mistaken, were - in my view - Albert Hirschman's first "half-truths" – 1983 pp. 218–19. Formally speaking this was undoubtedly the case (as a student intern, he had done volunteer work at the institute of statistics, and had graduated with a BA). But in actual substance? His articles on demographic statistics and his thesis show that his claim contains an element of truth. Working at the institute of statistics and on *The Poincarè Franc* (and especially conversing with Eugenio and his friends), he had in effect experienced much more than a simple doctorate. So in fact, I understand him, and I would add that, in my own small way, I had a similar experience as a young man in Cambridge UK…

75 Interview with Henri Hempel, a middle school teacher and old friend from his youth, cited in Ademan 2013 p. 115.

76 I have no difficulty believing this statement. Not least because it is a typical argument of Eugenio's, fitting with his anti-ideological and anti-systemic way of thinking. But, as we saw in the second chapter, Leibniz spoke of small perceptions rather than small ideas. Moreover, Leibniz's small perceptions, as we shall see later in par. 9, have a specific meaning that should not be confused with that of the small ideas that can be inferred from such perceptions. In other words: it is good to untie the knot in successive steps…

77 Adelman 2013 pp. 115–16 (based on the 1990 interview with Henri Hempel – cf. n. 75; and with Sarah Hirschman on 1st August 2005).

choices, but, rather, the other way around." "The Big Idea, which Hirschman associated with the 'claim to complete cognition of the world,' claimed 'to explain multi-causal social processes from a single principle.' The alternative was 'the attempt to come to an understanding of reality in portions, admitting that the angle may be subjective.'"

"With time this alchemy of an exploratory intellectual sensibility and voluntarist political dispositions would be one that Hirschman could cultivate and refine over the rest of his life—in many ways *because* it was so itinerant; it was an intellectual temperament that complemented a restless spirit. The petites idées was 'a really key thing throughout Albert's life,' according to his wife, Sarah, 'that he told me almost on the first day I met him, when we talked about Eugenio.' This was six years and several wars later, in early 1941—but it was as if he was still sitting beside his brother-in-law the previous day. In that first conversation with his future wife, Albert 'taught me not to think in big theories or big things, but to treasure small ideas.'"[78]

9 – So Colorni and Hirschman did indeed speak of small ideas. But this commonly used phrase can in practice be misleading. For in their intentions it does not simply mean the opposite of big ideas. It does not necessarily concern small problems, suggested by small personal perceptions. In Hirschman's experience, in fact, realizing the way things actually are through small ideas can be a shock (in relation to one's own previous 'theoretical consciousness' and/or to Economics), it can concern huge problems, induce major learning efforts, and even, after a considerable lapse of time, suggest significant corrections according to the logic of self-subversion…

Take the statistics on commercial exchanges between Germany and some of the Balkan states that—as we shall see below—led Hirschman to begin writing *National Power* in 1941. Think of the political correction of this early text that the same author presented in 1978 inaugurating a Conference on "dependencia." Or of Albert's observation on the Nigerian railways that lies at the origin of *Exit* (1970), and the 'equal relevance' of the model of mutual reinforcement between exit and voice with respect to the better-known hydraulic model,

78 Ibid. Thereafter, the affection for *petites idées* was also a bond, transmitted from Eugenio Colorni, between Albert and Sarah. "In our life," Sarah declared, "we have had these things that you say to each other, like all couples, and for us it was our petites idées: 'Wow, this is wonderful. It's small, but it's wonderful.' And his letters have a lot of petites idées. He will see a picture, a painting, and he would get a petite idée. He would see something going on in the street; he would get a petite idée."

which Hirschman finally acceded to in 1993 as an effect of his reflection on the fall of the Berlin Wall and the dissolution of the German Democratic Republic.

To argue, then, in the light of these examples (to which others could of course be added) that an understanding of reality is initiated by small ideas might almost acquire the sense of a deliberate (and somewhat self-deprecating) understatement of a stratagem, of a protective understatement[79]—as was certainly in Hirschman's style—rather than a true interpretive sense.

I also think that if I had found a way of bringing this aspect of the issue to his attention at the time, in the 1980s and 90s (and if he had wanted to answer honestly—not at all to be taken for granted), Albert would probably have observed that there was no need to get to the bottom of the question since, in the cultural conditions of the time, the small ideas thesis had actually performed a useful service....

This would be—in my view—an ingenious thesis, but one that would not meet the demands of the critics. Unless... Unless, in the Hirschman quotation recalled above, we implicitly attribute to these small ideas ("small particles of knowledge" that "do not stand in connection with any ideology") the significance of *gateways to new horizons*.[80]

79 Protective in the sense of promoting a calm work process, free of pointless—even damaging—polemics. For Colorni, on the other hand, I would say that his interest in genuine, grounded and true small ideas was instinctive opposition to any form of system as such—which would be intrinsically impossible and false. Note too how, in the conversations recalled by Hirschman in his 1990 interview (see above: sec. 8 and n. 75), Colorni's argument is conclusive, while Hirschman's would become so (conclusive) only with practice—in the sense that he would probably gradually go on to discover the great potential of "small particles of knowledge." Looking at Hirschman's formative process from this perspective, it seems likely to me that feeling that his back was covered (culturally and politically) by his brother-in-law's intellectual exuberance, and enjoying at the same time an unexpected freedom of thought were decisive elements in his education from a practical point of view, providing—as he wrote this explicitly—"the minimum amount of self-confidence everyone needs to get through life at all" (Hirschman 1990a p. xxx, 1995 p. 117).

80 The citation indeed develops the reasoning from the side of criticizing ideological-systematic thinking, but not from that of the practical construction of alternatives, even partial ones, that Albert Hirschman would go on to dedicate himself to. Over time, as we shall see further on, he developed several strategies of Colornian derivation for actually getting small ideas to grow—even though, from a programmatic standpoint, these never were and never will be exhaustive. Probably, Albert saw all this as a kind of trademark; a professional secret, a tool of the trade (*mestiere* in Italian, which in fact etymologically comes from *mistero*, mystery). He never undertook—to my knowledge—to investigate its source. For him it was enough to have learned it from Eugenio, and then gradually refine it through research on different planes, literature, social sciences, etc.

If this were then the sense of the reasoning, and not the notion of small ideas as such, in that case I think, on this specific point, it would be worth going back to Leibniz and to the "Anthological Exposition of the Leibnizian System" left to us by Colorni (cf. "A Conjecture," the second chapter).

In doing this we would learn that for Leibniz ideas have an intimate origin in the relation between the subject (his or her natural predispositions and accumulated experiences) and the surrounding world—both in the sense of cognitive acquisition and of premonition. We would learn that each of us is literally 'immersed' in a sea of perceptions, differing in texture and meaning, and that among these perceptions there are some that strike the heart and the mind, but *do not reach the consciousness* of the subject.[81]

The point is this—they are small in the sense that they are in part *unexpressed*. The subject feels them, perceives them, but does not truly understand them and thus cannot process them. They hide something unknown, something yet to be discovered, such perceptions. Often the subject does not really notice them, instinctively aggregates them, confuses them with others, loses sight of them....

10 – "With the idea of *confused perceptions*," Colorni wrote, "Leibniz once again takes up the concept of petites perceptions. But while the function of the latter was to show the presence in each soul—albeit unconscious and indistinct—of the entire content of the world, confused perceptions point to such unconsciousness and confusion as the cause of each monad's own imperfection."[82]

"Our sense perceptions, even when they are clear, must necessarily contain a certain confused feeling, for, since all the bodies of the universe are in sympathy with each other, ours receives impressions from all the rest, and thought our senses are in response to all of them, it is impossible for our soul to pay attention to every particular impression. This is why our confused sensations result from a really infinite variety of perceptions. This is somewhat like the confused murmur heard by those who approach the seashore, which comes

81 Cf. above, sec. 19 of the second chapter. "Leibniz," Colorni wrote (2023, p. 194), "appeals in this regard to *petite perceptions* or unfelt perceptions, which continue to influence the soul, even if they do not reach its consciousness."

82 For Leibniz, Colorni explains (Ibid, p. 198), the entire Universe, in short, is already inherent a priori in the soul. But the soul has no current knowledge of all this. The field of its knowledge is limited and extends only to what is most immediately in contact with it. Small perceptions belong to the soul's representation, but the soul is not aware of them. They allow Leibniz to conceive of the monad as both limited and universal.

from the accumulation of innumerable breaking waves. For if out of several exceptions which do not harmonize so as to make one, there is no single one which surpasses the others, and if these perceptions make impressions that are about equally strong and equally capable of holding the attention of the soul, it can perceive them only confusedly."[83]

"Differentiation in the clarity of perception," Colorni comments, "is thus what constitutes the individuality of each monad, and is what differentiates monads from one another."[84]

Perhaps, this is the source of Colorni's noted strategies for the identification and resolution of these perceptions—such as doubt, being on the lookout, a passive readiness (as in a spiderweb) to snap into action, the decision to focus on and probe the most promising perceptions, to capture the hidden meaning of those that interest us most, to turn them into small pathfinder ideas toward vast new acquisitions. And also, the idea of surprise as a litmus test for prior knowledge—in the sense that noticing incongruities, opening up and abandoning resistance to the new, shaking up, 'recording'

---

83 Leibniz 1686, now in Colorni 2023 pp. 201–02.

84 Colorni ibid, p. 202. Leibniz argued (1702, now in Colorni 2023 pp. 206–07) that "besides the perceptions which the soul remembers, there is a mass which is made up of an infinite number of confused perceptions which it does not disentangle. It is through these that it represents outside bodies and comes to have distinct thoughts which are unlike the preceding ones, because the bodies which the soul represents have suddenly changed to something which strongly affects its own. So the soul sometimes passes from white to black or from yes to no, without knowing how, or at least involuntarily, for what its confused thoughts and feelings produce in it we attribute to the body. So, we should not be surprised if a man who is stung by some insect when eating jam should, despite himself, pass immediately from pleasure to pain. For, in approaching the man's body before stinging it, this insect was already affecting it, and the representation of this was, albeit unconsciously, already affecting his soul. However, in the soul as in the body, little by little the insensible becomes the sensible. That is how the soul changes itself even against its will, for it is enslaved by the feelings and confused thoughts which occur according to the states of its body and of other bodies through their relation to it. These, then, are the means through which pleasures are sometimes interrupted and followed by pains, without the soul's always being alerted or prepared for it; as for example when the insect which stings approaches without making a noise, or, if it is a wasp, for example, when some distraction prevents our noticing the approaching wasp's buzz. Thus we must not say that nothing new happens in the substance of the soul which makes it feel the sting; for what happens is confused presentiments or, better, insensible dispositions of the soul, which represent the dispositions of the body with regard to the sting."

and reconstructing consciousness—a process that will inevitably follow such disruptions, etc.

11 – But back to the point. In this non-stop flood of small and confused perceptions, the subject may become aware of having stumbled across something that might be interesting. In such a case he or she will try to identify this "what?" and go back to the perceptions that have to do with it. Through mental experimentation, the subject will try to isolate those perceptions from the rest, aiming to relive them and understand their initially indistinct and/or hidden meaning. In this way, beginning in a condition of confusion, some small and partially unexpressed perceptions can be transformed into "distincts" (in Leibniz's terminology). And this could be the beginning of a research program that might even go places. Step by step, this process can be repeated in the mind, sometimes (almost) obsessively through a game that is partly conscious and partly not[85], until the subject finally feels satisfied with the small-big idea in hand that allows him or her to set sail.

If we trace this line of reasoning back to the young Hirschman's texts, it quickly becomes clear that the critique in the 1937 essay of the demographic campaign (via the in-depth study of the statistics on the subject that had unwisely been published by Fascism) was quickly dismissed for obvious reasons of political expediency. Instead, as we shall see more clearly in the following chapter, at the opposite end of the spectrum of possibilities, the small perception about the statistics on German foreign trade with eastern and southeastern European countries that Hirschman had brought with him on arriving in the United States in 1940 became an idea, and had such extraordinary potential for theoretical-practical rebellion that it finally suggested to Albert his first masterpiece—*National Power and the Structure of Foreign Trade*.

And his other youthful texts? I think that to decode them we need to see that the process described can give rise to a wide number of variations on the theme—in the sense that once one key to the puzzle has been found it becomes easier to find others. This was in all probability the source of Hirschman's satisfaction with "Les finances et l'économie italiennes" when he was able to intercept information that the regime would have liked to hide by going through Italian financial newspapers.

85 In the sense that while the conscious mind, having wrung itself out, would like to file the thing away, the subconscious can bring it back up and prompt the subject to think about it again.

Which is to say that in these texts documentation is never an end in itself—it leads to a series of mini-discoveries that are discussed and collated, often using other stratagems like decomposition-recomposition (e.g., sectoral analysis) or temporal sequencing (e.g., historical-economic analysis) as discussed in sec. 17 and 18 of the previous chapter.

12 – Demographic statistics, Italian finance and economics, monetary economics in France and Italy, foreign exchange control and foreign trade—young Albert proves that he can easily move from one topic to another, out of expediency (and necessity), adjacency, or a sort of "spillover" of curiosity. And not least in order to verify what will happen when an idea that worked well in one field is transferred, lock, stock and barrel to another, different in location, topic, resemblance, etc.

Moreover, in addition to sequences, he develops interactions and mirroring. Statistical skill is very useful in bringing other professional ideas into focus, monetary history can facilitate journalistic work and vice versa (thus establishing a novel and more practical attitude toward economics), the study of the Franc can mirror (to some extent) that of the Lira, and devaluation is studied as an alternative to exchange control—not to mention, of course, that research on international trade prefigures the study of national power.

In this way, 'going off on a tangent' also means 'going from strength to strength,' with the young Hirschman displaying a high level of analytical adaptability and flexibility. While absorbing Eugenio's lessons, he was experimenting, perhaps without fully realizing it, with a way of working that would propel him forward for life, an indisputable foundation for his extraordinary creativity.

It is true, then, that making Hirschman's 1937–39 texts available to critics, one after the other, confers the great advantage of finally enabling them to arrive at an overall assessment. Indeed, although conceived for different purposes, these writings collectively represent an early youthful effort to understand the wider world, starting with France and Italy.

His interest in 1931–36 French monetary history on one hand, and his step-by-step research on the Italian situation allowed Hirschman to acquire his own particular *modus operandi*, by which he laid the foundation stone of a broader interest relating to international trade, national power and thus, more generally, the structural verticality of the multi-dimensional system of the world—a process which, starting from individual papers, gradually shows the unfolding of Colornian logic over a very broad field.

At the same time, reading these writings from 1937–39, we can sense how Hirschman gradually formed his beliefs and also advanced them through interaction with the study of reality. We see how he qualified them, corrected them, developed them—a process that is here particularly easy to follow for Italy, because it involves examining one text after another, right down to the exchange control report (as against his thesis-report on France). It is a gradual, sometimes tortuous process, which later inevitably disappears behind the scenes.

The France-Italy dialogue is naturally not as direct as it would later become during the Marshall Plan, when Albert was asked to 'follow events' in the two countries. But it is always felt indirectly (Albert was still from Paris), and sometimes it comes out in the open.[86]

Finally, we already understand from these early texts the genesis of some of the *core beliefs* of Hirschman's thought—namely, respect for the effective/efficient functioning of the market and recognition of the role of the state for development purposes. Characteristically, concrete results would depend on both of these.[87]

---

86 For example, when Hirschman decides to write a paper on the changing fortunes of the Lira, after he had worked them out for the Franc in his thesis: cf. above, notes. 28, 49, 61, 66.

87 We should not forget, however, that these are still commissioned (or commissionable) texts that were needed to finish his studies and make ends meet. This was a factor which inevitably limited young Albert's capacity for expression.

· 4 ·

LONG LIVE *NATIONAL POWER*!*

Laudatio

1 – In the most important "laudatio" among Albert Hirschman's *Honoris Causa* degrees in the French language—the one awarded to him by l'Institut d'études politique de Paris on April 27, 1989—Prof. Jean-Claude Casanova stated that as early as *National Power and the Structure of Foreign Trade* (1945) a typical feature of Hirschman's work is evident: "uncertainty in classifying the book, exceptional longevity of the ideas. In effect, the book does not fit into any genre, nor any definite discipline—it mixes British conciseness with German erudition, economics with politics, history with ideas, notions of equilibrium with those of asymmetry and influence. It distances itself as much from economists who forget the nation as it does from politicians who forget markets.

* Remembering Marcello de Cecco. Earlier (and partial) versions of this paper have appeared (in English) in Meldolesi and Stame eds. 2017 and online in "Long is the Journey," nos. 3 (2017a) and 4 (2020).

All in one go," added Casanova, turning to Hirschman, "you discovered your road and defined your talent."[1]

Even with its limitations (which we shall see below), this is an important judgment that without doubt captures the importance, not to say *uniqueness* of this work in the context of Hirschman's intellectual output. It also has a particular role with respect to his writings of the 30s and 40s. The pages that follow aim to offer insight into both of these aspects.

In the first place, to argue that Hirschman discovered his intellectual vocation (let's call it) "all in one go" doesn't seem convincing, above all in the light of his prewar writings (recalled above in chapter 3). On the contrary, in my opinion, even compared to the earlier texts and then to those of the immediate postwar period, *National Power* really stands out. It rises with its own extraordinary intellectual force,[2] which needs clarification.

In the second place, well aware of Hirschman's long familiarity with French high culture, Casanova rightly stressed the longevity of the volume.[3] But then, in addition, he stressed only the German and English ancestry of his political

1 Casanova 1990 p. 10. "How were you able to do this in one go?" Casanova continued. "Doubtless, because of the complexity of your background, you can immediately make a synthesis of a German tradition and an English tradition. On the German side, you know how to distinguish the power order, and on the English side, the market order. You have learned that one does not absorb the other, and you have understood one and the other from a superior point of view. Doubtless, your perspicacity also stems from observing the world of the 1930s—the ruptures, the autarchies, the tensions that the international order was then experiencing. But more deeply I simply believe that regarding that era your blue eyes penetrated the clouds."

2 Because it finds a guiding thread in a well-known subject (foreign trade) that allows it to address a key theme (national power); because it is the first book which, while untangling a huge knot, reveals even greater potentialities; because although it concerns Germany in the 1930s, it has meaning for any "national power" (and, I would add, for any national-imperialist "verticality"); because while referring to the Second World War, it has a general validity of its own; because it talks about foreign trade, but it alludes to the numerous dimensions of the many relationships of domination/subordination/dependence in the great human pyramid we live with…

3 "Your book," Casanova continued, addressing Hirschman, "is still read today, and not only is it read, it's relevance has increased." And after listing some of the debates, reports, and international agreements that had unfolded since the 1960s, he added a question: how to think about all this "without advising our students to read the only international economics book in which politics and economics are harmoniously mixed?" Even with respect to what has happened subsequently up to the present, we could repeat (unfortunately endlessly) the same rhetorical question…

and economic arguments, while flying over the French influence and neglecting (or perhaps not even recognizing) the Colornian roots of the text—starting with the 'small idea' that, in a sense, brought things to a head.[4]

Thirdly, the mixture of economics and politics that impressed Casanova has not in any case been resolved, either on the economic or the political side—to the extent that the author himself (and Casanova should have remembered this) corrected it in 1978, thus inaugurating what he would later call his penchant for self-subversion.

2 – Let us take things in order.

As known, the starting point of his research was a "small idea" that (along with Montaigne's *Essays* and many other stratagems and stimuli) Hirschman had brought with him from Europe.[5] More precisely, that beginning was initially suggested by a 'confused perception' which, as he worked, had become 'distinct,' and had finally turned into a small enlightening idea. This was the accurate observation of certain statistics on German trade with eastern and southeastern Europe (in comparison with studies in London on the theory and practice of international trade) which had in a certain sense 'switched on a light bulb' in Albert's mind. In fact, generalizing the reasoning that began with these statistics, he devised the basic thesis of the book. This was that large and powerful states are able to manipulate commercial exchanges with smaller, poorer countries to their own advantage.

Naturally, we have to take into account the young scholar's precocious enthusiasm for demographic and later for economic and financial statistics. But this is still not enough to provide an answer for the inevitable question of

4 And therefore was in all probability not aware of the Leibnizian theory of small and confused perceptions (cf. above, ch. 3, secs. 8–12), and from which it is sometimes possible to derive small ideas—with virtue and fortune, as Machiavelli put it. In fact they can be generalized into bigger ideas (in dialogue with Colorni's theory of knowledge: cf. below, the Appendix). He was not aware, Casanova, of the sequence thesis that allows for such spatio-temporal generalization. Nor did he recognize, if I am not mistaken, the 'decomposition' which *National Power* springs from (and which from its very nature may later give rise to a process of recomposition – such as the one related to Hirschman's discussion of the theme of "dependencia": see later on).

5 Along with a statistical index of the concentration of the commodity structure of world trade (1943, 1943a) that he invented on his December 1940 voyage by ship to the United States (and whose authorship he vigorously defended in 1964). More broadly, it was from that now-acquired "expertise" that the statistical tools clearly arose to measure the many asymmetries and disparities analyzed in *National Power* (1945).

why, contrary to the case with other economists, such trade statistics 'spoke' as they did to Hirschman? Why did they suggest something so decisive? Clearly that seed of a small, confused perception fell on soil that was ready to receive it—from political, cultural, and economic points of view.

From here, then, more question marks spring up. How can it be explained that the observation of a few statistics gave rise to an intellectual earthquake such as the one we are about to discuss? How did it happen that from one small idea came numerous other, much larger ones? Also, how did it happen that the book was republished after a long period of oblivion?[6] And that the key political message that the entire text revolves around was abandoned by its own author—while the book itself, thanks to a new introduction, was published once again in 1980 and skillfully reinserted into Albert Hirschman's signature cultural frame?

Understanding all this requires that we proceed by degrees, first of all making another jump backwards. In other words, we need to excavate another level in the open-air mine provided by Albert's youthful experience. To this end, so as not to get lost in a sea of biographical anecdotes (and to stick to a succinct and useful discussion), we should focus first on two aspects: the discovery of 'verticalism' and the evolution of the economic discipline.

First, I have already mentioned Hirschman's crypto-Hegelian-Marxist political education, his militant commitment during his last year in Berlin (Ehrmann, Neu Beginnen, Miles, etc.[7]) and his intellectual development, in part critical, which followed. In this regard, it is worth looking at some of Demangeon's important lectures at HEC[8] (a judgment that Hirschman conveyed, as usual, in stages, a drop at a time, not to say reluctantly).

From those lessons, as he in fact wrote in *A Propensity for Self-Subversion*,[9] "we learnt a great deal about the location of economic activities and its determinants, the economic importance of rivers and natural resources for industrial development, and shifts in the flow of commerce between regions (I recall

6 The end of the 1960s "saw the reprinting of a long neglected study by Albert Hirschman, *National Power and the Structure of Foreign Trade* (1945/1969), now widely regarded as a classic. Written during World War II, the book highlighted the hidden politics of international trade: how relationships of domination and dependence between states can arise naturally from asymmetries in foreign trade; and how import and export policies can be used opportunistically by governments to exert political pressure and influence," (Cohen 2008 p. 21).

7 Cf. Adelman 2013 ch. 2.

8 Cf. above, ch. 3 n. 30.

9 Hirschman 1995 p. 116.

a superb lecture entitled "la concurrence entre Anvers et Rotterdam"). The lively green, brown, and blue colors of the geographical maps he displayed enhanced the effectiveness of his teaching."

It is an interesting passage, but one that (typically) still doesn't get to the point. In fact Jeremy Adelman, based on interviews granted him by Albert Hirschman was able to write[10] that "a lecture on the competition between Antwerp and Rotterdam provided a dramatic illustration of how underlying structural forces shaped economic rivalries. Another of Demangeon's lectures dealt with Russia's dependence on foreign trade before the First World War: the 'black soil' of the Ukraine was a breadbasket for the rest of Europe and a source of hard exchange for the tsar. As Moscow joined the war, Russia's minister of foreign trade was fond of exclaiming, 'Let's die of hunger,' though adding, 'but let's be sure to export!' Demangeon included his own addendum: 'And the minister was the more ready to say that *he* was not the one about to die of hunger!' Hirschmann was rapt. Demangeon was not just making fun of a tsarist official, but also making a point about the dilemma that some countries *really* faced.[11] [...] Demarageon laid some very preliminary grounds for Hirschman's thinking about trade and economic development."[12]

This passage, in the light of the dramatic current events of today, certainly resembles an incipient revelation. It shows us how Hirschman suddenly discovered an important aspect of the pyramidal, "verticalist" economic and political logic of the reality in which we continue to live—whatever we might hear from Marxism and Economics, which are instead structurally "horizontalist"—that is, founded on the simple opposition between entrepreneurs and workers.

3 – Now to the second aspect.[13] In the first chapter above I spoke about the cultural influence of romanticism which favored, in opposition, the development of Economics. In outline, however, it is important to keep the nineteenth-century

10 Adelman 2013 p. 91–2.

11 Note in this regard how already in this passage a social verticality within each country corresponds to the verticality between countries connected with international trade.

12 Adelman 2013 p. 91–2. It is likely that when Hirschman (1990a p. xxx; 1995 p. 118) declared that he had lost some of his youthful certainties even before he met Colorni in Trieste he was referring to experiences like this.

13 In this regard (as I have already mentioned: cf. above, ch. 3, sec. 5), the "landing" at the London School of Economics was crucial for Hirschman the economist. He confirmed this later (1998 p. 59): "In 1935," he wrote, "I received a fellowship for a year at [the LSE]. To understand my intellectual formation it is important to understand what was then happening in modern economics. For me this was a decisive year."

discovery (first gradual, then sudden) of the new marginalist economics, separate from its actual establishment—slow, and never complete—in the main cultural ganglia of the three linguistic worlds to which Jevons (English), Menger (German) and Walras (French) respectively belonged. Despite the innovative contributions of Stanley Jevons, in Britain the discipline of economics had long been dominated by the thinking of Alfred Marshall. In addition, between the two world wars a second and far more visible divide had been superimposed on this one—the split between the neoclassicists and Keynes. So that in the mid-1930s when Hirschman arrived in London these theoretical debates were in full swing.

There was not good blood between the general economic equilibrium advocated at the LSE by the "formidable Robbins"[14] (along with Hayek, Lerner, Hahn, Scitovski, etc.) and the Marshallian tradition at Cambridge. If anything, the Cambridge school was subtly leaning toward a return to the classics after Marshall's very long dominance.

Originally, Marshall had had a mathematical-philosophical-rational upbringing that sought truth in factual data, while at the same time he was always anxious to return as soon as possible to the "glories" of pure theoretical thought. Starting from the Ricardian tradition à la John Stuart Mill, he had gradually turned to marginalist ideas. He had maintained, however, the pretense of gradually reworking them in this or that aspect in the light of concrete observation and the cultural evolution of the time. After an extensive formative period, his many contributions had been merged by Marshall himself into Vol. 1 of the *Principles*, which over a thirty-year period were then 'tweaked' by the author himself over 8 editions followed by numerous reprints.

It also happened that the texts with which the *Principles* were to be continued in vol. 2 and 3, were instead published in stand-alone form. Many economists found inspiration—both positive and critical—in this vast 'prairie' of Marshallian reworkings. Apart from Keynes, I can personally attest to this for Joan Robinson, Piero Sraffa, Giacomo Becattini…

So the young Hirschman found himself in good company. But the big difference was that, while these economists (and many others) ultimately traced their economic reasoning (for or against) from *within* economics, Albert developed over time an original relationship that led *from outside* the economic discipline *into it* and then *out* again—so that he maintained that economics

14 Cit. in Adelman 2013 p. 121.

as such needed to be "complicated"[15] using some of the features of political science, sociology, anthropology, psychology, etc.

The London School of Economics, as mentioned, was at the time dominated by great neo-classical economists like Robbins and Hayek, who were also anti-Keynesian. Nevertheless, Hirschman added, "there were also some younger people, about my age, who had fled from Germany or Hungary. I joined these people spontaneously and we formed a group. They were all Keynesian and had been to Cambridge to hear the master. Among them there was a brilliant young economist, already well-known, by the name of Abba Lerner."[16]

At this point, the role that Lerner would go on to play in the genesis of *National Power* was still not clear. But it would soon become so. Probably Hirschman followed two paths: that of Barrett Whale (who, as we have seen, was helpful with his thesis on the Poincaré Franc), and that of Robbins-Lerner, which is perhaps the basis of *National Power*'s critique (part explicit, part implicit) of the orthodox theory of international trade.

Albert had become a tepid Keynesian. He had a nice chat in Cambridge with Piero Sraffa (via a letter of introduction from Eugenio Colorni, who happened to be Sraffa's cousin). "The man from whom nothing is hidden" (as Keynes called Sraffa), was already engaged *toto corde* in critiquing Alfred Marshall's *Principles* and was building an alternative Ricardo-Marx-Keynes

15 In particular I am referring here to Hirschman 1988a.

16 Abba, of course, was short for Abraham. He was a young Russian of Fabian socialist political inspiration. He had emigrated as a child to England, and had left rabbinical school to enter the LSE with full distinction. He was in fact "a brilliant, original thinker and was at work on a series of pioneering papers on concepts of international trade and the factor price equalization theorem" (Adelman 2013 p. 121; cf. also ibid. pp. 189–90)—so that, under the wing of Lionel Robbins, he had been entrusted with the economic theory course. Hirschman took the course, realized that he still had a lot to learn, and became friends with Abba. [Previously, Albert had never told me specifically about any of this (much as I had inevitably sensed it)—with the result that Abba Lerner does not appear at all in my 1987, 1993, 1994 and 1995 reconstructions, which Hirschman had even read personally—in advance!].

front, in part to stand up to the dominant theory of general economic equilibrium. Evidently Hirschman was not convinced by that project,[17] and he returned to London.

How to challenge (*cum judicio*) neoclassical economics, he would have asked himself, in such a way that would show how things actually are? Perhaps, to get different results, some assumptions might be changed—possibly only in one part of the theory of international trade, concerning a specific aspect of it. It is certain, however, that Albert never tried to set out to on a general current that was alternative to orthodox Economics (as did the present writer—thirty years later).[18]

Hirschman was a *sui generis* economist, who emerged from a singular sequence of theoretical-practical experiences and their progressive and ingenious 'distillation'—starting with statistics, economic journalism, some segments of the economic and monetary history of France and Italy, international trade, the partial acquisition of certain economic theories, and finally arriving at *National Power.*

Respectful (as I have mentioned) of the effective/efficient operation of markets, but an advocate, at the same time, of public functions, this volume initially found a breeding ground well adapted to what Albert intended in his reworking of a well-known theoretical-economic approach that was nevertheless considered obsolete by many avant-garde economists—that of Marshall.

Among Alfred Marshall's many texts there was one—*Money, Credit and Commerce* (1923)[19]—that interested Hirschman particularly, above all one key passage: "In broad terms, it may be said that the *prima facie* and direct gain which a country derives from her foreign trade consists in the excess of the value to her of the things which she imports over the value of her of the things

17 One might even speculate that it seemed a bit 'passé' to him. Not least because, as every student of economics knew at the time, Ricardian theory of international trade represented the first step in what would later become 'pure' theory—the theory that Hirschman was precisely about to learn in depth and then criticize indirectly, starting from a specific point in Alfred Marshall's 'gains from trade' theory.

18 Nevertheless, it is possible that, between Demangeon's lectures on economic geography and the Economics learned at LSE, Hirschman was already searching for his own path. What would later be, more consciously, the road agreed upon with Eugenio. On this point the two brothers-in-law understood each other very well—even though they came from different intellectual backgrounds, and even though they were absorbed in very different specific work programs.

19 A book which, originally conceived as part of a second volume of *Principles*, was instead published separately.

she could have made for herself with the capital and labor devoted to producing the things she exported in exchange for them: the costs of working of trade of course reckoned in."[20]

4 – So all this happened *before* 1936–40 (that is, before Albert's brief participation in the Spanish civil war, before the nearly two years in Trieste, the return to Paris, the outbreak of the war, the voluntary enlistment in the French army, demobilization, and the Marseilles saga with Varian Fry).[21]

It will be recalled[22] that after his "Triestine" period Albert realized "with great relief" that he could be a reasonably competent economist without having to decide in advance whether or not Keynes was absolutely right. Here we may of course detect a subtle thread of irony. It was the era of "for or against," whereas this way of thinking was foreign to Hirschman (and Colorni).

To understand this, it is enough to observe that John Maynard Keynes had been a student of Marshall's. So that, in order to decide whether or not every word of his *General Theory* was 'solid gold,' Hirschman would have had to immerse himself up to his neck in Marshall's vast scholarly output and even in his Cantabrigian milieu—to be able unravel, for example, points where Keynes attributes certain ideas to Marshall on the strength of his recollection of his lectures and conversations![23]

---

20 Marshall 1923 pp. 109–10; Hirschman 1980 p. 18. After that of Germany's trade statistics with central and southeastern Europe, Albert had in this way encountered a second gateway—this time theoretical—to his future treatment of the theme. Indeed, as we shall see, it was what allowed his decisive initial 'unraveling' of a truly tangled skein.

21 Understandably, with the outbreak of war, Hirschman was once again 'captured' by political commitment. He enlisted in the French army. After demobilization he took the name Albert Herman (using false documents: cf. Adelman 2013 ch. 5; the cover of Hirschman 1995; Tesnière 2020), and joined Varian Fry's group in Marseilles, working to save the very many intellectuals and artists in Europe whose lives were in danger. At the point of being found out, he managed to get away via one of the trails Fry's group had set up across the Pyrenees to rescue fugitives. From Lisbon he reached the United States by ship with a safe-conduct obtained through a two-year Rockefeller fellowship to be used at the University of California at Berkeley, where in the meantime Jack Condliffe had become professor of economics (Coser 1984 p. 164). The story of the initiatives on his behalf by his cousin Oscar, Max Ascoli, Jack Condliffe and others are narrated in detail by Adelman (2013 pp. 181–82).

22 Cf above: ch. 3 n. 44.

23 Keynes 1936; now 1973 pp. 175 and 177–78 – cf., regarding this, Becattini, 1975 p. LXI–LXII.

None of this took place. Albert's way of working never approached the reconstruction of an author's thought in its entirety (least of all Marshall's, given its vastness, labyrinthine afterthoughts, obsolescence, etc.). But this did not mean that the opposite was the case either—that is, that he repudiated Marshall's work out of prejudice. Hirschman looked for 'gateways' in order to argue his own point of view. He looked for them in the history of economic thought—mainly concerning currency and foreign trade—his major interests.

As happened in the case of other authors as well, Hirschman finally found the desired 'transit point' (for building *National Power*) in one specific aspect of Marshall's intellectual corpus. Evidently, the type of theoretical-practical issue alluded to above had lodged itself so deeply in his mind that it resurfaced *ex abrupto* (perhaps in 1940) just at the time when he had emigrated to the United States.

We know today that, as soon as his ship arrived in New York, he went immediately to the Emergency Rescue Committee, the support committee for Fry's work, and sent Fry a telegram.[24] We also know that he was able to obtain extra financing from the Rockefeller Foundation for his mother, who was living at the time in England. To save a little money he changed his train ticket from second to third class,[25] and since at that time it was possible, on the scheduled route, to get off and on the train at will, he used the same ticket to stop in Chicago to meet Abba Lerner (who had in the meantime moved to the university there)—presumably to discuss his project.

It is not unlikely that Abba advised him to demonstrate what he intended to argue with a mathematical model. In any case it would not surprise me, given that, as I wrote before, Lerner was at the time a leading exponent of the neoclassical theory of international trade.[26]

---

24 "Committee full confidence in you. Avoidance clash welcome. Love: Otto Albert" (Adelman 2013 p. 188).

25 Cf. above n. 21. It was undoubtedly an incredible journey, which finally (Hirschman confided this to his mother on February 8 and 11, 1941: see Adelman 2013 pp. 185–86), would lead him back to his studies. "I shall enter this country with the will of getting to something, of showing that I have merited the extraordinary chain of lucky incidents which have led me here" (note Hirschman's typical inversion of the cause-effect relationship, which later came out in the open in *The Strategy*—in the sense that an unexpected positive event could induce the beneficiary to try to deserve it).

26 Cf. above n. 16, and below n. 31.

Perhaps it was at this point that Albert decided not to confront such a monolithic conception head on, but to deal instead[27] with a specific theoretical aspect of the theory of gains from trade—inaugurated initially by one of the intellectual currents that had accompanied the rise of marginalist economics over time, that of Marshall. And perhaps this is why his friend Lerner suddenly departed from his intellectual horizon, to the extent that he was not even cited (unjustly, I think) in *National Power.*

5 – The rest of the story is better known. It made sense that after the intense period of political activism (let's call it) he had experienced in Europe, the personal and professional aspects of Albert's life should take precedence. In Berkeley (CA), he kept away from the chatter of the European "veterans" and their friends, fell in love with Sarah Shapiro and married her,[28] and resumed his collaboration with Condliffe. The latter had in the meantime published *The Reconstruction of World Trade. A Survey of International Economic Relations* (1940), and had drawn inspiration from it for a new collective study, a "Trade Regulation Project" looking at "how states manage their trade relations in ways that enhance or thwart cooperation between governments and thus keep peace or fuel conflicts."[29]

Hirschman thought seriously about what he should do, and by means of a stratagem, he managed to avoid enrolling in a PhD course in economics.[30]

27 Also with the help of chapters 8 and 9 – "Gains from Trade: the Doctrine of Comparative Costs" and "Gains from Trade: the Maximization of Real Income" – from *Studies in the Theory of International Trade* by Jacob Viner – 1937.

28 As noted, he discussed the importance of small ideas with his wife. Sarah, from a good family of Jewish-Russian-Lithuanian entrepreneurial and commercial origins and educated in Paris, was an expert on French and Russian literature, and was her husband's crucial partner and collaborator. Cf., in this regard, Albert's opening dedication of *The Rhetoric of Reaction* (1991): "To Sarah, my first reader and critic for fifty years" (that is, since 1941–42), which in the Italian version (following Machiavelli and Guicciardini) reads: "A Sarah, primo lettore e critico dei miei ghiribizzi." [To Sarah, first reader and critic of my whims].

29 Cf. Adelman 2013 p. 202. Albert's contract began with this project—and he in fact presented *National Power* as "an outgrowth of my collaboration with the Trade Regulation Project" (Hirschman 1945/1980 p. xiii).

30 Although well aware of the risks of such a decision, Albert did not follow the normally advisable procedure of enrolling in a PhD program in economics—because he maintained that he already had a doctorate from the University of Trieste (a claim which he repeated to the end of his days). Together with his putative position as "assistant" at the Institute of Statistics in Trieste—as mentioned previously (cf. ch. 3 notes 17 and 74)—this was probably what Hirschman later (1983) called a "half truth." Cf. below n. 81.

Instead, he made an agreement with Condliffe; and in 1941–42 he threw himself headlong into writing *National Power*, to turn small ideas into a big book, as I have already mentioned—even beyond what Albert himself then thought he could write.

National Power is an extraordinarily bold and enduring magnet-volume. In my view, it is striking for at least two reasons. First, because it succeeds in demonstrating that "power elements and disequilibria are potentially inherent in such 'harmless' trade relations as have always taken place, e.g., between big and small, rich and poor, agricultural and industrial countries—relations which could be fully in accord with the principles taught by the theory of international trade."[31]

Secondly, because "while the economics literature contained only scattered observations on the political aspect of international trade, life as it had been lived (during World War II) was all too revealing. In fact, *National Power* addressed this discrepancy at length and demonstrated significantly that the salient features of Nazi trade policy could be traced back to the principles of power politics."[32]

The book deals at the same time with the history of thought (in economic practice and economic theory) and the statistical analysis of international trade, and it can also be read retrospectively as a general logical background to Albert Hirschman's work.

In addition, it falls into that small group of books written by intellectuals from Europe for the purpose of clarifying for the educated American (and Anglo-Saxon) public what had actually taken place in the grand German imperialist expansion of the 1930s, and why.

Finally, its purpose was to combine a purely political desire (to contribute at an intellectual level to the positive conclusion of the conflict under way) and an individual need for professional self-advancement in the field of economics and statistics.

31 Hirschman 1980 p. 40. "To appreciate the boldness of this thesis," I wrote some time ago (Meldolesi 1995 p. 13), "it is worth remembering that a few years after the publication of *National Power*, Paul Samuelson (1948, 1952) would argue, based on traditional assumptions, that free trade leads to an equalization of the absolute returns on the factors of production of countries engaged in trade interchange. Thus, such countries would not only gain mutual benefits, as the relevant literature had long argued—they would also achieve equal levels of income from factors of production."(!)

32 Meldolesi 1995 p. 13; Hirschman 1980 pp. 34–9.

National Power over time came to embody the notion that the theoretical-practical demonstration of a small cognitive fact effectively hints at the undermining of the meaning of an entire construct (the standard structure of pure international trade theory, and beyond). In addition, by illuminating only one aspect of the national-imperialist nature of the pyramidal system in which we live, it indirectly clarified the existence of 'n' other 'vertical' dimensions. Casanova was right—it is the only book in existence to have actually accomplished such a feat.

With this volume (certainly challenging to conceive and construct) Hirschman boldly laid out his own innovative path (the road of intellectual discovery marked out for him by Eugenio Colorni) along with a particular way of developing it over time—based on reasons that, surprisingly, extend down to ourselves.[33]

National Power *and its economic structure*

6 – All right, the somewhat skeptical reader might object at this point, but what, in a nutshell, is the theoretical-practical sense of this work?

In the introduction—this is in 1941–42, when the book was written—Hirschman observed that the current discussion concerning the extensive use of international economic relations as an instrument of power "has not generally proceeded from an examination of the various theories of imperialism."[34] Most present-day investigations, on the other hand, "take as possible or as given

33 As noted previously, the book contains a technical-economic finding with far-reaching consequences, which at the time no doubt converged with the author's specific political intentions regarding the war and the prospects for the postwar period. The limits of the latter, however, would soon become evident—to the extent that Hirschman (as we shall see below) was eventually led to write a new and crucial introduction for the re-publication of the book in 1980.

34 Hirschman 1980 p. xv. "The proponents of these theories," the passage continues, evidently referring to the noted texts of Hobson, Kautsky, Lenin, Rosa Luxemburg, etc., "have tried to prove that the 'inner contradictions of capitalism' lead inevitably to a struggle for markets and sources of raw materials. This struggle has been pictured as the main underlying cause of the bellicose policy of governments and of the ensuing wars." One senses, scrolling through the text, that the author is attracted not so much to theories of imperialism as to current analyses. It is with reference to the latter that he intends, in fact, to address "a more fundamental problem"—the natural, inherent weakness of the international trading system with respect to national power.

a power-minded policy, whatever may be its political, economic, or psychological origins, and examine the use which such a policy make of the economic instruments at its disposal. [...] This type of analysis can make clear important intermediate links in the process of causation of modern war." For example, "the German trade offensive and economic penetration in such areas as southeastern Europe and Latin America has been thoroughly investigated by many economists. The processes and technical devices by which Germany achieved partial or total success and the political, social, and economic circumstances which favored her during the 'thirties have been given careful study."[35]

The present work, Hirschman added however, deals in any case with "a more fundamental problem. It is concerned with the nature of a system of international trade that can very easily be exploited for purposes of national power policy. Is there in the trading system some inherent weakness which makes it vulnerable to the will of any government so minded to use it in the pursuit of power?"[36]

National Power thus represents a return to theoretical basics. Its purpose is to reopen by this means critical research into national power (nationalism, in other words—the authentic *bête noire* of Albert Hirschman's discussions with Eugenio Colorni, and later decisive in the federalist political formulation of the well-known 'Ventotene group' animated by the young Italian philosopher together with Altiero Spinelli, Ernesto Rossi, Ursula Hirschmann and Ada Rossi).[37]

7 – *National Power* can of course be observed from numerous points of view. One of these might involve the analysis of the vast spectrum of international economic relations in order to deal with the economic and political problems of the time—perhaps beginning with the trail proposed by Condliffe in

35 Ibid. p. xv.

36 Ibid. p. xvi.

37 Cf. Colorni 2019; Colorni and Spinelli 2020.

Reconstruction of World Trade[38] Another way might be to begin a review of the literature on the question, which Hirschman clearly considered incomplete—considering that at a certain point he wrote that "practice has preceded theory."[39] Yet another might begin with the experiences of the author—and so on. Personally, my intention is to follow this last road, to suggest the exploration of two parallel readings of *National Power*—one 'centered' on the economic side and the other on the political.

To start out on this route, let us take in hand the third edition of the book—the one from 1980. It opens with an important "Preface to the Expanded Edition" (which we will come back to), followed by a pure and simple reprint of the 1945 edition.[40] That is to say:

Introduction
Part One – "Theoretical and Historical Aspects" (Thought on the Relationship Between Foreign Trade and National Power; Foreign Trade as an Instrument of National Power; The Question of 'Economic Aggression During World War I; Problems of Reconstruction).

38 "This volume," Condliffe clarified (1940 p. 9), "falls naturally into three parts. The first [ch. 1–3] analyzes the collapse of the international trading system that was restored, on the prewar model, after the last war. The second [ch. 4–8] examines the challenge now presented by totalitarian methods of bilateral trade. The third [ch. 9–11] surveys the problems that must be faced in any attempt to reconstruct world trade after the present war comes to an end. [...] It is a study in political economy rather than in economics or political science." It is a personal interpretation of the conclusions drawn from a large body of original research [including the preparation for the Bergen Conference: cf. above, sec. 7 and n. 64 of ch. 3] carried out in a spirit of cooperation by scholars from many different countries. The chapter titles are "The Background of Economic Policy," "The Process of Disintegration," "The Causes of Breakdown," "Regulated and Unregulated Trading Systems," The Complication of Tariffs," "Quota Politics," "The Monetary Weapon," "Commercial Diplomacy," "The Limits of Regionalism," "New Aspects of International Organization," "The Conditions of Economic Co-operation."

39 Actually, he opened the "Introduction" to *National Power* with the following statement: "A textbook for the modern prince should indeed contain, in addition to Machiavelli's classic chapters, extensive new sections on the most efficient use of quotas, exchange controls, capital investment, and other instruments of economic warfare. In this respect, *practice has preceded theory*. The extensive use of international economic relations as an instrument of national power policies has been, together with the 'war of nerves,' one of the main characteristics of the period preceding the outbreak of the present war," (1980 p. xv. Emphasis added).

40 Cf. below (in sec. 25) the explanation for this.

Part Two – "Three Statistical Inquiries into the Structure of World Trade" (Introduction; The Preference of Large Trading Countries for Commerce with Small Trading Countries; Concentration upon Markets and Supply Sources of the Foreign Trade of Small or Weak Nations; The Commodity Structure of World Trade).[41]

Actually, if we keep before us the author's trajectory as outlined so far, one glance reveals that the Leibniz-Colorni lesson had been fully absorbed.

First, we see that the *small idea* sparked by the perceptive observation of the trade statistics between Germany and east and southeast Europe was developed in Part Two in successive bursts ("Three Statistical Inquiries into the Structure of World Trade"). And then that, in their turn, these factual studies support the presentation in Part One ("Theoretical and Historical Aspects").[42]

Part One itself, as we shall now see, begins with an interesting *sequence* on economic thought and the relationship between foreign trade and national power.

In addition, the key chapter that follows is based on the multiple *decomposition* of a highly tangled theme (and skein).

And finally, the rethinking contained in the "Preface to the Expanded Edition," reveals that these decompositions can gradually be set on a path of *recomposition*—a process which (perhaps only instinctively at first) in the end arrived at the idea, recalled above, of *How Economics Should Be Complicated*.[43]

8 – Thus, by careful theoretical-practical analysis, *National Power* (unlike much of the economic literature on international trade) comprehensively addresses what its title promises. Namely, how national power can actually be increased

41 This—statistical-economic in nature—is the second pillar on which the book is built. "So far as I am aware," Hirschman wrote with pride (1945, p. 86), "the methods which have been used for the analysis of these questions are new." The book closes with two appendices: 'Note on Statistical Methods' and 'Resolutions of the Paris Economic Conference of the Allies, June, 1916.' (The last chapter of *National Power*—"The Commodity Structure of World Trade"—had been published earlier in 1943. Moreover, in 1951 and 1952, in addressing his emerging interest in underdevelopment, Hirschman took up some of the book's final analyses—Meldolesi 1995 p. 25–9).

42 Following the approach already pioneered in Hirschman's dissertation, *The Poincaré Franc* (cf. above, sec. 6 of ch. 3).

43 Hirschman 1988a; cf. above, sec. 3 and n. 15.

through foreign trade.[44] The first chapter provides an agile survey of the history of economic thought on this topic.[45]

Oft-repeated phrases in the literature of the liberal tradition between the wars about power politics, "like 'the perversion of normal economic activities' or 'the diversion of national wealth from its true economic purposes' indicate that [...] the pursuit of power was still largely considered as a subordinate or exceptional aim of economic policy." But it was not always this way. Indeed, Hirschman adds, "if the proposal to make the power of the state a primary aim of economic policy was a shock to many contemporary minds, it nevertheless formed the basis and even the *raison d'être* of earlier schools of economic thought"—mercantilism first and foremost.[46]

In general, the aim of increased national power at the expense of rival states, on the one hand, and the aim of increased wealth, on the other, were brought into complete harmony by the balance of trade doctrine, which led the Mercantilists to assume that in its external economic relations a nation can increase its wealth only be decreasing the wealth of other nations. The instrument of the shift was thought to be a balance of payments leading to an influx of gold and silver."[47]

44 "While the proposals put forward by various schools of economic thought were usually aimed at strengthening the power of a nation, Hirschman worked against the grain, taking national power as given and studying at a theoretical level the characteristics of foreign trade that can be exploited by the politics of power. This is why his book is called *National Power and the Structure of Foreign Trade*, not *The Structure of Foreign Trade and National Power*." (Meldolesi 1995 p. 12). The opposite causal path, on the other hand—from political to economic asymmetry—is not analyzed here. But this alone implies that such 'decomposition' of that interactive relationship, as we shall see later, may suggest the start of a reversed process—that of 'recomposition'—precisely by overturning that relationship.

45 Already emerging here is Hirschman's ability to navigate *pro domo propria* in a vast literature on the history of thought. In fact, to the regular Hirschman reader, this chapter calls to mind the more detailed discussions on the subject that would follow—such as those on politics and economics in *The Passions* (1977) and on political thought in *The Rhetoric* (1991).

46 Hirschman 1980 p. 3 and pp. 3–4. The reference in this regard is to Heckscher 1935 and 1936, and Viner 1935.

47 Hirschman 1980 p. 4. "An increase in the stock of precious metals," the passage continues, "would contribute indeed to the power of the state either directly by the accumulation of treasure or indirectly by enriching the country, which would thus be in a better position to contribute to the power of the state by taxes and services."

On the other hand, this was the background against which the debate over the wealth and power of nations later developed, engaging great economists such as Smith and Hume, which suggested free-market and protectionist policies and their eclectic combinations in the practices of states, and which provided economic and non-economic arguments to German and English internationalists, philosophers and economists, etc., up to John Stuart Mill—"one of the first to show that the material benefit derived from international trade is *not necessarily divided equally among the various trading nations.*" It thus happens—and this is the point—that some of mercantilism's main conclusions concerning the balance of trade "were rehabilitated, not as a certainty, but as a *possibility* by the theory of the terms of trade."[48]

It is clear what intellectual path Hirschman decided to take. By dealing with national power and foreign trade (and not just the latter) he accepted the criticisms of classical economics of mercantilism (as in the standard reconstructions of the genesis of international trade theory). At the same time, however, he focused attention on the re-emergence in English and German literature of the theoretical-practical exigencies that, in its time, had inspired mercantilism. And after examining a number of suggestions present in the debate, he found—as just mentioned—the theoretical opening he was looking for at a specific point in the process of transition between the prevalence of classical thought and that of neo-classical thought—from which, in fact, Marshall's thesis of gains from trade would arise.

9 – Let us take a close look at some passages that open the second chapter of *National Power.*[49]

"In trying to expand its power a nation must take account of many factors—historical, political, military, psychological, and economic." In concerning himself only with the last of these, Hirschman clearly carries out an *initial decomposition.*

"Among the economic determinants of power," he adds, "foreign trade plays an important part"—*second decomposition.* And the text continues: "In order to analyze the way in which foreign trade contributes to a certain distribution of power among the various nations, it must be *isolated* temporarily from the other determinants; for the purpose of our inquiry these other determinants

48 Ibid. p. 10 and 11. (Emphases added).
49 Ibid. p. 13 and 26. (Emphasis added).

may be impounded in a vast *ceteris paribus* upon which, for the sake of rendering our analysis more realistic, we shall have to draw from time to time."

"It will then be our aim to understand why and how relationships of dependence, of influence, and even of domination can arise out of trade relations. We are not concerned with the opposite line of causation *which also exists* and which may even have had a greater historical importance: the question of how a given distribution of power influences trade relations"—*third decomposition*.[50]

Having thus carefully narrowed down the scope of his research, Hirschman presents the two effects of foreign trade—supply and influence—which he then illustrates with the role of foreign trade in the rise of Nazi Germany.

The supply effect "is certain to be positive: By providing a more plentiful supply of goods or by replacing goods wanted less by goods wanted more (from the power standpoint), foreign trade enhances the potential military force of a country. [And also] it uses the threat of war as a weapon of diplomacy."[51]

The influence effect resides instead in the provision of its own, peculiar method of coercion in relations between sovereign nations. "We must concede," Hirschman explains, "that the explanation of the great power held in the past by Great Britain was the fact that she possessed strategic bases, such as Gibraltar, Suez, and Singapore. The possession of these bases had two consequences: First, it guaranteed the security of British trade; second, as a welcome by-product, it enabled Great Britain to cut off the trade of other countries passing through these points, be it trade with Great Britain or trade between two other countries. This second consequence gave her considerable direct power over, and influence in, other countries. [...] But every sovereign nation has some influence of this kind, since [...] it can at any time interrupt its own export and import trade."[52]

---

50 Ibid. p. 13. (Emphases added). The author later comes back to this last point (ibid. p. 26), writing, "We are here concerned only with the methods and conditions leading to this [national] power, not with its possible uses which may be the reaping of advantages of any kind—military and political, as well as economic." "It will, however," he had clarified earlier (ibid. p. 13), "be well for the reader to remember that frequently the adoption of certain economic policies leading to greater power for a given nation is possible only if there exists an initial power disequilibrium in favor of that nation. Colonial trade often gives us the opportunity of observing this type of cumulative effect." This is the beginning of a *recomposition* that sets in motion a commercial interaction between nation and colony that increases the wealth and power of the former at the expense of those of the latter.

51 Ibid. p. 14.

52 Ibid. p. 15.

10 – There follows in the text an extensive discussion of the influence effect of foreign trade (which we can necessarily account for only in part).[53] To me it is interesting to look for the significance of this indirectly—starting with Marshall's affirmation (anticipated at the end of sec. 3) that the direct gain that a country derives from its foreign trade consists of the excess of the *value* attributed to imported goods over the *value* attributed to the goods that the country could have produced domestically with the capital and labor dedicated to producing the goods exported in exchange for them.

"This definition," Hirschman maintains,[54] "brings out clearly that the gain from trade cannot be measured either by comparing the satisfaction derived from the consumption of the imports with the satisfaction which could be derived from the consumption at home of the exports, or by comparing the hypothetical domestic cost of the imported commodities with their actual cost."

No statistics are available, Marshall had continued,[55] "for making a near estimate of this excess [of value]: and consequently the gain which a country derives from her foreign trade is often stated on another plan, which suggests more definite ideas: it is not strictly correct; but it serves fairly well for some purposes. On this plan, it is tacitly assumed that the country would make for herself those things which she imports, if she could not get them by trade: and accordingly her gains from her trade are taken to be the excess of the cost to which she would be put if she made her imports herself, over that to which she is put by making other things and exporting them in exchange for her imports."

The importance of this passage lies, in my view, in the assertion that strictly speaking the calculation *is not correct*. For it is one thing to compare the objective cost of different products, another to compare the satisfaction of consuming different commodities, and yet another, quite different indeed, to compare the *value* ascribed to them by a nation.[56] Fundamentally, it is among these discrepancies that Hirschman's reasoning moves.

53 This is a kind of theoretical-professional tête-à-tête with some of the literature of the time on gains from trade (ibid. p. 17 ff.) necessary to complete his own argument.

54 Ibid. pp. 18–9.

55 Marshall 1923 p. 110.

56 Because "if a country was shut off from trade it would normally neither continue to produce the goods formerly exported nor try to produce at home all the goods formerly imported, but, given the reduced resources, an adjustment would take place toward the production of the goods most desired." (Hirschman 1980 p. 19).

In fact, "the inquiry into the factors which determine the amount of the subjective gain from trade has to be made directly. It has been undertaken with the help of diagrammatical illustrations by the neoclassical writers [...]. Marshall's conclusion [...] is that 'the surplus (of country G) is the greater, the more urgent is G's demand for a small amount of E's goods and the more of them she can receive without any great movement of the rate of interchange in her favor.' In other words, with a given volume of trade, the subjective gain is smallest if the supply-demand schedule of a country maintains a high elasticity throughout its relevant part; whereas the gain would be largest if a country's demand, after having been very elastic for small amounts of the other country's goods, becomes inelastic in its later (and relevant) stages."[57]

11 – The focus of the reasoning is thus on the demand elasticity of imports and exports. What is the meaning of the expression "*elasticity of national demand?*" Marshall asks. And he answers that "the elasticity of her effective demand for foreign goods is governed not only by her wealth and the elasticity of the desires of her population for them, but also by her ability to adjust the supplies of her own goods of various kinds to the demands of foreign markets." It is from here that the noted argument arises on the exchange between rich and poor countries: "The rich country can with little effort supply a poor country with implements for agriculture or the chase which double the effectiveness of her labour, and which she could not make herself, while the rich country could without great trouble make for herself most of the things which she purchases from the poor nation: or at all events could get fairly good substitutes for them. A stoppage of the trade would therefore generally cause much more real loss to the poor than to the rich nation."[58]

This means that in a poor country demand elasticity for imports (capital goods and consumer goods desired by its élites) is often relatively rigid because the country is not in a position to produce them domestically, while the products it offers on the external market are elastic in demand, i.e., undesirable and/or easily replaceable.

57 Ibid. p. 22; Marshall 1923 Appendix J, p. 338–40.

58 Marshall 1923 p. 167 and 168. (Emphasis added.)

Hirschman drew from this the conviction that "tariff wars and interruptions of trade rarely occur, but the awareness of their possibility is sufficient to test the influence of the stronger country and to shape the policy of the weaker."[59]

12 – At this point the book begins gradually modifying the assumptions of the theory to bring the reasoning little by little closer to the observed reality. In fact, along with impoverishment, the eventual disruption of trade would impose on the punished country a difficult process of 'adaptation'—reuse of the factors of production employed in the goods no longer exported, and making up at least in part, perhaps with substitute products, for the loss of imported goods. Of course, the immediate effect of this would be different from the ultimate effect. "The classical theory of international trade was aware of this distinction, but it concentrated upon the ultimate loss," considering the adjustment difficulties to be short-term. In contrast, "modern theory insists that this is not necessarily true; and even if it were true," Hirschman adds (beginning to encroach on political and social science), "our analysis would have to take into account the fact that harassed statesmen generally have a short-run view."[60]

And furthermore, "with a given quantity of exports the problem created by an interruption of trade will be the more difficult, (1) the smaller the mobility of resources within the country, (2) the more the economic activities leading to exports have been concentrated in certain lines of production or in certain regions." In fact, "the actual going volume of trade, indeed, produces *its own vested interests*"—with respect to both the danger of losing a supply and the danger of losing a market. "Aside from the purely commercial groups, [...] the vested interests will consist of the producers for export and of the industries using imported raw materials." For example, "if exports are concentrated in some region or some industry," these "will exert a powerful influence in favor of a 'friendly' attitude toward the state to the imports of which they owe their existence"[61]—not to speak, of course, of the workers and their families, etc.

---

59 Evidently, along with Demangeon's course (see above, sec. 2), reading some of Marshall's work on foreign trade lay in the background of Hirschman's interest in the development economics of less advanced countries, which, as we know, would be vigorously asserted later in his work.

60 Hirschman 1980 pp. 26–7; cf. above, sec. 9. "Given a certain ultimate loss, the influence which one country exercises upon another through foreign trade is therefore likely to be larger the greater the immediate loss which it can inflict by a stoppage of trade."

61 Ibid. pp. 27–9. (Emphasis added.)

13 – "We must now drop a simplifying assumption under which we have worked hitherto," Hirschman continues, "and allow for the possibility of alternative markets or sources of supply."[62] "In the old colonial system a colony was not permitted to turn to other buyers or sellers, even though the mother country had no obligation at all to provide the colony with goods or to buy from it. Under modern conditions, subtler methods must be devised in order to arrive to a similar results."[63]

Apart from monopoly or monopsony conditions (natural or artificially produced), one of these methods concerns the greater or lesser concentration of exchange. "German-Bulgarian trade in 1938, for example, represented 52 and 59 per cent of Bulgarian imports and exports, respectively, but only 1.5 and 1.1 per cent of the German imports and exports. Under these conditions it will obviously be "much more difficult for Bulgaria to shift her trade with Germany to other countries than it will be for Germany to replace Bulgaria as a selling market and a source of supplies."[64] In other words, a basic principle of power politics for large and rich nations is to direct their trade toward countries that are small and poor. These, on the other hand, have the opposite interest—to diversify their commercial relations.

Another way of reaching these results has to do with a general condition of incomplete resource utilization at the macro-economic level—such that countries are far more inclined to sell than to buy. It thus happens that, for reasons of power politics, bilateral agreements that ensure the export outlet of the dominated country at the same time produce the technical impossibility for the latter to replace its imports by turning elsewhere. "In this way the device of bilateralism is seen to be an important link in the policies by which the aim of maximum power through foreign trade may be attained."[65]

Finally, if, due to geographical, technical or contractual conditions, transit trade cannot be replaced by direct trade, it then becomes an ideal tool

62 Ibid. pp. 29–34.

63 Ibid. p. 30.

64 Ibid. pp. 30–1. On this issue we may note the typical Colornian-Hirschmanian reasoning process. A well-founded observation that contradicts current thinking has to be taken seriously (rather than being set aside so as not to challenge the status quo—including, of course, the personal 'comfort zone'). This is the thesis of the *petite idée* that needs to be explored gradually, Hirschman said, like a Chinese paper flower that opens little-by-little when it's put in water. In this case, as we shall see, this happened through robust intellectual efforts and subsequent self-subversions.

65 Ibid. p. 33.

enabling the intermediary country to exert its influence—both on the country of origin and the country of final destination of the goods in transit. Which is to say that "provided only that its services are indispensable, the country handling the transit trade acquires [...] a twofold influence and at the same time evades almost entirely any dependence of its own economy."[66]

This is where things finally come to a head, because the author inserts at this point in his reasoning "an illustration: German trading methods under National Socialism." After presenting a table summarizing "the conditions or policies which have been described as being conducive to increased national power by means of foreign trade," Hirschman states that, "practically all the outstanding features of German foreign economic policy since 1933 can be subsumed under this scheme. This does not mean [...] that Germany has consciously worked out such a master plan." On the contrary, "it seems probable that the amazing coherence of German policies was due only in part to detailed planning springing from economic analysis and that an important role was left to experimentation in the elaboration of actual policies. But if we assume only that in every decision of commercial policy the political power standpoint was given due consideration, the coherence of German policies need not surprise us, for, in every case, this power, so far as it is based on foreign trade at all, goes back in the last analysis either to the strength which foreign trade lends to the German war machine or to Germany's power to menace her trading partners with a stoppage of trade (influence effect)."[67]

An intriguing (and unexpected) debate

14 – In the early 1980s, Albert Hirschman proposed to a mutual friend, Marcello de Cecco, an economist with expertise in monetary theory and international economic history, that he edit the publication in Italian of an anthology of Hirschman's works written at around the time of the Second World War. Probably on the recommendation of Hirschman himself (who already had the project in mind), Marcello was then a temporary member of the Institute for Advanced Study (Princeton, NJ), and decided to accept. Together with a former student of his, Pier Francesco Asso, he undertook the 'curation' of what

66 Ibid. pp. 33–4.
67 Ibid. p. 35 and 39.

eventually became *Potenza nazionale e commercio estero. Gli anni trenta, l'Italia e la ricostruzione* by Albert Hirschman (1987).[68]

Therefore, along with "Mémoire sur le contrôle des changes en Italie"(1939)[69] and five papers on Italy (from 1947–48),[70] Asso and de Cecco published in Italian "Part One: Theoretical and Historical Aspects" of *National Power and the Structure of Foreign Trade.*

In offering these youthful writings of Albert's the two editors wanted "to present a contemporary interpretation of the period able to inspire an analysis of current international economic history based on assumptions 'alternative' to those of the theoretical orthodoxy that continues to permeate the study of economic reality of today's economists."[71] "Nevertheless," they added,[72] "we must say that the texts proposed here seem important to us precisely because they transcend the historical frames that they immediately deal with. What primarily interests us, and we hope interests the reader, is their methodological message." This is a reference to their firm stance with regard to three foundations of then-dominant economic policy theory: "the orthodox analysis of 'gains from trade,' exasperation with the logical-deductive method and the associated heuristic value losses, and the identification of economics as an end and not as an instrument of statecraft."

The idea, if I'm not mistaken, was to learn first of all to navigate between economic history and theory as a way of exploring once again, à la Hirschman, the relationship between national power and foreign trade. Thus the two editors skillfully surveyed some of the essential terms of their analysis: the emergence of bilateralism in the evolution of international trade between the wars; their relation to the policies in support of domestic demand provoked by the

68 Asso and de Cecco – "Introduzione" 1987 p. 8 – asserted, among other things, that the collected texts had special significance for the Italian reader because "they concern, for the most part, facts about the economic history of our country, of which Albert Hirschman, from a very early age and since then as well, has proved himself a most acute and passionate observer." (A point of view, which, as I mentioned in the introduction, requires, however, some further study and clarification.)

69 This report was written for the League of Nations: see ch. 3, sec. 7 above.

70 "Exchange controls in Italy" (Part I and II) – 1947; "France and Italy: Patterns of Reconstruction" – 1947a; "Italian Exchange Rate policy" – 1947b; "Inflation and Deflation in Italy" – 1948; "Economic and Financial Conditions in Italy" – 1948a.

71 Asso and de Cecco 1987 p. 8. (This laudable intention was then put in practice in "Bilateralism, Trade Agreements and Political Economists in the 1930s: Theories and Events Underlying Hirschman's Index" by Pier Francesco Asso - 1988).

72 Asso and de Cecco 1987 p. 8.

'29 crisis; the exercise of power politics in various projects of trade integration; the acquisition of positions of control over supply sources, import composition, and their uses; the divergent results obtained by the main countries involved; the reception in later periods of the writings of Hirschman's presented in the book; and the ability of the latter to interpret the historical facts in the light of the existing literature.

But they focused particularly on the specific aspect of Albert's work that concerns "gains from trade." Hirschman's analysis, they argued, "conducted using the Marshallian theoretical apparatus, manages to reach different conclusions from Marshall's. This is an analytical operation of the same kind as Keynes conducted with respect to orthodox theory, and which serves the same purpose—to make plausible to orthodox economists considerations and reasoning that arise from philosophical foundations that are opposite to their own."[73]

In conclusion, Asso and de Cecco maintain that "in the few years that passed between the drafting of *National Power* and the writings on Italy [some of which are included in *Potenza nazionale*] a methodological break took place which the latter writings attest to and which brings them much closer to more celebrated works"[74] – like *The Strategy* and *Exit*.

In contrast, in their view, the Hirschman of *National Power* seems to be an "economist more sensitive to the appeal of the power of economic theory, and to an enriched but systematic use of it to understand and describe changes in the real world. His is a rigorous if at times naïve attempt to provide an alternative vision, crowning an intellectual process that starts from within an already established theoretical tradition, and which carefully takes into account the economic lessons of the 1930s and, in general, the post-Versailles innovations."[75]

15 – Having been a (long-time) friend of Marcello de Cecco, and then of Albert Hirschman, I was surprised re-reading these criticisms after so much water had

73 Ibid. pp. 25–6. In doing this, the two scholars maintain (p. 33 and 34) that Hirschman, like Keynes, "seems intent above all at this stage on showing that on the same instrument as Marshall's one can play quite different music, and that such music is not only typical of Germanic folklore, but belongs to the common tradition of modern states." "In effect," they add, "in this work, the main desire seems to be to identify stable relationships between magnitudes, so as to crystallize the analysis in a modeling that is alternative to the traditional one, but which is still a mirror image of it."

74 Ibid. pp. 34–5.

75 Ibid. p. 37.

passed under the bridge, first and foremost because of their imperfections (let's call them) I am dealing with below. Moreover, I was even more surprised, as we shall see later, by the response our author gave to the two editors.

In the first place, Asso and de Cecco's contention that "Hirschman became Hirschman" from a methodological point of view only with the postwar texts does not hold to a careful examination of Albert's writings from the 1930s (cf. above ch. 3)—as indeed de Cecco himself ended up admitting implicitly (although not *apertis verbis*[76]) in his introduction to the 2004 publication of Albert Hirschman's graduation thesis *The Poincaré Franc and its Devaluation*.

I suspect, however, that the responsibility for this 'misunderstanding' (so to speak) should be divided equally between Marcello and Hirschman because, knowing the latter's typical behavior, it seems likely to me that he did not provide all his prewar papers to the two editors beforehand.[77]

For me this explains how, as economists, Asso and de Cecco could take a standard interpretive path—the author's methodological change. This path *seems to me to fit better with their own experience* (reflected here anthropomorphically on Hirschman's), rather than with Albert's actual "life and work"—which includes, of course, his Colornian roots.

If this is well founded, it nevertheless remains to be understood why, even in the context of a continuity of inspiration that is today substantiated by the availability of the texts, *National Power*—written by the young Albert in the midst of the world war—has come to take on (methodologically) distinctive characteristics, with respect to both his prewar and postwar writings.

It is in fact true, as we have seen, that while at times taking into account certain political and social considerations, Hirschman essentially found in Alfred Marshall's economic work on international trade an important guiding

76 Probably so as not to retrace his steps and out of (Abruzzese!) pride.

77 What makes me think this, among other things, is a note of Asso and de Cecco's (1987 p. 20 n. 20) that reads: "It will be recalled that Hirschman presented the Italian case to the International Conference on Economic Policies and Peace organized by the International Institute for Intellectual Cooperation in Paris" organized by Jack Condliffe. Aside from the already mentioned "Mémoire sur le contrôle des changes en Italie," however, the fact is (see ch. 3, sec. 7) that for this international conference (which was supposed to be held in Bergen, Norway, and partially failed to convene), Hirschman wrote the important "Étude statistique sur la tendence du commerce extérieur vers l'equilibre et le bilateralisme," which contains indices of bilateralism for five countries (but not Italy).

thread, very useful in unraveling his own reasoning.[78] And it is true as well that, utilizing certain Leibnizian-Colornian strategems, he carried out the "decomposition" of Marshall's treatment to the point of basing achievable national power on foreign trade—rather than vice versa.

So why did this happen? A first answer is already contained in what we have written so far—the interpretation Hirschman came up with starting from a small idea and a specific rib of economic theory was decisive in explaining what, with regard to foreign trade, enabled the rise of Nazi Germany in the 1930s.

But there is a second, more challenging reason, which needs to be brought to the foreground. Re-reading Hirschman's 'Preface' to the 1987 book[79]—I have already mentioned it—held a maxi-surprise for me. For Albert does not address the somewhat problematic aspect of the editors'"Introduction" discussed so far; rather, as we shall see, he praises the critical remarks of Asso and de Cecco, almost taking for granted the validity of their thesis on the 'methodological break' characterizing his developmental process. In contrast, after a brief preamble, he points without hesitation to the positive side of the story.

16 – It must be borne in mind that Hirschman's clarifications in this "Preface" are part of a small series of fine-tunings—not to say 'revelations'[80]—by means of which (inter alia) he intended to revisit (and revitalize) *National Power.*

Indeed, "Beyond Asymmetry: Critical Notes on Myself as a Young Man and on Some Other Old Friends," was published in the 1980 edition of *National*

78 Something that had also happened to other famous economists. It is true, however, that (compared to, say, Keynes or Sraffa) Hirschman's elaboration deliberately (typically) followed path that was collateral, not overtly antagonistic, to orthodoxy.

79 A "Preface" to be seen as a sort of (partial) 'private word' in Italian, since it was not republished in English, unlike his contemporary, "I, Detective of the Fascist Economy." Actually, the "Preface" is from May 1987, while "I, Detective" was Hirschman's response at the conferral of his honorary degree in political science at the University of Turin on 12 November 1987 [later in Hirschman 1990a p. xxix–xxxi, and republished in English in 1995, ch. 9]. Consequently, the statements in this "Preface" should be considered as addressed to an educated Italian audience, but *not* to an international audience.

80 A process that continued later with his autobiographical communications at his numerous "honorary" degrees conferrals during that period; with his "Introduction" to the new edition of Varian Fry's *Autobiography* (1993); with *Crossing Boundaries* (1994; 1998 ch. 3); and with the "On Self" section of *A Propensity* (1995).

Power as the "Preface to the Expanded Edition," and reproduced in the 1987 book as a sort of "Prologue."[81]

Moreover, it is well-known that in "A Dissenter's Confession" (1984b), setting aside the most famous of his "half truths,"[82] Hirschman had recalled *coram populo* his work with the Federal Reserve Board during the Marshall Plan period (1946–52). "The enormous economic power in the hands of the United States at that moment in history," he added in the 1987 "Preface,"[83] "made even my position, seemingly only dedicated to research, surprisingly influential, both within the US government and in economic relations with Western Europe."

Therefore, it is easy to see at this point how Asso and de Cecco's argument might "back up" Hirschman's reasoning. In fact, after briefly summarizing his exploits, he wrote, "these biographical notes can help explain the differences between the prewar and postwar writings that Pier Francesco Asso and Marcello de Cecco astutely capture in their introduction."

Reading this led me to wonder—does it also refer to his dissertation (*The Poincaré Franc and its Devaluation*)? No, I thought—that can't be right. It seemed to me, rather, that, contrary to what he wrote, Hirschman had actually decided to 'gloss over' the methodological question of the relationship between *National Power* and *his pre-war writings*, and to focus instead on the difference between *National Power* and *the post-war texts*.[84]

---

81 As we will see, this important, 'self-subversive' essay (out of which a new 'slant' in Hirschman's thought later emerged, leading up to his well-known composition of *A Propensity to Self-Subversion* – 1995) reworked the relationship between economics and politics that sustains his early monograph.

82 "There is nothing quite like a good story, to lend authority to a half-truth" [like the one on the origin of *The Strategy of Economic Development* Albert Hirschman was used to tell – 1986 p. 4–5].

83 Hirschman 1987 p. 42.

84 Using for example by way of '*viaticum*' some of Asso and de Cecco's (1987 p. 31) statements such as: "In postwar Hirschman [...] we see with greater clarity the anti-paradigm developed 'in the field,' according to which the practical application of a theory's coherent conclusions is never painless. On the contrary, in suggesting recipes and formulating predictions and interpretations, '*a priori* deductions, while instructive, can only yield extremely rough guesses and are not able to replace as yet the method of trial and error'"—as noted, in "Economic and Financial Conditions in Italy": a 1948 essay included in this collection.

After 1945 the political tension – Hirschman wrote – "was reduced, with consequences of various kinds. First of all, there was no longer the same need as before to always reach definitive conclusions capable of inspiring action."

"What is more," he continued, "in my new role in postwar Washington I found myself in an ironic position. If just a bit earlier I was a political refugee with no power whose most ambitious work at the time [*National Power*] had criticized the political use of economic power, I could now not help but note that the economic power of the country of which I was now a citizen and representative, gave my opinions and those of my colleagues undeserved weight and resonance with the US government. My reaction, perhaps excessive at times, was to suppress the use of whatever power I had; but above all I worked hard to *undermine* the certainty of my colleagues (whether pro-market or pro-planning), many of whom saw no harm in using the fullest extent of their power in the service of their opinions and beliefs."[85]

His conclusion: "Such an attitude perhaps explains the 'caesura' noted by Asso and de Cecco, which may even have become a methodological habit underlying a great part of my successive work."[86]

---

85 Hirschman 1987 p. 42. (Original emphasis).

86 Hirschman 1987, p. 42. At this point the reader may have noted an unusual peculiarity that can be deduced from the reasoning just given. When Hirschman confessed to his rather amusing "half-truth" (cf. above, n. 81), he still did not take on the responsibility of telling "the whole truth" (through a "more complex story," like the one concerning the Marshall Plan). So that later, in the "Preface" to the book edited by Asso and de Cecco, he felt it necessary to add to his initial "confession" some crucial considerations. The fact is, Albert was always particular about deciding case by case what to say and not to say, what to write and not to write. Thus it happened that often, in retrospect, his "more complex stories" actually seem *partial*—so much so that, in my opinion, (favorable) critics inherited in this regard a problem to be solved, that of making the developmental process of his 'point of view' more understandable, convincing, and (within certain limits) more complete. Albert, on the other hand, always displayed a certain reluctance to 'tell all,' to clarify completely exactly the way things were—perhaps because of a mixture of the shrewdness typical of his character, and caution of a relational and political origin. Almost as if he enjoyed observing the perplexity of those inquiring about his intellectual world. Almost as if he liked maintaining an aura of the unspoken, the intangible, the indecipherable. Almost as if, as a stateless person, he was always concerned about 'watching his back,' of being in reality a 'blessed one-eyed man' (in the land of the blind). And it was from this, in my view, that the issue of his half-truths arises—which, however, as he approached his seventies, Hirschman decided to 'unveil' in stages, with difficulty, and never fully—but with a touch of self-irony.

17 – It is an enlightening piece, no doubt about it. But nevertheless (I insist!), *not enough* to explain the methodological question about *National Power* raised by Asso and de Cecco. In fact, it is perfectly clear that from observing the statistics regarding Germany's trade, Hirschman took a small idea and managed to make it big by leaning on a specific aspect of the theory of international trade. But what is still not clear is *why* he stopped there—even while maintaining, as we have seen, that the argument *could* have been continued by inverting the relationship between foreign trade and national power.

In other words, *why* at the time did Albert deny himself the possibility of exploring a general characteristic of his work—namely "the tendency to study an experience in its 'becoming,'" as Asso and de Cecco observed, "leaving its imaginable conclusions completely open and highlighting the dialectical phases of the experience itself."[87]

Of course, a first reason inevitably has a professional flavor—in the sense that given the situation he was in, Hirschman first and foremost had an absolute need to make himself understood by the experts in his discipline.[88] But in all likelihood there is a second, perhaps more important reason. As we shall now see, along with the explanation of the international trade aspect of Germany's rise, *the general political message* entrusted to the book flows (*sic et simpliciter*) from the theory—at first glance almost making its further elaboration seem unnecessary.

Is this really the case? Is it an enticement to the unknown, a forbidden fruit?

18 – This hypothesis needs to be tested, perhaps by going back to excavating the text. All of this fascinated me—until I discovered that even the "Preface" to the 1987 book itself contains a "half-truth."[89] So—I said to myself—Wow: *repetita iuvant*!

87 Asso and de Cecco 1987 p. 35.

88 It reminds me of my friend Giacomo Becattini, for example, who did not advise young economists to bother with Hirschman. Because, he said, "it's bad luck" from the point of view of their university careers (!).

89 Actually, several things attracted me: the dialogue with this interesting book edited by Asso and de Cecco; the discussion they provoked with their idea of Hirschman's pre- vs. post-war methodological break; and finally, the process of Albert's successive

Let us recall: as already mentioned, Albert's conclusion of the passage quoted above refers, in my view, to the relationship between *National Power* and Hirschman's later texts, but not to the relationship between *National Power* and the prewar writings. So that in light of Hirschman's *Early Writings* (discussed above in chapter 3), the thesis of the "methodological caesura" argued 'en gros' by Asso and de Cecco does not seem to have any real basis *from the standpoint of the relationship between National Power and the prewar writings*—in the sense that along with the inevitable discontinuity due to the war, there is between the two groups of writings—those from before the war and those from after—a remarkable continuity of inspiration.

Moreover: going back in our minds to the early 1980s, this appears understandable for the two editors—especially if (as is possible) they did not have Hirschman's prewar writings at their disposal when preparing their "Introduction" and based their reasoning on the texts chosen for the volume. However—and this is the point—it is less intelligible for Hirschman, not least when one examines in detail the beginning of his "Preface."

'confessions' along a single trajectory. Indeed, all of this favored my research into the different developmental stages of our author—a young, promising economist who later became a researcher and public servant, and then an academic. This is the extraordinary and influential social scientist we have come to know and appreciate. It was this inspiration that sustained me for a long time, until I realized a confused perception that turned into a small idea: what it is that Hirschman's "Preface" to this anthological selection edited by Asso and de Cecco *does not say*. My interest turned first to distress, and then to the opposite feeling: to gratitude in approaching an author who, to put it the old-fashioned way, scattered several 'sibylline riddles' among his essays. He bequeathed them to the critics, implicitly suggesting that they gradually find their own solutions (a kind of 'treasure hunt'), so that they could collaterally grasp the importance of Hirschman's work, and then re-propose it (in part) from different points of view, and in this way create an intellectual tendency compatible with it. This sentiment finally convinced me to frame a new and even more comprehensive discourse on Albert's work. As seen in the previous chapters, it ultimately took the "Triestine" path (and Colorni's *opera omnia*).

Actually, after thanking the two editors and the publisher for the "wave of pure joy" he felt in "suddenly finding himself in front of these collected, carefully drafted and elegantly published early texts," and after briefly recalling some of the phases of his intense early life, Hirschman argued, as I have already mentioned, that such biographical notes can help us understand the thesis of Asso and de Cecco's "methodological *caesura*." And he added: "up until the final defeat of Fascism and Nazism, everything I wrote was somehow bound to fit into that struggle."

Of course it might be objected that some of the writings from before the war take into account the very serious darkening of the European and world political situation that preceded the Second World War, but this does not shed light on the difference in approach between those texts and "Foreign Trade as an Instrument of National Power," the second chapter of *National Power*, examined in depth by Asso and de Cecco.

What would be required, in other words, is an answer to the following question: Why didn't Hirschman, once he had seen the two editors' introduction, take the road that in my view would have been the most natural—that is, supply them with the 1937–39 papers (which he later delivered to me personally)? He could have requested a small "adjustment," or at the least that they distinguish (even with a simple caveat such as 'conceived in a different way') the approach in *National Power* from that of the prewar texts.

The only explanation I can find is binary. On one hand Albert was attracted by Asso and de Cecco's 'methodological break' argument for its valid side (pointing out the huge leap between *National Power* and his successive work with the Federal Reserve Board of the United States) and for the opportunity it offered by that route of adding in Italian (and thus in a separate venue) a number of important aspects of his "Confession."

But on the other hand, perhaps just to get by (*se debrouiller*) in the brief period before the book's publication, Hirschman did not see the need to go back to the 1930s. He found it expedient simply to write what he wrote.

The conclusion therefore is that even this "Preface" is itself a "half-truth," and making it more complete will require linking it to the itinerary I followed in the previous chapter.

From here a general observation arises. Since it is not unusual—let us say—to run into questions of this type in examining Hirschman's writings in depth,[90] it is worth speculating that the author used such stratagems—first instinctively and possibly temporarily, and then increasingly consciously—perhaps from the moment he first stepped onto American soil. So that having finished the militant phase of his life—the one spent with German, Italian and French anti-Fascists (and anti-Nazis) and culminating in his Marseilles exploits with Varian Fry—of which he was most proud, Albert began to adapt his daily professional routine to some of the many ingenious devices he had invented or acquired during his heroic period—including the use *pro domo sua* of the relative isolation of Italian culture and language from the Anglo-Saxon world…[91]

90 And recalling the many personal conversations I had the good fortune to have with him. I remember, for example, asking him face-to-face what he thought of the 1968 protests (which his daughter Katia had taken part in along with Alain Salomon, her fiancé and then husband). Albert's answer was that he couldn't give an opinion because during that year, as guest of a famous institute at Stanford, he was absorbed in writing *Exit, Voice, and Loyalty*. This was true, of course, but only halfway—in the sense that such an answer also helped him dodge a question that in that moment he didn't want to answer.

91 If I'm not wrong this was the same inspiration that gave rise to the numerous 'focuses of attention'—let's call them—that I came to notice over time: how to put silence on the same level as speech; emphasizing or setting aside his personal experiences, even minute ones, according to convenience; learning always (and in every case) to choose between voice and exit; speaking little and in a low voice, so as to nudge the interlocutor to 'step back and think'; deciding carefully (specifically for the visitor/s of the moment) what topics to discuss and what words to use—so as to draw from them, as far as possible, the desired effect (short- and long-term); never conforming to another's point of view, though without needing to explicitly contradict it—even to the point of appearing reticent; circumspectly unveiling the part of his own 'disclosures' that might lead to useful results *pro domo sua* without ever actually spilling the beans; carefully delimiting the scope of the discussion so that he could get useful feedback from the interlocutor for his own purposes; proceeding cautiously, prudently, and with a smile on his face, etc. A series of attitudes and ways of behaving that bring to mind 'Beamish' Hirschman of Marseilles (cf. above, ch. 2, sec. 6), and that led Andrea Giznburg to say that Albert was one who "knew it all…." They suggested (and suggest) the conclusion (cf. above, n. 85) that even for a great stateless Western intellectual of Jewish origin, as Albert undoubtedly was, the continuous search for truth in facts *did not automatically translate* into telling the truth, the whole truth—to the extent that critics are sometimes forced to search hypothetically, cautiously, patiently, laboriously for keys to numerous puzzles…. His Harvard students nicknamed Hirschman "tricky Albert." Perhaps they were not just referring to the intellectual stratagems he carried around with him….

National Power and its Political Inspiration

19 – Let us return to *Potenza nazionale e commercio estero*. Asso and de Cecco—and it is no small thing—managed to open the way for new thinking on the part of the author himself (an unusual occurrence for such an elaborate and well-constructed work). In addition, they suggested an interpretive-cognitive perspective that is in my opinion worth examining again, in detail—starting with a question that may have surfaced in the reader's mind.

That is, if the above interpretation of *National Power* makes sense—if the book is actually so different from (on one hand) the prewar texts and (on the other) those from after the war, how do we explain such differences?

My idea is that, once having grasped the *Marseillais* way of operating "à la Beamish"[92] (and evaluated what he wrote from that standpoint, but also what he kept quiet about), it becomes clear that *National Power* is a child of the war, of the subjective and objective conditions in which Hirschman found himself in California, and, at the same time, of his courageous decision to 'put himself on the line' as an intellectual, with everything he could reasonably conjure up at the time.

"Given the opportunity to become fully aware not only of their own methods," Colorni had written in his 1938 "Program"[93] (which Hirschman could have discussed with him in depth before leaving Trieste), "but also of the necessary premises underlying each of their constructs, the sciences are stimulated to overcome this necessity and to create new premises for themselves. The task of the mind here is not restricted to intellectual research. It also includes attitudes that may be brought together under the general term 'moral.' These require violent resistance to a way of seeing things that we are all bound to, a striving for liberation, a leap out of the world we are part of. The goal is to create a 'new mindset' for ourselves, to see things with different eyes, to simplify, to reject prefabricated constructs. We must rely on imagination, invention, and intuition to conjure worlds that are different from the one we are used to seeing."

It is the determination, in fact, the ability to lift himself up, the interior drive toward progress (in the emergency of war) of an extraordinarily gifted combative young economist in exile like Albert Hirschman which in my view (first and foremost) clarifies the genesis of *National Power*. It explains, that is,

92 Cf. n. 85 and 90.

93 Colorni 1938b; now in 2021a p. 89.

how "in one go," as Casanova put it, he was able to raise himself "au dessus de la melée"—the now mature fruit of his theoretical and practical experience, to the point of unwittingly ensuring the "exceptional longevity" of his book.[94]

This therefore (retrospectively) clarified Albert's decision, mentioned above, to keep his distance from European political veterans and instead concentrate on this book and, in accord with Jack Condliffe, to tread the Colornian path of small certain understandings which in and of themselves bring down large acquired systemic points of view—positions which, while manifesting ironclad theoretical coherence, do not actually match reality (specifically including general economic equilibrium theory and the attached 'pure' theory of international trade).

Hence the sequential development, through a few Marshall's suggestions, of the small starting idea on German foreign trade with the countries of eastern and southeastern Europe so as to trace out a different point of view on national power and the structure of foreign trade, one which is certainly incomplete in view of the complexity of all creation, but is nevertheless solid.[95]

Hence the decision to express *apertis verbis* the political reason behind the entire work (which, using a self-mocking expression—in my opinion only partly justified—he later labeled "infinitely naïve").

20 – Hirschman constructed a 'unicum' in comparison with his writings from before and after the war—a fundamentally political text, undoubtedly linked to his time, but one that still interests us a great deal today, and for more reasons than one. For one thing, it lifts the veil on one part of the immense inequalities that continue to characterize human affairs (and thus on the vertical, pyramidal structure of the planet's places, peoples and countries). And it implicitly suggests the existence of many other inequalities to be corrected. Furthermore, it teaches us similar ways of exploring the way we live (while also alluding to others that are very different), and it helps us decipher their difficulties and dangers. It recognizes that the world changes over time and we must be able to adapt to that process. And it points (in part) to a Colornian

94 In the sense that it stands as a 'unique piece'—a bit like what happened later, *mutatis mutandis*, with the writing of *Exit, Voice, and Loyalty* (which, not surprisingly, Hirschman dedicated to Eugenio Colorni).

95 And more useful therefore than theories of imperialism and 'dependencia,' which nevertheless contained a kernel of truth. This is clear from Hirschman's participation in the debate on the subject in the 1970s.

perspective that, in practice, a different planet, more people-friendly, is indeed possible.

This multiplicity of unsolved problems thus crowds the mind as soon as we delve into the book—especially the third chapter of the first part of *National Power*, where we read: "The Nazis have done nothing but exploit to the fullest possibilities *inherent* in foreign trade within the traditional framework of international economic relations. This is the general lesson which should emerge from the experience of economic penetration of such countries as Hungary, Bulgaria, Rumania, and other countries less successfully penetrated by 'bloodless invasion.' What are the conclusions which can be drawn from this experience when the present war will be won by the United Nations?"[96]

This is the question that at this point accompanies Hirschman's research, starting with the title of the chapter "The Question of Economic Aggression during World War I"—a sort of retrospective glance so as to get a better run-up to the future. "The literature on the commercial and economic policies of Nazi Germany being rather voluminous, it is surprising not to find in it—so far as the author is aware—a single reference to the parallel and equally copious literature which was published before and during World War I."[97]

This is an egregious error, Hirschman seems to suggest, at least for those who would like to find ways to prevent the recurrence of such world tragedies. The book therefore offers a quick overview of the economic-political events relating to national power and foreign trade that preceded, accompanied and followed the First World War.

"The accusations voiced against Germany at that time were in their substance very similar to those we hear today [1941–42]. The intellectual level of the writings on this subject, however, compares rather unfavorably [...]. In addition, the *methods* by which Germany was said to achieve her end of economic conquest before World War I were different from those which she has used more recently." At the same time, the (often alarmist) attitude of the analysts was conditioned by the immediate interests of their respective nationalisms (and rivalries). "Only at a later stage was Germany accused of consciously using her foreign economic relations as an instrument of domination" through dumping (as a way to monopsony), economic penetration (for the 'conquest' of Italy: Preziosi), economic warfare in the midst of peace (Hauser).[98]

96 Hirschman 1980 p. 53, (Original emphasis).

97 Ivi.

98 Ibid. pp. 53–7, (Original emphasis).

"In general," Hirschman comments, [these works] were entirely lacking in systematic analysis of the connection between national power ant international economic relations." And yet the possibility of employing the latter for objectives of political power was clearly recognized; "it had become a very strong subjective reality. For many persons it turned into an obsession" destined to perpetuate itself during and after World War I.[99]

There were, in the main, "two schools of thought. The writers who had aroused the public to the danger of 'silent economic penetration' were ardent advocates of preparing defensive or offensive weapons from the arsenal of economic nationalism. Aligned against them were the defenders of the virtues of free trade who ignored or denied the danger to which their adversaries had pointed."[100]

We can see at this point how Hirschman is (once again) seeking an interpretive path between two predictable, biased, ideological attitudes and thus harbingers of new tragedies (which, unfortunately, we cannot dwell on here). Moreover, Albert's is a discussion that winds its way through the 1916 Paris economic conference of the six allied nations,[101] through the debate that their resolutions generated in Russia, England, the United States, and France, and through the Versailles Peace Treaty, which represented a compromise between the nationalist and free trade currents—and was later defeated by the economic and trade policies developed during the peace years that combined the principle of full economic sovereignty with policies of restriction and discrimination. Evidently, the purpose of the discussion was to prepare the ground for the "denouement" in the chapter that followed—"The Problems of Reconstruction," which would have to be faced after the victorious end to the Second World War.

99 Ibid. p. 58.

100 Ibid. p. 59. From this singular tussle ("between those who ignore the danger of external economic relations becoming an instrument of national power aims and those who see the danger but try to remedy it by the defensive and offensive weapons of economic nationalism") Hirschman spares (ibid. p. 70) only Francis Edgeworth…

101 England, France, Italy, Russia, Belgium and Japan, in whose Resolutions (reproduced in Hirschman 1980, Appendix B, pp. 163–65) "we find enumerated all the fundamental policies of refined economic nationalism with which we have become so well acquainted in the period between the two wars." Conclusion: "Even a cursory view of this amazing Pandora's box raises doubts whether these measures were devised for defense only" (Hirschman 1980 pp. 61–2).

21 – This brings us finally to the heart of the problem. Hirschman anticipated it in some of his questions:[102] "Should we, because of its evil potentialities, try to limit international intercourse? Should special safeguard or boycott measures be erected against German trade once the war is over? Should we be content with prohibiting certain practices and technical devices, such as bilateral clearings, differential exchange rates, etc., which have been a prominent feature of German policies in the 'thirties'? Or should we rather endeavor to build a new framework of international relations in which this use of foreign trade for purposes of national power would encounter more difficulties than hitherto? And how could this end be achieved?"

Here we understand what Albert was thinking (retrospectively) when, in the 1987 "Preface," he wrote that right up to the final defeat of Fascism and Nazism, "what I wrote was in some way forced to fit into that struggle." He was obviously not thinking of his numerous 1937–39 writings, but of *National Power*. In fact, the book is consciously constructed, as a whole, to reach a (final!) conclusion—one that Hirschman presents after examining "three possible attempts to solve the question: (1) the imposition of certain restraints upon the commercial and economic policy of Germany and her allies; (2) universal free trade; and (3) the abolition of discriminating practices and the restriction of state intervention."[103]

In the first case we run the risk of setting in motion "a vicious circle" similar to what occurred after the end of World War I. In other words, "more economic nationalism, more restriction, and more discrimination"—with all the economic, political, and military consequences that we might imagine.[104]

In the second—dear, as we know, to liberal economists[105] (classical and neoclassical)—"the conditions which were supposed to lead to a neutralization of the power aspects of international economic relations are not merely 'unrealistic,' but *entirely fantastic*. They presuppose, indeed, a multitude of states of approximately equal importance each with approximately the same volume of foreign trade, the trade of each country being spread equally over all the other

102 Ibid. p. 53.

103 Hirschman 1987, p. 42; and 1980 p. 71.

104 Ibid. pp. 72–3.

105 According to whom (ibid. pp. 74–5) "the political or power aspect of foreign trade could be neutralized efficiently by a universal free trade system, because the trade of every country would be so nicely spread over the various markets that it need not worry about the interruption of the trade with any particular country."

countries and no country possessing a monopoly with respect to any peculiar skill or natural endowment."[106]

In the third case, the abolition of discriminatory practices implicitly refers to President Woodrow Wilson's program regarding the reconstruction of international trade.[107] This, as Hirschman points out,[108] "seems still to be the only official postwar aim of the United Nations. This program is generally coupled with some attempt to limit restrictive state intervention and state trading in general. No doubt can exist," he continues, "that the use of discriminatory methods as well as the power of national governments to determine directly the direction and the composition of foreign trade enables them to make the most of the power potentialities of their external economic relations." Nevertheless, he argues, this is not enough: because even "protectionism without discrimination" increases the existing inequalities of natural and human resources and thereby creates for some nations conditions of privilege, because "every tariff implies a certain amount of discrimination against a particular country or group of countries,"[109] and because the "politicization of trade" has its roots primarily in the power of the nation-state to block trade. "This power is an attribute of national sovereignty whatever may be the degree of positive state intervention."[110]

22 – In concluding, Hirschman proposes that we distinguish between the "economic *policy* of welfare" and the "economic *policy* of power." "The economic relationships existing in a society dedicated to the pursuit of welfare inevitably give rise to various forms of economic power; and this is by no means

---

106 Ibid. p. 75. (Emphasis added). "Actually," Hirschman continues further on, "the division of the world into big and small, rich and poor political units combined with the fact that the poor and small countries trade but little among themselves renders this solution [universal free trade] completely impracticable."

107 Ibid. p. 76. In the third of its 14 points, his program (which was defeated at Versailles) called for "the removal, so far as possible, of all economic barriers and the establishment of an equality of trade conditions among all the nations consenting to the peace, and associating themselves for its maintenance."

108 Ivi.

109 Ibid. p. 77, "By skillful coordination and timing of tariffs, prohibitions, and exchange manipulation," the passage continues, "it should be possible to obtain, with respect to the direction and the composition of trade, effects similar to those which can be reached more easily by quotas, bilateral clearings, etc."

110 Ivi.

necessarily an evil, since such a society must develop power, both political and economic, against those who do not agree with its aim of welfare."[111]

So the economic and political aspects are not separable. "An economic system guided by the objective of welfare," Hirschman had written earlier,[112] "must also provide for and organize the use of economic power. At present we see that the 'economics of power' may use the welfare analysis to great advantage. And moralists may well ponder over the fact that concerns about the trading partner's satisfaction becomes relevant for economic analysis when it is considered as a step toward eventual domination."

Coming back to the "leitmotif" of the book, Albert finally states:[113] "The Nazis, have merely shown us the tremendous power potentialities inherent in international economic relations, just as they have given us the first practical demonstration of the powers of propaganda. It is not possible to ignore or to neutralize these relatively new powers of men over men; the only alternative open to us is to prevent their use for the purposes of war and enslavement and to make them work for our own purposes of peace and welfare. This can be done only by a frontal attack upon the institution which is at the root of the possible use of international economic relations for national power aims—the institution of national economic sovereignty."[114]

The Current Relevance of National Power

23 – This, then, is the 'ultimate conclusion' capable of inspiring the action the author wished to focus on. No need to add that the world did not follow such an approach. The predominant position that the United States assumed during the entire postwar period, its liberal inspiration, the UN, decolonization, the Communist system, the cold war, the gradual formation of the European Union, etc. did not require a frontal attack on national sovereignty. Yet, with the passage of time, it cannot be ruled out that the gradual decline

111 Ibid. pp. 78–9, (Original emphasis).

112 Ibid. p. 48.

113 Ibid. p. 79.

114 "More than seven decades later, in his speech to the United Nations General Assembly in September 2017, the President of the United States [Donald Trump] argued the opposite 21 times. Because the recognition of unrestricted sovereignty is, in his view, the key to the world order he wishes to promote. This is no mere coincidence. There is something important and profound about this." (Meldolesi 2017 pp. 365–66).

of American dominance and the simultaneous rise of new large and medium-sized powers in a world that is quickly taking on a multi-polar character will end up rediscovering, in other guises, the initial problematic of *National Power*, and vice versa. Which is to say that reading this durable volume may help us look with different eyes at some of the economic and political processes we observe in the world around us.

In order to move ahead in this direction it seems necessary, however, to return to our narrative and summarize its argument as simply as possible. Written in 1941–42 (and published in 1945), *National Power* inevitably refers to the situation of national power and foreign trade structure during the first half of the last century when, in a multi-polar European context torn by great rivalries, an emerging national power—first Prussian-imperial Germany, then Nazi Germany—twice had aimed to obtain a dominant position by military means.

In that context (in which the economic policies preceding the two world wars respectively had long been debated) Hirschman directed his magic lantern on a specific issue that had hitherto been little understood—the fundamental relationship between national power and foreign trade. To this end, he took up one aspect of the economic theory of international trade (national gain from trade) and ultimately came to a far-reaching policy conclusion.

It is thus a work in which politics and economics cannot be separated by a Chinese wall, and in which it is politics and not economics that 'rules the roost'—something that normally occurred to some of the young people who decided to study economics (including evidently Albert Hirschman). They thought that knowledge of economics represented the necessary basis for a life dedicated to studying, addressing and (hopefully) solving some of the vital problems afflicting humankind.

The position argued in *National Power*, Hirschman instead suggested, does not reside solely in a reformulation of a specific aspect of the theory of international trade which then leads to a determined policy conclusion, but also the reverse. In other words, it was anti-Fascism and anti-Nazism that led the author to construct the illuminating theoretical-economic exercise (in itself, and for economic thought in general[115]) that is *National Power*. The real purpose of the volume is embodied, then, in the 'federalist' proposal to drastically limit the postwar sovereignty of states in order to bring international trade under control.

115 Whose exponents, proud of their profession, of course wish to verify their reasoning along lines of economic logic, perhaps accompanied by tables and figures.

Indeed, if we reread the book with this interpretive key in mind it quickly becomes clear that its re-proposition of the theory of national gain from trade fits perfectly into the great battle that was then under way. This is the text's recurring theme: in the introduction, at the end of the first chapter, and throughout the second—in which young Albert amuses himself by ingeniously going through the maze of literature on the economic theory of international trade—sometimes 'fishing' for important insights into national power, correcting others, patiently constructing still others, and so on.[116]

What is more, he also recognized the existence of the opposite relationship (politics as the basis of economics), but did not delve into it. Because the theme of his book was about the fact that trade with small and poor countries was manipulated by large and rich countries to increase their own national power. It was an interpretation of what had happened, what was happening. It was a 'memento,' concerning the future need to harness the national sovereignty of the great powers to avoid going from one world war to another.... Ultimately, all this is perfectly in line with Eugenio Colorni's political theses. It can be said that it drew inspiration from his activities (perhaps even in order to contribute to a general federalization of humankind).

24 – The backdrop to all this, as I have mentioned, was an extremely unstable multi-polar world, with several powers contending for predominance. As we know, with the end of the Second World War this situation was superseded by two opposing rival blocs of countries and a vast Third World. Among the many consequences, this upheaval also silently generated a temporary eclipse of *National Power* and an inevitable 'purgatory' for an important part of its argument.[117]

This is an issue that jumps out at us. In fact, after the interlude of the Marshall Plan (in which evidently Hirschman had in fact already abandoned the very idea of a frontal attack on the sovereignty of the great powers in favor instead of an attitude that was more sheltered, but very useful), he once again

116 Specifically, in fact, Hirschman had the advantage of being able to 'track' the classical and neo-classical economists who had underestimated the problem of the relationship between foreign trade and national power. So that even the few who had allowed for it had not adequately worked out the consequences.

117 Asso and de Cecco, who had read some of the elusive reviews of *National Power*, did not mention this. Instead, Cohen (2008 p. 21: cf. n. 6 above) mentioned that afterwards, since the first reprint in 1969, the themes of *National Power* "have also been echoed in the literature of International Political Economy."

took up the study of international trade in twin articles.[118] Following this, as we know, he worked at length on the economics of development and on Latin America. Already in Colombia in 1952 he came into conflict with the World Bank and later with other Western-dominated international institutions—a troubled relationship that nevertheless had a positive side.[119] In addition, during the Kennedy administration he took part in a study group, where he argued that the US should not have intervened in the internal affairs of Latin American countries.[120] He dealt finally with the issue of development aid and the 'repatriation' of foreign investment.[121]

In spite of this, as we shall now see, in 1976 Hirschman reasserted the founding logic of *National Power.* He recalled the key argument of the book, according to which "elements and imbalances of power are potentially present in 'harmless' relationships that have always been in place, such as those between large and small countries, rich and poor countries, industrial countries and agricultural countries." To which he added, "of course, it is precisely this position that explains the enduring vitality of my book: the political dimensions and side effects of international trade and foreign investment are a feature that is still massively present in today's situation (think of the obvious examples of the relationship of the United States with Latin America and the Soviet Union with Eastern Europe)."[122]

Yet it was precisely at this point, out of the long period just mentioned that, as we shall now see,[123] *a second life* of *National Power* emerged in the mid-1970s.

Hirschman had been invited to preside over the plenary session of the Latin American Studies Association in 1976, whose title was "Dependency Theory Reassessed." "In my remarks as session chairman," he later wrote in "Beyond Asymmetry: Critical Notes on Myself as a Young Man and on Some

118 Hirschman 1951 and 1952.

119 So much so that it ultimately found expression in *Development Projects Observed* (1967).

120 Meldolesi 1995 p. 128 and ff.

121 Hirschman 1962, 1968 (with R. M. Bird) and 1969.

122 Hirschman 1987 p. 46.

123 "While doing research for *The Passions and the Interests*," Hirschman later wrote (1981 p. 141), "I found, to my considerable surprise, that the essentials of the economic theory of imperialism, usually associated with the names of J. A. Hobson and Rosa Luxemburg, are anticipated in Hegel's *Philosophy of Right.*" An essay arose from this recognition (Hirschman 1978), originally written for a volume of essays in honor of Felipe Pazos (Diaz Alejadro C. F. et. al. 1976) and now in Hirschman 1981 ch. 7. It may be that this renewed interest in Hegel's work (which Albert had been concerned with in his youth: cf. above, ch. 3 sec. 4) facilitated the self-subversion that followed.

Other Old Friends,"[124] "I presented some of the speakers, such as Fernando Henrique Cardoso and Osvaldo Sunkel, who were among the first to discuss 'dependencia' in the early or mid-sixties. Then I proceeded to introduce myself as the frequently unacknowledged founding grandfather, on the strength of my book *National Power and the Structure of Foreign Trade*." His intention, he stated, was "not to substantiate this claim; it seems more useful to spell out my present critical perspective on that Jugendschrift of some 35 years ago [...] and, in the process, to criticize as well some aspects of the dependencia literature."

It was precisely this *propensity to self-subversion*[125]—also undertaken "pour encourager les autres"—which then enabled Hirschman to publish *National Power* (until then little known) for the third time, using "Beyond Asymmetry" as the "Preface to the Expanded Edition." To this end, he[126] borrowed the following remarks from the foreword to the second edition of Erwin Panofsky's classic text, *Idea: A Concept of Art Theory* (1924). "The suggestion to republish a little book that appeared more than thirty-five years ago and has been long out of print is uncommonly flattering to the book's author. But at the same time it presents him with a problem of conscience. It is only too clear that in such a long time not only has scholarship as such gone forward, but also the opinions of the author himself, even if fundamentally unchanged, have been altered in many details. To take this development into account would be possible only if the author could bring himself to write a completely new book probably three or four times as big; but for this he lacks the time, the strength, and—to speak frankly—the inclination."

"Any 'updating' of this old essay of mine," Albert commented, "would indeed be a formidable undertaking. My main object of study was the politics of *foreign trade*, the possibility of using trade as a means of political pressure and leverage. During the first two decades of the postwar period, foreign aid and capital flows largely replaced trade as the principal arena for the political

124 Hirschman 1980 p. v and pp. v–vi.

125 Which would later, as we know, become the title and leitmotif of Hirschman 1995. Note specifically how, with this decision, Albert may have reconnected ideally with a famous letter from Colorni to Spinelli in May 1943 (2019a, part III, ch. 3) that opened an important political path for the postwar period. He obviously could not have known of it in 1941–42 while he was writing *National Power*. But he may have read it after Colorni's death, when he arrived in Italy with the U.S. military and tried to collect Eugenio's writings.

126 Hirschman, 1980 p. v.

element in international economic relations.[127] More recently [that is, in the 1970s], with the negotiations at the United Nations Conferences on Trade and Development and the discussions about the New International Economic Order, trade and the institutional framework within which it is carried on have come back into the picture. Time and inclination apart," he concluded, "an attempt to refurbish or modify the book's analytical tools so as to have them come to grips with these experiences could easily become an exercise in self-importance"[128] (which obviously did not interest him).

25 – However, Hirschman added, "I recently had the occasion to return to the book with the simpler purpose of criticizing one of its features that has become unsatisfactory to me."[129]

In fact, having decided—as I have previously mentioned—to reintroduce *National Power* using "Beyond Asymmetry" as a new preface, he reviewed some key aspects of the book and ultimately observed: "Having explained how relations of influence, dependence, and domination arise right out of some 'mutually beneficial' trade I let matters rest there except for some, in retrospect *infinitely naïve*, proposals to 'arrive at an internationalization of the power arising out of foreign trade.' In other words, I invoked a *deus ex machina*; I wished away the unpleasant reality I had discovered instead of scrutinizing it further for some possibly *built-in* modifier or remedy."[130]

127 So that Albert could allude here, indirectly, to his work in this area (cf. above n. 120). Specifically, as he states in a note (1980 p. v), "I have dealt with the politics of foreign aid in two articles which maintain, I believe, a certain continuity with the analysis of the present book."

128 Ibid. pp. v–vi.

129 Ibid. p. vi.

130 Hirschman 1980 pp. vii-viii. (Emphases added). "Infinitely naïve"? Was it, really? "In the first place, the doubt in question has ('Colorni-like') a certain foundation. The thesis did not spring from the mind of Zeus: it responded, as mentioned, to a political and intellectual need that Hirschman felt deeply, and it dovetailed with the collective efforts developing around Condliffe toward the regulation of international trade which should be established after the war as a bulwark against new conflicts. Moreover, it had led to a significant analytical result regarding a mainstream economic literature proud of its scientific approach, but *de facto* out of touch with the real world. Finally, it was perfectly in line with and drew inspiration from the federalist theses of Albert's sister Ursula and Eugenio Colorni which—while *National Power* was being written—were advanced (*sub speciae unitatis europee*) at Ventotene in a work group that also included Altiero Spinelli, Ernesto and Ada Rossi. Why dominate? – Albert wondered at Berkeley. Why dominate? – wondered his California colleagues. Why dominate? – wondered his relatives and their friends in Italy. The importance of *National Power*, first and foremost, is its straightforward posing of this question," (Meldolesi 2017 p. 4).

It is worth pausing for a moment on this self-subverting mode in the reasoning to ask why he stopped at this point when he had already carefully observed Eugenio Colorni searching for avenues of possibility in Trieste. First of all, one must recognize, in my opinion, beyond the specific proposals, the importance of pointing out the danger of the situation that might arise after the conclusion of the war. This is Albert Hirschman's distinctive participation in the ongoing struggle—the political reason, the moral duty that without a doubt motivated the great effort of thought made by the author in writing *National Power*.

Moreover, I think it is safe simply to assume that, at that particular juncture, Albert (young, exiled, still with little experience) just "did not feel like" proceeding any further—not least because it would have required, in a sense, an encroachment into political science, and this might have alienated him from the few certainties he held, such as the connection with his own discipline (which *ipso facto*—as I have already mentioned—had been strained by what he had written), and perhaps even the connection with Condliffe, his patron. In other words, exposing the situation had already been an uncommon act of intellectual courage.

But 35 years later the situation had changed profoundly. Beyond the "infinitely naïve proposals," the reader will realize (from the passage just quoted) that, as part and parcel of his lifelong work, Albert had by then practiced and acquired an interactive conception of dominance/subordination/dependence relationships. Viewed retrospectively, he was now able to complete the general pattern of *National Power* and thus open to view the vast field of the possible.[131]

With this in mind, he sought an illuminating theoretical example, perhaps evocative of the myriad skirmishes that typify the asymmetrical interrelationships that affect every aspect of life—and one that was also *memorable*, so that it would never again be lost sight of. This he found, as he told me personally,

131 An area that in turn contains a broad spectrum of issues and behaviors—such as proposals and ways forward, support for positive trends, participation in ongoing processes, setting them in motion and guiding them, and so on.

in a youthful memory—a well-known page from Hegel's *Phenomenology of the Spirit* on the relationship between master and servant.[132]

"It may be instructive to indicate," as Hirschman accordingly continued in his new "Preface," "how this common defect of my original treatment [invoking a *deus ex machina*] and of most *dependencia* writings could be remedied by taking as point of departure the very situation of asymmetry previously noted: an identical trade flow that represents the bulk of the small, poor country's total trade while occupying only a small percentage of the large, rich country's trade. The straightforward inference from this observation is that the large country, having a much smaller stake in this common trade than the small country, is able to bend the latter to its will by subtle or not-so-subtle hints that the benefits of this trade might otherwise be withdrawn. But the next question is now: how solid or stable is the resulting relation of domination and dependency?"[133]

New observation (or rather a new series of observations) is required for a more reliable picture of what emerges from this simple recognition. "Perhaps," Hirschman suggested, "such a relation can be made to arise out of the following conjecture, based primarily on the observation of United States-Latin American relations. A country whose trade or investment is dominated by ties to a large and rich country is, at some point, likely to devote its attention with single-minded concentration to this uncomfortable situation and to attempt to loosen or cut these ties. But the large rich country which carries on only a small portion of its international economic relations with the country it dominates is normally preoccupied with its more vital other interests, for example, with its relations to the other large powers. Hence our basic economic disparity generates a disparity of *attention*, or at least of high-level attention [...], and this disparity now favors the *dependent* country: that country is likely to pursue its

132 Hegel 1977, pp. 111–19. (This is the book that he had studied as part of a work group at the Französische Gymnasyum in 1932–33 - Meldolesi 1995 p. 4; Adelman 2013 p. 96). However, he decided not to make this ancestry explicit (perhaps to respect the [hyper-]sensitivity of his audience). He confined himself to the essence of the reasoning—a "self-subversive" procedure in which the specific case alludes to a broader hypothesis. In a sense, it seems similar to that of "Melding the Public and Private Sphere: Taking Commensality Seriously"—Hirschman 1998a. (It is likely, in fact, that with time [and use] this particular propensity for self-subversion became clearer and more explicit—up to and beyond Hirschman 1995).

133 Hirschman 1980 p. viii.

escape from domination more actively and energetically than the dominant country will work on preventing this escape."[134]

This is a thesis that lends itself to further consideration. In the first place, this conjecture, arising from the concrete observation of relations between the United States and Latin America, shows how the original relationship (in which an economic opportunity implicit in international trade can foster the political strengthening of national power) can suggest the appearance of its opposite—a political opportunity that can lead to an economic re-balance of some kind.[135] In this way, the new preface in fact explores the political terrain that can exist "beyond the economic asymmetry."

At the same time, in doing this, Hirschman implicitly shows that the Leibnizian-Colornian logic of decomposition (cf. above, sec. 7) can be reversed into a tendency in the direction of recomposition (partial though it may be). It is like a ladder. In this particular case (as happens in life, we might observe with a hint of irony) it is undoubtedly easier to go down than up.

Finally, as I have already written, the fact that in order to develop the dialectical logic manifested here Hirschman found it useful to reread a page from Hegel on the relationship between master and servant seems to me to suggest, as a consequence, that this reasoning can also be turned on its head. What I mean is that: given the great dissimilarity between the two cases examined (master-servant relations on the one hand and U.S.-Latin American relations on the other), the approach discussed here of setting up dominance/dependency relations could also prove useful in a hundred other circumstances,

134 Ibid. p. ix. "From the point of view of Latin America's aspirations," Hirschman goes on to clarify (p. x), "the advantage of day-to-day policy being in the hands of lower-level diplomats heavily influenced by an intrusive business community is precisely that policies so formed are usually short-sighted as well as reasonably predictable. (Occasionally they become so inept and conflictual that they have to be corrected by a salvage operation staged at a higher level of policy making). For these reasons they are no match for a determined adversary."

135 This does not mean, however, that small and poor countries necessarily enjoy political asymmetry, while large and rich countries enjoy economic asymmetry (otherwise, what would then happen to the political-military asymmetry?). In effect, the economic and political aspects of the issue cannot be completely separated. When we speak of economic and political disparities, we mean the *predominance* of one aspect over another (or vice versa). These are circumstances that exist, moreover, in certain conditions within a general relationship of dominance/subordination that has many facets and evolves over time.

each of which, however, needs to be broken down and reassembled in order to be analyzed in detail.[136]

In other words, this development of the argument also has the merit of inviting readers to re-propose it in other situations (perhaps by constructing the appropriate "castelluzzi" [little castles][137] themselves); and even invites them to generalize it cautiously—*cum judicio*. This is the source of the important heuristic value of the conclusion reached by "Beyond Asymmetry."

26 – In saying all this I certainly do not mean to deny that in relations between the United States and Latin America "wise and salutary neglect" by the dominant country[138] and "correspondingly concentrated attention on the part of the dependent country" are inscribed in the "asymmetrical trade percentages just as much as the facts of dependence and domination themselves."[139] I do want to emphasize, however, that—as Hirschman himself makes clear—there are limits to the maneuvering space that the dominated countries have[140] and

136 Actually "the possibilist policy against international trade asymmetries advanced by Albert in the new 1980 introduction to *National Power and the Structure of Foreign Trade*, ingenious as it is, is not the only one in sight. There is, for instance, another useful démarche opened up by Eugenio and later practiced by Albert that needs to be recalled. The public opinion and institutions of the dominant power may be influenced by individual or collective actions, from below or from above, from outside or from inside, such that the working policy of that power would become more favorable (or less harmful) to the dominated peoples (countries). Eugenio did precisely that within the Resistance in Rome: collectively, from outside, and from below. Later Albert creatively rediscovered it within the Marshall Plan: individually, from inside, and from above. In my view, keeping in mind what is happening in the world of today, this possibilist horizon should be further explored." Meldolesi 2017 p. 169.

137 As Hirschman at one point referred to his small constructions (Adelman 2013 p. 146).

138 "Which Burke long ago recognized as a basic cause of the growing strength of England's North American colonies," (Hirschman, 1980 p. x).

139 Ivi.

140 "The point I have been making," Hirschman adds (ibid. p. x-xi), "can be reformulated as follows: because of the disparity of attention dependent countries are in a favorable position to utilize what room for maneuver they have and may be able to widen this room."

that many other cases of change in a dominance/dependence relationship need to be taken into account, such as those led by economic performance.[141]

In fact, moving "beyond asymmetry," as the title of the essay we are discussing states, undoubtedly leads into a complex analytical and propositional field, that implicitly guides us in two different directions. In one of these, the focus of the argument remains on dominance/dependence relationships that take different forms as they go along, all of which need to be decoded. In the other, there is a need to understand in depth—and in an articulate, subtle and perceptive way—the specific nature and developmental processes of the *dispute* between these forms, through *in corpore vili* probings, comparisons, cautious generalizations, etc., in order to focus attention on their potential for change and thus for inspiring concrete action.[142]

It is a concern that today, after another 45 years, seems increasingly urgent to us. It only takes a moment's reflection, in fact, to realize that the major economic and political events that have affected foreign trade in the intervening period—such as the establishment of the WTO, so-called globalization, the fall of the Berlin Wall, the eastward expansion of the European Union, the great rise of China, the 'refocusing' of the United States, the Russian invasion of Ukraine, the strengthening of NATO, the Hamas-Israel war, etc.—have been accompanied by processes of reallocation and relocation of horizontal and vertical national powers. And what is more, after a genuine era of trade liberalization, we now observe an oscillation between such policies and the

141 "For example (ibid. p. xi). when a country which dominates the world market of one commodity or product raises its price and thereby eventually loses its monopoly [...]; or when a country, that initially has little bargaining power in relation to a firm wishing to exploit its natural resources, increases this power over time both because the firm's installations, once built, are captives of the country where they are located, and because the country is likely, in due time, to insist on training its own technologists and other experts."

142 "It will be noted," Hirschman wrote (ibid. p. xi), "that the mechanisms by which such counterforces arise are very different from case to case: they range from purely economic reactions [...], to purely political considerations [...]. To ferret out such mechanisms is anything but easy, particularly when [...] initial asymmetry and dependency relations are grounded in economics while the counter tendency relies on a certain kind of political reaction coming into play."

gradual, but often triumphant, rediscovery of protectionism and bilateralism (often in the form of direct negotiation).[143]

We in fact need to recognize that our own time is very different—both from the first half of the last century and the second half as well.[144] And that in a world in which innovations and communications are growing at a dizzying pace, the day-to-day interactions between the great powers and those of the multiple relationships of domination/subordination around the planet are taking on unprecedented, often unstable and worrisome characteristics, linked at times to very long historical-cultural-religious-psychological legacies.

The impression, then, is that those who seek to cautiously explore "National Power's *third life*" will have to emphasize "the economic *policy* of welfare" (et alia[145]) over "the economic *policy* of power" (et alia[146]) - and not only vice-versa.

Of course, this will have to be done in the light of the lessons of the new Preface "Beyond Asymmetry." That is, from within the human community's existing dominance/dependence relationships and the alignments that

143 I must add specifically that it was the emergence of this attitude and the consequences it immediately produced for U.S. trade relations with Mexico that led me to reconsider the entire question. In particular, reading an article by Azam Ahmed in the *New York Times* of 26 March 2017, I realized that the President of Mexico was forced to ask for a rapid revision of Mexico's trade agreements with the United States in favor of the latter (!)—to dispel as quickly as possible the great economic uncertainty created by the Trump administration and the resulting investment freeze; and also, of course, to avoid losing the upcoming election. It was at this point that I said to myself, "I've got to get back into *National Power*!"

144 It belongs neither to the game of traditional European colonialist imperialism, nor to the Cold War balance of terror, nor even to the American dominance of yesteryear. It follows dynamics (and wars) that are largely still to be decoded.

145 Namely, fair competition, peace, freedom, equality, fraternity, democracy, federalism, gender, environment, health, civility, etc.

146 That is to say, rivalry, low blows, militarism, war, violation of international law, extermination, subjugation, barbarism, etc. See above, sec. 22.

divide it.[147] Because if this really does fail to materialize, a terrifying chasm may open, as we are well aware.

So it becomes imperative to adjust thinking to reality, first of all, as our author proposes, exploring "the contradictory character of social processes."[148]

Actually, as Hirschman had previously written, "The failure to discover the countertendencies is not due only to difficulties of crossing interdisciplinary boundaries; to a considerable extent it must be attributed to an intellectual orientation that is both un-dialectical and what I would call anti-possibilist. For many of the countertendencies that can be discovered are *possibilities* rather than certainties, and social scientists often consider it beneath their scientific dignity to deal with possibility until *after* it has become actual and can then at least be redefined as a probability."[149]

To conclude

27 – We can now answer the implicit question we left open above (in sec. 26)—whether *National Power*'s original proposals were indeed "infinitely naïve". The most correct answer seems to me to be that they undoubtedly were, but only up to a point.

The fact is that the solution the young Hirschman suggested of a frontal attack on national sovereignty over the issue of foreign trade was simply not effectively practicable on this planet. While the mature Hirschman's idea of skillfully and persistently exploiting the room for maneuver that actually exists

147 Note, in this regard, that while it is true that "the economic *policy* of welfare" can be used as a footstool by "the economic *policy* of power," it is also true that sometimes "the economic *policy* of welfare" can override "the economic *policy* of power." In fact, in the case of a shifting (but stable) equilibrium that does not degenerate into generalized confrontation as was the case during the Cold War, "the economic *policy* of welfare" ended up prevailing over "the economic *policy* of power" through the great collective motor of the fall of the Berlin Wall and the dissolution of the European Communist system. In other words, since we do not possess a crystal ball fit for the purpose, we can hardly predict what might occur under the new historical conditions mentioned above. But based on past experience, we can inquire about it by observing reality with the eyes of *National Power*—not least to understand from time to time, on the small and the large scale, where the road of "the economic *policy* of welfare" runs and how to successfully pursue it.

148 Hirschman 1980 p. xii.

149 Ibid. pp. xi-xii. Emphases added.

within the same dominance relationship is indeed valid, and has a long concrete history behind it that would be well worth exploring.

It is also true, however, that aggressive cases of nationalism and imperialism, and relations of oppression and domination have by no means disappeared from our world. On the contrary, growing rivalries, whether persistent or new, are going through a period of 'resurrection' in large countries such as Russia, China, India and the United States, and also in medium-sized countries such as Turkey, Iran, Saudi Arabia, North Korea, etc., and even in Europe—from Brexit to the surreptitiously sub-imperialist behavior of some countries[150] (not, of course, forgetting Germany).[151]

This then begs the question: given today's world in which, not surprisingly, we see neo-mercantilism (even within the EU[152]), politico-commercial restrictions, tendencies toward bilateralism, etc. resurfacing again and again, wouldn't it be appropriate to have another look at *National Power*?[153] Perhaps it is too early to tell. But I make no secret of the fact that the idea of contributing to such a rediscovery is part of the present writer's wishes—as a way of opening the door to a new kind of thinking. Indeed, it is clear that the situation cannot remain static. We must learn to come to terms with a sort of "sliding equilibrium" (or controlled developmental imbalance).

Put another way, on one hand we must as far as possible avoid dangerous ruptures. But on the other, even with some unexpected backlash, we need to channel emerging energies toward positive changes (locally, regionally, continentally, globally)—thinking about and fostering such processes, starting from where we are. And never losing sight of future prospects.

So we welcome anything that enables us to see clearly and act accordingly. If only because naïvety and even innocence undoubtedly play an important

---

150 In this respect, Italy is in a different position: it has fewer relationships, but is also less contested (due to the shorter colonialist experience later repudiated by popular outcry with anti-Fascism and the Constitution).

151 Hirschman was so aware of this that he argued in an interview (1995a) that Germany should remain "saddled" with the European Union.

152 Cf., concerning this, Fisher 2012; Ginzburg 2013; Vianello 2013; Visco 2014; Meldolesi 2015 ch. 4.

153 Or possibly parts of it. Along with the question of aid (cooperation) and investment that Hirschman referred to later (see above, n. 120 and 126), the very issue central to *National Power* might return to relevance, along with Albert's 'memento' to economists on the relationship between welfare and national power (now completely forgotten, if intensely practiced). Here, too, the sliding equilibrium of change for good must be set in motion.

role as points of departure in the overall intellectual development of Eugenio Colorni and Albert Hirschman—ever since Colorni wrote in 1937, referring to his students, that young people see the world "with eyes that are naïve, and therefore without prejudice."[154]

Moreover, if we look back and reflect on what has been going on in these parts over the last couple of centuries we can't help noticing that the overall record of domination/subordination relations at every latitude is far from reassuring. Gradual as it may be, the battle for federalization, for de-verticalization and democratization of the system—as Eugenio Colorni and Albert Hirschman envisioned it in Trieste in 1937–38 and which they began to practice, each in his own way (Eugenio with and beyond the Ventotene group and Albert with *National Power*)—remains crucial. It continues to be the pole star (the shining star, the Phoenician star, the red star of the ancients) of any democratic action intelligently planned as an alternative to rampant nationalism and 'sovereignist' imperialism.

Viewing from this angle, at this point we need to invert our hourglass and defend the young Hirschman from the (corrosive) retrospective irony of his adult self. Of course, recognizing that the frontal attack proposal was infinitely naïve—indeed, it must be added that the absolute conviction with which it was formulated was certainly erroneous.[155] But at the same time, it needs to be reaffirmed, even in hindsight, that while it should have been presented as a *possibility* and not as a certainty, the denunciation of the state of affairs it referred to was not wrong at all.

---

154 Colorni 1937b; now in 2019, p. 43. Cf., also, Colorni 1998, Hirschman 1963. Effectively, it was a vigorous political need to promote change, ingenuous as it was initially (cf. Hirschman 1963 pp. 271–75), that was the real driving force behind the author's personal journey. From the theoretical crystallization of *National Power*, to its interactive breakthrough in the 1970s, to the still largely unexpressed process set in motion with the end of the Cold War and the exhaustion of so-called globalization (first version). The concrete facts of the different eras thus suggest theoretical advancements which in any case—as Asso and de Cecco observed (1987 p. 8)—in a certain sense transcend the events themselves and assign tasks to humanity that need to be pursued relentlessly, but which, it would appear, can only be carried forward positively in part, in stages, over time. In effect, we may conclude, 'the path of improvement' (we might call it) can take a hundred different forms; and can at the same time suggest incredible, meaningful and exciting adventures…

155 Notably, after having written *National Power*, Hirschman enlisted in the U.S. armed forces. Perhaps he was hoping to discuss his book with Colorni before publishing it. But he learned in Algiers that Eugenio had been killed.

This therefore indicates the necessity of sticking to a clear *point of view in terms of values*—something that the Albert we know evoked concisely (but also somewhat enigmatically) when he said we needed to work "for a better world"—without which it is easy to lose one's bearings. That is to say, it is essential to split the discourse—on one hand we have the long-term goals that need continually to be argued and reiterated, and on the other our daily, perceptive, relentless attention to seeking and positively exploiting every concrete opportunity, large or small, to move intelligently in the intended direction.

This means consolidating past achievements and effectively building new ones on them, however limited they may be—starting, for example, with the United Nations and, more generally, with the international community (first and foremost for humanitarian emergencies) as well as with the federalist and solidarity-based pressures that have arisen (and are arising) at the local level in different continents.

At the same time, every process of liberation from relations of dominance requires the careful study of the specific concrete conditions in which it develops—an analysis that seeks to bring into focus the famous "constellation of favorable circumstances" (if and when it exists) to be gleaned wisely in favor of the desired change.

With this in mind, it is also essential to refer to overall dominance relationships, and not consider only the immediate aspect(s), the ones we generally tend to keep in mind. This means going beyond the simple intelligent use of the elbow room that the relation of subordination generally allows to the dependent country. Through multiple initiatives (from below and/or from above, from outside and/or from within) this space must be expanded, so that the political choice most favorable to the subject populations prevails in the dominant country. This is what Eugenio Colorni began to think about (and put into practice) beginning in May 1943.[156] And it is what Albert Hirschman pursued a little later in the second phase of his Marshall Plan experience.[157]

156 Colorni 2019a, part III, ch. 3.

157 Hirschman 1998 ch. 2 and Meldolesi 2013 ch. 2.

· 5 ·

A CRITIQUE OF ECONOMICS: FROM SAINT-SIMON TO HIRSCHMAN*

Saint-Simon and the Economy as Base

The critique of political economy that I intend to consider in this paper is not generally addressed by economists. It is not internal to the discipline (like Keynes's), nor it is it partly internal and partly external (like that of Marx). It stems from the "social philosophy" of Auguste Comte in the wake of the formulations of his mentor, the Comte de Saint-Simon, and has had a significant influence on French sociology and historiography up to the present day.

As is well known, Claude Henri de Rouvroy, Count Saint-Simon (1760–1825) thought that in place of the old political system of feudal origin, a new society should be formed based on productive, scientific and artistic "skills." He therefore set himself the task of devising a system of thought corresponding to the needs of the new order, conducting a comprehensive struggle against the old ruling classes (the nobles, the clergy, the military), and creating a party of "industrialists" capable of taking over power from the hands of the "legalists" and "metaphysicians" (jurists and literati) who had temporarily seized it.

During the French Restoration, Saint-Simon associated with many members of the Liberal Party and succeeded in convincing a group of bankers, industrialists, deputies, and scientists (including Jean Baptiste Say) to finance

* *Economia Politica*, 1990, n. 2.

L'industrie, a series of publications that came out between 1816 and 1818.[1] In the second volume, in the context of an (imaginary) "political and philosophical correspondence" with "an American," a striking line of reasoning appears on the relationship between politics and economics—and is also quite complimentary to the latter.

By birth, the count had been committed "irrevocably" to a military career, and in this capacity he took part in five campaigns of the French expeditionary corps in the American War of Independence. But at some point, seeing that peace was fast approaching, he was gripped by revulsion for the profession of arms and realized that the study of the "path of the human spirit" was his true calling. He therefore decided to devote the remainder of his time in America to "foreseeing the consequences" of the momentous events he was witnessing, and quickly arrived at the conclusion (later confirmed by the facts) that the Americans would create a much more liberal and democratic regime than the Europeans—one that was tolerant in matters of religion, free from feudal vestiges, fond of peace and productive activities, and a champion of individual freedom.[2]

France, on the other hand, was a nation "divided into many castes," characterized by the presence of "privileged bodies." The revolution—which erupted out of a passion for equality—had shown that the principal castes were transient, but it had also shown that the French people were "children" when it came to managing public power. It was a question then, Saint-Simon reasoned, of stimulating a new passion—for a "*more industry-friendly form of organization*"—understood in the most general sense of the beneficial, spiritual and manual labor inherent in all economic activities.

---

1 The initial two volumes were favorably evaluated by the funding group; the third provoked a backlash (and the end of funding) because it argued for "a system of earthly morality" as a basis for the new society. The fourth was written in a (failed) attempt to regain contact with the backers (Manuel, 1956 ch. 16 and 17).

2 "I understood," he writes (Saint-Simon, 1816–18; 1975 p. 275), "that the American Revolution marked the beginning of a new political era and that this revolution would necessarily bring about a major advance in the whole of civilization and would soon cause great transformations in the social order then existing in Europe" (Saint-Simon, 1816–18; this important prophecy—see below, sec. 3 and note 9—would, however, take almost a century and a half to be definitively affirmed).

This construction project, the count continued, could only arise from a fundamental principle: "Of all those who have dealt with it, it seems to me that the most useful work has been done by the learned men who have written about economics, and Say's treatise on political economy seems to me to be the book that contains the greatest number of coordinated positive ideas" (Saint-Simon, 1816–18; 1975, p. 293).

Economics emphasized the production of useful goods, the limitations of government action, the central role of producers, the damage produced by wars and monopolies, the need to spread education and strengthen moral ideas favorable to production, and the existence of goals and interests common to all working people.

But these "general truths" set forth by Say are also the compendium of "facts observed by political science." They lead in their turn to a central idea—that there is a "class of interests" that relates to the preservation of life and welfare on which people need to agree, deliberate, and act in common. This is the unique scope of politics; it is the "sole standard" of criticism of institutions and the construction of the new order.[3]

In this way Saint-Simon brought to light a relationship between economics and politics that has resonated deeply in our culture. It is the economists, he maintains, who indirectly establish the "*general political principle.*" And it is Jean Baptiste Say who comes closest to the goal because, at the beginning of his *Traité d'économie politique*, he delimits the field of economics and reproaches the economists of the past (including Rousseau for his "Economie politique" entry in the *Encyclopédie*) for confusing, in their research, the constituent principles of good government with those on which an increase in wealth is based.

What interests the count is precisely the separation of economics from politics. He sees this as the end of previous confusions and the birth of a new

3 Note the central place given to this reasoning within the "correspondence." Under the title "Search for a General Political Principle," it appears in the eighth virtual letter out of a total of ten. The third, fourth and fifth are not deemed "fit for publication," while the answers "[...] will be published as they are received by us from America." (!) (Cf. Saint-Simon, 1816–18; 1975 p. 283, 297 and 303).

relationship between the two spheres—which Say foreshadowed without intending to, and established without saying as much.[4]

Later, in the fourth volume of *L'industrie*, discussing the political history of industry, Saint-Simon returns to the subject (perhaps with the help of Comte[5]) and credits the "immortal Smith" with enunciating the principles that had so long been missing from industry.[6] Smith had presented the science he had founded "with much modesty," "as a secondary, auxiliary science, an appendage of *politics*." But Say then took up his ideas,[7] classified them systematically, and took a step forward from a philosophical standpoint in establishing that "*political economy* is distinct and independent from *politics*." (Saint-Simon, 1816–18; 1975, p. 386).

As we can see, Saint-Simon does not go into the merits of economic reasoning, nor can it be said that he ever really mastered the subject—he merely observes some general conclusions and poses the problem of their political consequences.

Before Smith, economics had "shrewdly" blended in with politics, while afterwards it had taken on a "clearer and more resolute" character. "Now it will

4 Understandably, this viewpoint did not displease Say who praised the style of *L'industrie* and called Saint-Simon a true friend of the public welfare (cf. Péreire, 1912 p. 111). "Anyone who has read Say's book or attended his public lectures," the count made clear, "knows full well how much importance he attaches to the science he is concerned with and how many times he has stated that it is to this alone that morality and politics owe everything they both possess that is certain and positive. This contradiction shows that the author felt vaguely, almost in spite of himself, that political economy is the one and only true basis of politics. Nevertheless, he did not see this with sufficient assurance, for he makes it as clear as day in the details of his work, but denies it in his general considerations." (Saint-Simon, 1816–18: 1975 pp. 294–95).

5 Cf. Comte's letter of 17 April 1818 (Comte 1870 p. 35) in which he states that he continues to be interested in political economy on behalf of Saint-Simon, even though, given the situation (see footnote 1) "the work is unpaid."

6 "Smith's work," writes Saint-Simon, (1816–18; 1975 p. 385), "contains the most direct, most comprehensive" critique ever made of a feudal regime, "a collection of detailed refutations" of the actions of governments, a demonstration of the need to change "the principles and the nature" of governments. To achieve prosperity a nation must act like manufacturers and merchants—it must formulate its budget like that of an enterprise and produce as much as possible at the lowest administrative costs.

7 "The emphasis Say gave to Smith's thought," Bernard wrote, (1963 pp. 99–100), "amounts to an enhancement of the hopes of the industrialists. His whole art consisted in disguising and distorting Smith's doctrine sufficiently so that it seemed to guarantee the business of the industrialists."

be politics that leans upon economics, or rather it will encompass all politics. This moment," wrote the count, "is not far off" (1816–18; 1975, p. 295).[8]

Of Saint-Simon's many prophecies that have miraculously made their way down to us like messages in bottles,[9] this last one cannot be said to have found a safe harbor. It is true, though, that it has sailed for a long time because, contrary to expectations, its vitality has stemmed from the presence of a multiplicity of different economic theories and political viewpoints.

While Smith was a leading figure in classical economics, Say was (in reality) a major exponent of the economics of "appearance"—to which marginalist economics would later be linked. The followers of Saint-Simon, on the other hand, developed the master's political thought in a radical direction (and following this route came to criticize many economists on the issue of private property: Bazard *et al.* 1928–29; 1924, pp. 289–96). Marx, for example, wrote *Capital. A critique of political economy* as the foundation of his own political conception, which can in part be traced back to that of Saint-Simon (Meldolesi 1982), and Walras thought he could derive precise indications for societal reform from his *Éléments d'économie politique pure* (Walras, 1896, 1898).

Finally, to complicate matters even more, it is possible (fortunately) for economists from the same school to argue different political theses, and for like-minded political scientists to refer to different economic theories—regardless of whether they belong to the conservative or progressive camp.

There can be no doubt about it—the very existence of an entire series of relations between economic theories and political arguments belies Saint-Simon's basic position. Simply put, economics did not discover the "general political principle" on which to base political science.

8 Summarizing the crucial aspects of the political clash at the end of *L'industrie*, Saint-Simon argues that since the lawmen—the lawyers of the old classes—are on one side, on the other side the industrialists must call upon their own lawyers: the economists. "Let us consecrate the memory of the important services they rendered; the mistakes they made are now no longer a problem, because they have been totally lost sight of" (!) (1816–18; now 1975 pp. 393–95). (For possible further development see note 12).

9 Some of them, as Ghita Jonescu (1976) explains, did come true. Think, for example, of the following theses: industrial society will be based on the consensus and organization of the various interest groups of productive workers; privileges of feudal origin will disappear; people who demonstrate their abilities in the sciences, arts and industry will enjoy a high degree of social esteem; meritocracy will assert itself in the various fields, whatever the starting position of the participants. (See also note 2).

It remains true, however, that the repetition—in different areas of the discipline of economics and different sectors of the political spectrum—of the claim that economics is at the foundation of politics has ended up entrenching this idea in our culture, so much so that it has not yet ceased to haunt us.[10]

So that reasoning in hindsight, it seems to me (paradoxically) true that Saint-Simon's merit lies precisely in having raised the issue in general terms. What sustains a good part of the economic and political ideas around us—the count seems to suggest (with a hint of irony)—is the notion that the economic discipline identifies the individual and collective interests of a large part of the population and that policy based on these, becomes *ipso facto* "positive."

Comte and the Critique of Economics

It is interesting to note that this pattern of thinking, still so popular today, was already being challenged by Auguste Comte. Having graduated brilliantly from the École Polytechnique, Comte became Saint-Simon's secretary in August 1817 and collaborated on the third and fourth volumes of *L'industrie*, dealing with (among other things) political economy.

After the third volume was reviled by the financial backers (cf. note 1) the young Comte wrote two letters to Saint-Simon (Péreire 1912, pp. 41–46) arguing that for various reasons, the journalists, scientists and industrialists would never really take their side and that they therefore needed to change track—abandoning political activity altogether and working on a purely theoretical scientific system that developed (among other things) the philosophical foundations of economics in such a way as to yield a positive political science. Comte later actually took this route and when he arrived at the question that interests us here he no longer followed the line of economics as the basis of politics.

Comte's ambition was to embrace the knowledge of his era, and in a very broad and systematic work, he constructed a long intellectual journey which, through mathematics, astronomy, physics, chemistry, and biology, finally arrived at social physics—or *sociology*. I am referring, of course to his *Cours de Philosophie Positive*, in which "philosophy" is used in its ancient meaning

10 "Out of the agony of the great French Revolution," wrote Ferdinand Braudel (1980, p. 6), "the meditations of the count de Saint-Simon were born, and then those of his disciples and adversaries, Auguste Comte, Proudhon, Karl Marx—meditations which still have not ceased to torment the minds and reasoning of men."

of "the general system of human ideas," and "positive" refers to the particular way of doing philosophy which "has as its object the coordination of observed facts." As such, this positive or experimental approach was set against theology or imagination—the starting point of human intelligence—and against abstraction or metaphysics, in which supernatural agents are replaced by personified entities. All the sciences under consideration, Comte maintained, had to pass through these last two ways of philosophizing to move in the end toward the positive.[11]

Of course, a modern discussion concerning "stages of development" cannot but lead to an attitude of caution toward Comte's overall construction. Nevertheless, this should not stand in the way of an understanding of the specific contribution of this "French Hegel," as Manuel (1979 p. 346 and ff.) calls him.

As a complex discipline requiring a broad experimental basis—this founding ancestor of sociology thus argued—social physics arrived last at its appointment with positive philosophy. Order and progress, the two cardinal concepts that support it, were still monopolized respectively by theological and metaphysical thinking. The latter in particular played an indispensable role as a revolutionary way of thinking. But then, by reintroducing the dogmas of unlimited freedom of conscience, equality and popular sovereignty in absolute and abstract terms, it unintentionally hindered the consolidation of the new system, the "intimate and indissoluble" combination of order and progress that must distinguish it.

This was the origin of the need to alter the orientation of political thought and thus, in the 47th lesson, of a "brief examination of the main attempts so far to establish a social science." Economists, the text tells us, have endeavored to portray the object of their studies as independent of political science as a whole. But this particular feature, which Saint-Simon had valued positively, now takes on a negative connotation. "In spite of this decisive admission," Comte continues, "these philosophers have persuaded themselves, in good faith, that they have managed, in imitation of proper scientists, to finally subject what they call economic science to the positive spirit, and every day they

11 The *Cours* was published between 1830 and 1842 (Vol. IV covering the 47th lesson on political economy came out in 1839). It is a development of preexisting ideas—the youthful pamphlets of the decade 1818–28 (attached as an appendix to Vol. IV) and the lecture courses given by Comte to a group of distinguished scientists and disciples in 1826 and 1829. Comte's work has long been studied: see, for example, Lévy-Bruhl (1900), Gouhier (1933–41, 1965), Lacroix (1956), Bréhier (1932), Aron (1965), and Coser (1971).

propose their manner of proceeding as the basic model on which all social theories must finally be regenerated" (Comte, 1830–42; 1967, p. 186).

Detaching economics from politics—the author seems to want to say, reversing his teacher's reasoning—instead of giving birth to a fundamental political principle, has created a "way forward" that economists can propose to political scientists and other social scientists.

Actually, in his *Essay on Government*, James Mill had already formulated the first economic theory of politics in 1820. Saint-Simon, as noted above, believed that economics had identified the collective interests of producers, on whose solidarity the politics of the industrial system could be built. Mill, on the other hand, in the same years, suggested that politics should be analyzed like economics—that it should be based on the hypothesis of the rational action of participants motivated by their individual interest—just as Schumpeter, Downs, Olson and many others would do in our time.[12]

Any observer of the development of the American social sciences in recent decades will be well aware that this "'encounter' of economics and politics called 'public choice' amounts to an invasion of the political field—something that has also happened in history, sociology, etc. In this way, in others' home territory, economists have gained considerable public and critical acclaim and have created a vast current that in the various social sciences points to the standard behavior of *homo oeconomicus*.

But this is not the only school of thought—as the absolutist economists would often appear to claim. There are many other approaches, in different disciplines (including, of course, political economy). Among them I would like to point out the approach of many French-educated social scientists, who even today invoke—more or less explicitly—Comte's critique of political economy.

In the first place, as Comte argued, the scientific claim of economists has no reasonable basis—their discipline lacks observational regularity, a systematic search for the laws of society and thus any true proof. What is more, economists purport to separate economic phenomena from the 'social whole,' while the different aspects of society are in reality 'inseparable.' "These two

12 On the other hand, when looked at from a different angle, Saint-Simon's and Mill's texts don't seem so far apart. The count, as noted (sec. 3), had argued in one of his characteristic forays that economics should encompass "all of politics." Does this not mean, James Mill might have interjected, that politics should be measured by the yardstick of economics? Needless to say, it is unlikely that Saint-Simon would have appreciated such interference—but that does not detract from the fact that it draws him in and in a sense places him "upstream" of this well-known intellectual démarche.

criticisms," writes Raymond Aron (1965; 1972, p. 94), "were taken up by most French sociologists of the Durkheimian school and have led to the attitude of semi-hostility, at least in French universities, of those who call themselves sociologists toward those who call themselves economists."

Perhaps there is more to be said. As we shall see below, this attitude has been transmitted from sociology to the other social sciences, above all to the historiography of the *Annales* school, which in the 20th century has long held a prominent place in proposing to 'do history'—economic history included—independently of theoretical economics. In addition, the exceptional continuity of this type of criticism within French culture in a certain sense makes it possible to take it as a significant example of a larger movement that includes important intellectual branches, such as the German historical school, American institutionalism, various schools of political thought, and so on.

Political economy—this, then, is Comte's thesis—is by nature "purely metaphysical." Destutt de Tracy, with his characteristic philosophical candor, spontaneously confesses to a similar construct by situating his treatise on economics between logic and morality, as the fourth part of his general treatise on ideology. When current works do not present themselves as the gradual refinement of previous works but take on a personal character, so that the most fundamental concepts are continually called into question; when the dogmatic constitution of the discipline results in a sterile reproduction of illusory controversies that never take a step forward, one can be sure that this is by no means a positivist discipline. This, in the eyes of Comte, is precisely the case with political economy. Considering "impartially" the sterile disputes existing in the discipline on the most basic notions of value, utility, production and so on, he has the impression that he is witnessing "the most absurd debates of the scholastics of the Middle Ages on the fundamental attributes of their pure metaphysical entities." (Comte, 1830–42; 1967, p. 183).

This would have been seen by economists as complete incomprehension of the state of the discipline, especially those with a thorough knowledge of classical economics which—thanks to Ricardo and his followers—was then coming into its maturity. Viewing things from this point of view, an undeniable 'rejection effect' arises spontaneously in reaction to Comte's accusing the debate during the first decade of the 19th century of deeply distorting the indications of common sense, converting them into notions so radically confused as to force wise people who prize exactitude to "employ painful circumlocutions"...

What thus emerges from Comte's work is a rift within the social sciences that even today remains unresolved. Economics, in the view of many sociologists, historians and political scientists, is a discipline that is abstract, conceptual, speculative, absolutist, metaphysical—a discipline that is not based on the systematic observation of the facts of this world.

In addition, according to Comte, the economists' confession regarding the necessary isolation of their discipline constitutes an involuntary recognition of this state of affairs. "In fact, due to the nature of the subject [...] the various general aspects are of necessity mutually supportive and rationally inseparable, to the extent that they can only be properly clarified in relation to each other." (Comte 1830–42; 1967, p. 190). An economic analysis of society cannot be positively accomplished by excising the intellectual, moral and political analysis of the past and present.[13]

Economics, he concludes, was a "last essential part" of the critical philosophical system. It performed a revolutionary task through criticism of the old social regime. But precisely for this reason it is not suited to the creation of a new order. Liberal economics claims, for example, to set up as dogma the absence of any regulatory intervention. Faced with a serious eventuality—such as unemployment produced by the introduction of machines—it seems to forget that human life does not go on indefinitely.

The Passions and the Interests

And so we come to the point. Apart from the extension of the economic paradigm to politics (which has only recently occurred in any systematic way), it can be said that Saint-Simon's and Comte's theses represent two poles of thought around which the problem of the relationship between economics and politics has long been debated. Placing economics at the center of politics (and of sociology and history) in the end produces a critical reaction against abstractness, partiality, impotence—that is, a challenge to the veracity and

13 Say, whom Comte knew well but who is not even mentioned here, is evidently not spared from this tirade. Adam Smith, on the other hand, would be to a large extent spared. This "wise and illustrious philosopher," Comte maintains (1839; 1967 pp. 187–8), did not 'in any way' claim to be founding a new distinct science. He had set out only to clarify several essential points of social philosophy (on the division of labor, money, banking, etc.). Although he was inevitably linked to metaphysical philosophy, he tended to distance himself from such a speculative method. In essence, neither of the two objections to economics is properly applicable to Adam Smith's work. It is a thesis separating Smith and political economy that overturns Saint-Simon's viewpoint and is, in a way, emblematic (see below).

relevance of the analysis. By contrast, basing politics and other social sciences on autonomous assumptions completely independent of economics leads economists to think that there is a fatal misunderstanding of the analytical contribution that this discipline is capable of making. Theoretical analysis would come at the cost of a loss of contact with reality and realism at the cost of descriptivism.

How to get out of this awkward bind? One approach is to re-examine the ideas of Saint-Simon and Comte from this standpoint as unsatisfactory solutions to a real problem. It might be argued that if economics cannot be the basis of politics but, on the other hand, it cannot be completely separated, then economics must inevitably contain some aspects that are necessary to politics, but are not exclusive and fundamental. Such a relationship will not be able to leave things as they are—it will have to get to the bottom of both economics and politics.

On closer inspection, it is this latter aspect that is notably lacking in the reasoning of Saint-Simon and Comte. Unable, in either case, to delve into economic reasoning, they are led to solve the problem of the relationship between economics and politics from the outside,'*en gros*,' following an acceptance-repulsion model.

Now, if we look at how such a 'transformation' could have occurred, we find ourselves facing the origin of the fracture—call it the total lack of understanding—between the disciplines. Our thoughts naturally turn to Ricardo's *Principles* and the ensuing discussion. It is likely the first chapter "On Value" which is at once, emblematically, a *locus classicus* of the thinking of many economists (such as Marx, such as Sraffa: cf. Meldolesi 1967, 1982 Appendix) and the bête noire of many social scientists.[14] What seemed to many economists to be a decisive step in the formation of their discipline (through the

14 In recent decades this attitude has perhaps been diluted by the influence of Marxist thinking. This does not detract, however, from the fact that the traditional view in French sociology and historiography clearly distinguishes between the Physiocrats and Smith on the one hand and Ricardo and the later economists on the other, thus putting the onus (rather than the honor) on Ricardo for the change that took place. Furthermore, once the scientific validity of economics had been denied, this tradition solved the early economists' problem through the sociology of ideas. (Cf., for example, Simiand 1930, vol. III, lesson 40; and 1934). For Bernard—author of a text on economic doctrines that Fernand Braudel was kind enough to pass on to me—it is a matter of "*grasping the meaning of these doctrines as an expression of the political, economic and social reality of their time and their significance as an expression of human aspirations and moral values*," (Bernard 1963 p. 7) (Cf. Meldolesi 1990).

kind of abstract reasoning that "calls to science: Halt!"[15]) was instead for just as many social scientists the irrefutable demonstration that economics was extraneous to their problems.

Without doubt, encountering a contradiction like this leads to bafflement (if not shock!). But fortunately, one further thought can save us. It is well known that, as Ricardo writes in the 'Preface' (Ricardo, 1821; 1976, p. 4), his *Principles* linger particularly on the passages from Smith that he has reason to disagree with, while for the rest he shares "the admiration that the profound work of this illustrious author so justly inspires." This begs the question: do the characteristics of political economy, so 'indigestible' to many social scientists, actually originate with Ricardo or have they been part of the discipline as a whole since its inception?

This in turn leads to a particular aspect of the question as a whole. There is a traditional consensus among economists that attributes to Adam Smith the title of founder of the discipline. *The Wealth of Nations* is generally considered the first systematic account of economics (so much so that for some it remains the best).

This does not mean, however, that the problem has actually been solved. Schumpeter for example (1954, p. 9) wrote that "as regards economics, bias or ignorance alone can explain such statements as that A. Smith, or F. Quesnay, or Sir William Petty, or anyone else 'founded' that science." Sraffa, in contrast, drew Gramsci's attention "to a possible approximation of Machiavelli to an English economist of the 1600s, William Petty, whom Marx calls the founder of classical economics," (Gramsci 1953 p. 211).

Apparently, the different solutions are linked to different assessments of the current state of the discipline and lead to divergent accommodations regarding the history of thought and its relation to the evolution of the West. The development of political economy thus presents itself as the result of a long gradual process which, according to Schumpeter, began in ancient Greece (and much earlier, according to Keynes – 1930; 1979, vol. I, pp. 22–5), or as a phenomenon that developed in parallel with the Renaissance creation of capitalism, or as the product of its triumph at the end of the 18th century, and so on.

15 The first two chapters of Ricardo's *Principles*, Marx continues (1905–10; 1955 p. 13 and 17), "contain his whole critique of previous political economy [...] and achieve some altogether new and surprising results. Hence the high theoretical pleasure derived from these two first chapters [...] because of their originality, unity of basic conception, simplicity, concentration, depth, novelty and comprehensive conciseness."

Even taking this into account, I still think there are some good reasons to distinguish between the (ancient and Renaissance) discipline's formation process and its actual establishment, and to attribute to Adam Smith the title of progenitor of political economy.

Such reasons stem from the work of two authors, Louis Dumont and Albert Hirschman who, in contrast with what is generally the case for histories of economic thought, discussed the genesis of the discipline from within the development of ideas in the Western world. Their contribution, while born of present-day concerns, emerged from reflections on the thinking of the past[16] and came to identify the emergence of economics as a *separation from the political science* produced by *The Wealth of Nations* (Rosen, 1978).

In 1964 the French anthropologist Louis Dumont, scholar of traditional India, initiated a long comparative study of the modern system of ideas and values aimed at identifying the phases in the genesis of Western individualism (Dumont 1966, 1977, 1983). He analyzed the transition from the "individual-out-of-the-world to the individual-in-the-world" that took place in religious thought and "concepts of politics and the state beginning in the 13th century," maintaining that "Machiavelli's politics was perhaps the first practical science to emancipate itself from the holistic network of human goals," (Dumont 1983 p. 79).

He also examined the genesis of economic ideology through "a series of surveys or rather of partial or intersecting slices" (Dumont 1977, 1984 p. 12) showing that, just as religion had generated 'the political,' so the latter had given birth to 'the economic,' and that Adam Smith's book, *The Wealth of Nations*, effectively represented the birth of this new 'category.' It is therefore a genesis by offshoot (from political science) that occurred at the end of the 18th century.

At the same time, following a completely independent intellectual path, Albert Hirschman (1977) came to convergent conclusions in *The Passions and the Interests*. Long committed to development issues, he decided to devote himself to the history of ideas in the wake of a series of political disasters in underdeveloped countries following the 1964 coup d'état in Brazil. In the hope of indirectly solving some of the major puzzles in the relationship between economics and politics, he went back to a time when scholars "could range freely and speculate without inhibitions about the likely consequences

16 Paraphrasing Marx (1939–41; 1968 p. 33) one might say that in this case it was more useful to study the anatomy of a monkey than of (economic) man.

of, say, commercial expansion for peace, or of industrial growth for liberty." (Hirschman 1981 pp. V-VI; and 1977 p. 3).

To this end, the Euro-American economist ventured into the great edifice of political and social thought of the 17th and 18th centuries and emerged with a more comprehensive result than expected—a sequence of interconnected ideas about how interests were used to cope with passions, with a "vision" based Montesquieu and Steuart's view that economic expansion would improve the political order, and with certain observations on this episode in intellectual history.[17]

For our purposes it is enough to realize that this line of thought that grew up at the center of the political scene goes all the way back to Machiavelli, effectively asserts itself in the 17th century through 'the principle of passion as counterweight,' and culminates in the mid-18th century in the conception of 'doux commerce.' It testifies to the existence of the centuries-old issue of the opposition between different passions, and then between interests and destructive passions, that later fell into disuse—precisely in the era of the creation of political economy.

The Smith Problem

The question is therefore how this change came about. Hirschman argues in this regard that "Adam Smith abandoned the distinction between the interests and the passions in making his case for the unfettered pursuit of private gain; he chose to stress the economic benefits that this pursuit would bring rather than the political dangers and disasters that it would avert" in resisting destructive passions (Hirschman 1977, p. 68).

17 Included in these reflections is a new interpretation of the 'spirit' of capitalism and its controversial origin. I tried personally to explore this last point by comparing it with a key chapter of Fernand Braudel's *Civilization and Capitalism, 15th–18th Century* (1979, vol. II, ch. V). I realized that the long sequence of thought that unfolded 'in the court of the prince' that Hirschman brought to light can also be extended and can find solid parallels in other aspects of reality—in different areas of the spirit (or spirits) of capitalism, as well as in economic and social history (Meldolesi, 1985, 1991–92).

The reader of *The Wealth of Nations* would have no great difficulty accepting this argument.[18] But it should be noted that this volume was to be part of a larger work, consisting of four texts—on natural theology, ethics, jurisprudence and political economy—corresponding to the parts of Smith's course in moral philosophy at the University of Glasgow following in the footsteps of his teacher Hutcheson. It is well known, however, that the course produced only two major works, *The Theory of Moral Sentiments* (Smith 1759) and *The Wealth of Nations* (Smith 1776).[19] Whereas in the latter, Smith predominantly bases his analysis on the pursuit of individual self-interest, in the former he examines in detail a range of moral sentiments.

It cannot be said that this double contribution appealed to economists, who were very likely gratified by the achievements of *The Wealth of Nations*. It is true however that "Das Adam Smith Problem"—to recall the title of Oncken's (1898) well-known essay—gave rise to a long discussion. Many authors saw a contradiction between the Smithian formulation that "it is not from the benevolence of the butcher, the brewer, or the baker that we expect our dinner, but from their regard to their own self-interest" and the theses contained in *The Theory of Moral Sentiments*. And yet it is undeniable that in Smith's time great importance was given to this "essay on the analysis of the principles by which men naturally judge conduct and character, first of their neighbour and then of themselves."[20]

---

18 This seems to me to be true despite the occasional presence in the text of the opposition between calculating interests and impulsive passions, and despite the opposition between interests and pride in topics such as colonialism, ancestry, slavery (Holmes 1988). The overriding pursuit of material interests is behind the Saint-Simon and Say affair I recounted earlier, as well as the modern claim of 'public choice' encroaching on politics (Stigler 1975). In the first case, since politics is in traditional hands, a normative indication is drawn from the intellectual revolution of *The Wealth of Nations*; in the second, the intention is to go beyond Smith's text and deduce an interpretative hypothesis (which in some central aspects, however, does not seem to stand up to the scrutiny of criticism—Hirschman 1982, Meldolesi 1987b).

19 These would have been the second and fourth parts of the original program. A copy also exists of a manuscript of notes taken in the classroom by a student (perhaps in 1763) concerning part three, published by Cannan in 1896. As for the first, see Morrow's comments (1928 p. 170).

20 This is in fact the subtitle of *The Theory*. It is well known that a popular argument of the last century held that Smith's great works represent two different stages in the development of his thought—the first a stage of altruism and the second of selfish materialism.

There is, however, a second interpretive tradition—constructed in the 1920s by Glenn Morrow (1923, 1928) and later taken up by Macfie (1967), Raphael and Macfie (1976) and in Italy by Vittorio Dini (1974)—according to which Smith's overall oeuvre has to be positioned within the intellectual horizon of his time in comparison with the English moralists. Rather than immediately addressing the relationship between the two main works, as if to presuppose a necessary separation between ethics and economics, it is proposed here first to focus on *The Theory of Moral Sentiments* and then move on to a comparison with *The Wealth of Nations*.

What thus emerges—already in Morrow's work, in fact—is an appropriate reading of *The Theory*. The basis of this theory of moral judgment is 'sympathy,' i.e. the ability to connect to the situation experienced by others and feel emotions similar to their own. By means of this participation the subject enters into contact with the feelings of others and can thus judge such feelings with respect to both their motives (the cause that arouses them) and the effects they produce. The subject positively values related actions out of sympathy for the feelings behind them, judging them appropriate, useful or fair – because they are in part shared and under similar circumstances would be similarly felt.

Utility, Smith argues in his dispute with Hume, is therefore not the source of ethical judgment. Utility concerns the individual relationship between persons and objects, while the nature of morality is social. The virtues that inspire love (the kind, loving virtues of sincere courtesy and forgiving generosity) are based on the subject's effort to empathize, and the virtues that inspire respect (the austere, majestic virtues of self-mastery required for dignity, honor and decorum) are based on the judged person's effort to bring his or her emotions into line with those of the spectator. Various types of passions can conform to the 'propriety' or convenience

This change is attributed to Smith's encounter with French intellectuals in the years 1764–66. But the publication of the manuscript of his lessons (cit. in note 19) undermined this interpretation (and reduced Smith's intellectual debt to the Physiocrats: Cannan 1896). It should also be noted that Smith edited no less than six editions of *The Theory of Moral Sentiments*, two of which came after the publication of *The Wealth of Nations*. A comparison of the first and last of these—Macfie (1967 p. 82)—leads to the conclusion that the alterations and new additions were considerable but that "there occurred no fundamental change in his beliefs on ethical and social (including economic) theory."

of feelings, such as the passions of the body and imagination, asocial passions (hatred and anger), social passions (characterized by sociability and benevolence), and selfish passions (pain and joy connected to individual circumstances).

Now, this construction in the first part of *The Theory of Moral Sentiments* (and the following parts, concerning the judgment of the merit of human actions, the "foundations of our judgments concerning our own sentiments" etc.) has to be read with reference to the "systems of moral philosophy" of the time—a topic that, significantly, occupies the last part of the volume. Here, Smith takes a position with respect both to the tradition of Shaftesbury and later Hutcheson, and to the work of Mandeville, and positions his own construction somewhere between the one and the other. His theory of moral judgment based on "sympathy" and the "propriety" of sentiments allows him to distance himself from the idea of a "moral sense" and from "systems that make virtue consist of benevolence" without thereby subscribing to "licentious systems" such as Mandeville's that do not take into account the possible impropriety and demerit of selfish impulses. It also allows him to emphasize the mercantile virtue of prudence—and with it safety, caution, skill, commitment, frugality, and thrift—while recognizing the existence of superior virtues such as justice and benevolence.

This line of interpretation thus leads the reader into *The Theory of Moral Sentiments*, situates the text within Smith's intellectual horizon, and advances the thesis that this problematic should in turn be seen as the starting point of *The Wealth of Nations*—a 'prudent' person would also be a person drawn to economic activity by their own self-interest and the 'natural inclination to exchange and barter.' Nevertheless, having reached this point, one cannot help but question whether, on an analytical level, the 'Smith problem' has actually been solved.

With this question in mind let us return to Hirschman's contribution.[21] As mentioned above, this author reconstructed an expanded intellectual horizon which allows Smith's work to be approached from a point of view that is

21 *The Passions and the Interests* received a (generally favourable) reception from a very wide range of social science journals. For political economy, Nathan Rosenberg (1978) observed that "one of the many strengths of this highly provocative essay is that, through its examination of intellectual developments in the pre-Smithian world, we are led to see the *Wealth of Nations* itself (and to understand its triumph) in a very different light. In bringing intellectual skeletons out of the closet, Hirschman has performed a fascinating task given that Adam Smith's victory was so decisive that we have almost erased from our collective memory any real perception of the rather tortuous path we have traveled."

unusual today. The position based on the counterbalance between passions and interests is lost, and along with it the eclipse of Montesquieu's and Steuart's conception of 'doux commerce,' according to which commercial expansion was believed to curb the passions of sovereigns. This brings into focus two important aspects of our question.

In the first place *The Wealth of Nations* addresses "the great mass of humanity." According to long tradition, only the aristocracy were capable of experiencing superior passions (positive and negative), while the common mortal was a much simpler creature. This would mean that the spectrum of sentiments in a work dealing with ordinary people could be much narrower than in *The Theory of Moral Sentiments* (e.g. it could be about the virtue of prudence more than that of justice and benevolence[22]).

Hirschman also calls attention to an important page of "The Origin of Ambition and the Distinction of Ranks," a chapter in the first part of *The Theory*.[23] We seek wealth and flee poverty, Smith argues, in reference to human feelings. The goal to which all the labor and toil of this world is directed—the goal of avarice, ambition, power and the pursuit of wealth—is not the satisfaction of natural needs, which could be secured by the most modest wages. "From whence, then, arises that emulation which runs through all the different ranks of men, and what are the advantages which we propose by that great purpose of human life which we call bettering our condition? To be observed, to be attended to, to be taken notice of with sympathy, complacency, and approbation, are all the advantages which we can propose to derive from it. It is the vanity, not the ease, or the pleasure, which interests us" (Smith, 1759; 1974, p. 74). So it is that in all social classes, the various vanities are driven by the improvement of material conditions.[24] If it is true, Hirschman comments, that

22 It is not by chance that Morrow (1923 pp. 49–50) argues that the lower virtues can be treated with scientific exactitude, whereas the higher ones can only be determined less precisely.

23 Cf. also the first chapter of Part IV. "The pleasures of wealth and greatness," Smith writes (1759; 1974 pp. 124–5), "when considered in this complex view, strike the imagination as something grand and beautiful and noble, of which the attainment is well worth all the toil and anxiety which we are so apt to bestow upon it. And it is well that nature imposes upon us in this manner. It is this deception which arouses and keeps in continual motion the industry of mankind." Other convergent passages are cited in Rosenberg (1968).

24 With respect to people's 'changing involvements,' Smith refers here to an era of deep 'aversion' to the condition of the lowly laborer and of admiration of wealth (and thus of the shame of the poor and satisfaction of the rich)—it is this era that is 'immortalized' by political economy's pursuit of material interests.

individual interest—the drive to increase personal wealth—becomes simply a vehicle of the desire to be appreciated, it is also true that the urges of the various vanities fall into the category of economic motivation and lose their autonomous existence.

What we therefore have—according to this thesis—is a twofold path of *reductio ad unum*. It is through this means that certain modest passions of the great mass of humanity are satisfied by the improvement of each person's material conditions. The process becomes, in Smith's words, "a natural endeavor" on which to base economic analysis—within wide margins of latitude, economic improvement can stand on its own two feet, without interacting with developments in the political and moral spheres.

A not insignificant consequence of the analysis in *The Theory of Moral Sentiments* is to create the premises for the construction of *The Wealth of Nations*. It stands to reason, Hirschman observes, that after analyzing a vast arc of human sentiments and passions and coming to the conclusion that for the common man an important part of them is resolved in the pursuit of self-interest, Smith should then devote himself to an in-depth study of the conditions for the improvement of material conditions, the wealth of nations.

Hence the tradition of the opposition and counterbalance between interests and passions is lost—this line of thought suddenly becomes incomprehensible, if not nonsensical. From here, finally, political economy is born. The delimitation of its field of inquiry was what permitted the specialization and professionalization of the discipline. We have finally managed to grasp the nub of a truly knotty problem, but perhaps it should be added that economists have taken the reasoning beyond Smith's own intentions.

In fact, precisely because Smith stands at the origin of the discipline of economics, his work springs from a confrontation with an earlier world of thought, which he separates himself from. This undoubtedly contributes to the work's charm and elusiveness. As Saint-Simon had observed, there is no explicit split in Smith between economics and politics, just as there is (clearly) no explicit split between economics and morals. In both cases we can speak, if at all, of a separation 'in the making.'

The economic analysis of *The Wealth of Nations* plays out, as is well known, through lengthy political and historical passages. And as far as morality, it must be said that "the Smith problem" holds in store another surprise. Once the genetic relationship between *The Theory of Moral Sentiments* and *The Wealth of Nations* has been (as far as possible) explored, we cannot help but look at the other side of the coin. If utility is not an end in itself and the pursuit of material interest is motivated by the satisfaction of a series of vanities, then these and thus the acquisitive impulse itself should be subjected to the moral judgment of the subject—that spectator that the Smith of the theory of sentiments claims to be impartial and armed with general rules of morality that are "justly held to be divine laws."[25]

This is an (inverted) expression of the traditional opposition between passions and interests. In developing the idea of interests as the *reductio ad unum* of a multiplicity of passions in *The Wealth of Nations*, Adam Smith, rather than himself producing the ultimate collapse of passions into interests, showed the way by which such a collapse could occur.

In this regard it is worth noting that some reviewers of *The Passions and the Interests* were perplexed by the Hirschmanian hypothesis of this collapse. Ronald Meek, for example, pointed to part VI of *The Theory of Moral Sentiments* (written long after *The Wealth of Nations*) in which passions reappear with no possibility of error in their original un-collapsed form and where a highly significant emphasis is placed on how they can be counterbalanced or curbed by 'prudence'—the characteristic *par excellence*, according to Smith, of a person pursuing their own economic advantage or interest. Thomas Kaiser, on the other hand, cited Smith's assertion that "passions are restrained [...] by prudential considerations of the bad consequences which might follow from their indulgence" (*The Theory of Moral Sentiments*, VI, concl., 3); cf. also, in this respect, the opposing views of Lewis Coser (1978) and Andrew Skinner (1979).

Now, these observations do not seem at all in conflict with our line of reasoning—with the idea, that is, that *The Wealth* is the offspring of some of the "collapse" arguments in *The Theory* and at the same time must be brought back into the intellectual context of the parent work. In any case—whether one considers Adam Smith to be the last of the great moralists of the 18th century or the first scientific economist (or, more appropriately, a mixture of the

25 This is particularly evident in the controversy with Mandeville. Vanity in the negative sense, Smith explains, should only be understood as the desire for praise for qualities and behavior that are not worthy of praise (or insufficiently so); conversely, the desire that corresponds to the exercise of genuine virtues is morally right and socially useful. A part of Mandeville's defect is thus transformed into virtue: the property of the sentiment depends on the degree of desire relative to the actual behavior. In this way, moral judgment—along with justice—should temper and regulate human vanities and thus also the acquisitive striving that underpins them. The natural impulse to improve material conditions in *The Wealth of Nations* finds a counterpart in the virtue of prudence (thrift, industriousness, etc.) in *The Theory of Moral Sentiments*, and through the action of a myriad of independent agents gives rise to the 'Invisible Hand'—a notion significantly present in both works.

two)—the crux of the problem highlighted by Hirschman remains decisive. This is the demonstration (arising from both the reconstruction of a long intellectual journey and the in-depth examination of an episode in the history of ideas) that at the origin of scientific economics lies a distinct break in the thinking of the social sciences.

To Conclude

So this—as far as I can understand—is what the situation looks like. With the overwhelming success of *The Wealth of Nations* and the decline of *The Theory of Moral Sentiments* in the collective consciousness, the link between economics and morality that connects the two works quietly fell into abeyance. Out of the door opened by Smith, platoons of economists burst onto the scene, increasingly explicit advocates of an isolated discipline, independent of politics, morality and the other human sciences—a discipline which in fact offered itself as an example for these other disciplines' scientific reformulation. Following an initial period of interest in the intellectual achievements of the new science, this produced, as early as the 1830s, a reaction and a rift which we continue to experience today. The great cultural progress represented by the birth of economics brought with it a significant narrowing in the field of investigation and thus a serious impoverishment of the concept of human nature on which its analysis has since been based.[26]

26 To get an idea of the issue, it seems useful to keep in mind the list of the most frequent antinomies to self-interest compiled by Stephen Holmes (1988 pp. 15–16) after consulting many 17th and 18th century works (including those of Adam Smith and David Hume): "1) animosity, enmity, and hatred; 2) affection, attachment, and love; 3) the relish of telling people what to do; 4) the relish of being told what to do; 5) excessive pride, megalomania, the passion for superiority, and the desire to eclipse others; 6) self-deprecation, dejection, spiritlessness, and a failure to take an interest in oneself; 7) the love of spewing vilifications on others; 8) extreme touchiness about social slights; 9) primordial inertness or the desire not to work; 10) primordial restlessness or the desire to do something, anything—to be where the action is; 11) the need for consensus; 12) the relish of conflict—it clarifies life—and the spirit of contradiction; 13) the hatred of change; 14) the love of change; 15) the hatred of uncertainty; 16) the love of uncertainty; 17) instinctual imitativeness—monkey see, monkey do; 18) the desire to be different; 19) the obsessive desire to follow rules; 20) the obsessive desire to break rules; 21) identification with the victors; 22) identification with the victims; 23) envy for merited or unmerited success; 24) pity for undeserved misfortune." Clearly, with the advent of scientific economics, the analysis of these passions (and many others) has disappeared.

It is an end point that can lead to discouragement. But if it is true that becoming aware of a problem is the first step in solving it, this could instead initiate an intellectual process capable of pulling together the threads of an ancient way of thinking (using in the analysis the knowledge that has accumulated in the meantime), and thus usher in a new flowering of the interrelationship between economics, politics and morality. Some of Montesquieu's and Steuart's key propositions come to mind, along with the revival of the problem of passions and interests that Hirschman put to work in many directions[27]—almost as if, having rounded a 'cape of good hope' in his work, as Giovanni Satori observed,[28] he needed to appeal to antiquity to proceed further.

27 That is, in analyzing the causes of the authoritarian turn in Latin America in the 1960s and 70s (1979a), in explaining the decline of modern development economics (1981), in constructing an important theory of the rival interpretations of the market economy (1982a), in bringing down to us (from euphemism to tautology) the history of interest (1986a), and finally in offering some basic categories (and a vast background) for a conceptually more complex political economy (1984, 1988a).

28 Personal conversation at Columbia University (March 1988).

APPENDIX
A COLORNIAN DECALOGUE *À RETENIR**

1 – It is an intellectual style, a construction of ideas based on an "essential balance" between past and present, between the humanities (first and foremost philosophy) and the natural sciences (especially physics), a style that should be extended, in my opinion, to the social sciences and, more generally, to every area of life.

2 – Its starting point is a "conventionalist" conception of knowledge based on the five senses and on the forms, categories, and associative and interpretative criteria that we use (in science and conscience, without realizing it), "without which it is not possible for us to attempt or pursue anything."

3 – Specifically, under the pressure of historical circumstances Colorni arrived at his point of view by maneuvering between his initial subject, philosophy (Kant, positivism, idealism, irrationalism) and those that followed—physics, mathematics, geometry, psychology and psychoanalysis.

* Appendix, "Introduction": Eugenio Colorni, *"The Philosophical Illness" and Other Writings*, L. Meldolesi ed., New York, Bordighera Press, 2021.

4 – He argued for abandoning the use of capital letters so as to progressively dethrone the anthropomorphic "idols" of contemporary views of the world (Space, Time, Causality, Number, Reality, Truth, etc.) and gradually achieve new specific cognitive acquisitions. Knowing for Eugenio means taking possession of a certain phenomenon (human, natural, social, etc.)—and knowing how to break it down and reassemble it in such a way as to be able to use it for one's own ends.

5 – Women and men can never get outside themselves, even in the process of cognition. But the refutation of some aspects of their own theory of knowledge allows them to simultaneously acquire new ways of seeing and therefore new types of proficiency. For this reason, it is necessary to relentlessly question past knowledge in the light of the evolutionary processes we experience and of our own observations regarding our surroundings. That is to say—it is essential to learn not only from books, but from experience.

6 – To profitably intercept stimuli from the external world it is useful to deploy our senses in a receptive position, reducing as much as possible our anthropomorphic projection onto the observed phenomenon. Furthermore, it is necessary to actually embrace messages that challenge what we have acquired previously. Indeed, we ourselves need to develop an acute sensitivity that will allow us to glimpse the openings through which this process of new understanding can manifest itself.

7 – The aim, therefore, is to arrive, case by case, at an awareness (short and long term) that places the subject in a relationship that corresponds as closely as possible to "how things actually are." Discoveries, innovations, and individual and collective changes concern every aspect of human life. For each event, positive or negative, the outcome depends on the circumstances, as well as on intuition, imagination, the ability to find an access point, and learning in other fields, along with mobility and the capacity of the person or persons involved to pull things together.

8 – As this transformative process becomes better understood and more conscious, it can become commonplace, routine. But it can also suggest new stimuli both near and far, even very far removed from the usual ones. It can engage and infect other subjects through love (as in "do unto others what others would like"). It can spread, suddenly setting in motion unexpected economic, political, and social processes. It can inject into our societies, all at the same

time, freedom, development, democracy, federalism, fraternity, social justice, peace, respect for the environment, art, beauty etc. It can promote a process of "becoming civilized," a "magnet effect" that attracts the attention of peoples and promotes the evolution of humanity.

9 – Knowledge (with its consequences of discovery, innovation and change) can therefore release a powerful individual and collective force capable of holding back (and gradually taming) the aggressive tendencies that have long bloodied humanity's violent past—up to the appalling nationalist tragedy of the Second World War (and beyond).

10 – On scales both large and small, the art of the possible (possibilism) involves continuous efforts to widen the spectrum of opportunities and choices, along with "optimal imbalance" initiatives (intentional and/or incidental) that can play a cutting-edge role and providentially correct existing negative trends.

BIBLIOGRAPHY

Adelman J. (2013) *Worldly Philosopher. The Odyssey of Albert O. Hirschman*, Princeton, Princeton University Press.

Ahmed A. (2017) "Renegotiate Nafta? Mexico Says Get on With It. Economy Is Hurt By Uncertainty", *The New York Times*, March 26th.

Aron R. (1965) *Main Currents in Sociological Thought*, New York, Basic; Milan, Mondadori, 1972.

Asso P. F. (1988) "Bilateralism, Trade Agreements and Political Economists in the 1930s: Theories and Events Underlying Hirschman's Index", *Political Economy* n. 1.

Asso P. F. and de Cecco M. (1987) "Introduzione," Albert O. Hirschman, *Potenza nazionale*, cit.

Auerbach E. (1946) *Mimesis* mimeo; Bern, Francke, 1956.

Bazard S. A. et al. (1828–29) *Exposition de la doctrine de Saint-Simon*, (First Year); new ed. Bouglé C.-Halevy E. eds. Paris, 1924.

Becattini G. (1975) "Introduzione. Invito a una rilettura di Marshall", Alfred and Mary Marshall, *Economia della produzione*, Milano, Isedi.

Bernard M. (1963) *Introduction à une sociologie des doctrines économiques des Physiocrates à Stuart Mill*, La Haye, Monton.

Bobbio N. (1975) Introduzione a Eugenio Colorni, *Scritti*, cit.

Braudel F. (1969) *Écrits sur l'Histoire*, Paris, Flammarion.

Braudel F. (1977) *Afterthoughts on Material Civilization and Capitalism*, Baltimore, Johns Hopkins University Press.

Braudel F. (1979) *Civilisation Matérielle, Économie et Capitalisme (XV-XVIII Siècle), Les Jeux de l'Échange*, Paris, Collin.

Braudel, F. (1980) *On History*, Chicago, The University of Chicago Press.

Bréhier E. (1932) *Histoire de la philosophie*, Paris, PUF.

Bumbaca M. P. ed. (2004) *Eugenio Colorni 1944–2004. Dalla guerra alla Costituzione europea*, Roma, Municipio III.

Cannan E. (1896) "Introduction" to A. Smith *Lectures on Justice, Police, Revenue, and Arms*, Oxford; reprint New York, A. M. Kelley 1964.

Casanova J. C. (1990) "Éloge du Professeur Albert Hirschman", *Doctorats Honoris Causa*, Paris, Institut d'études politiques.

Cohen B. J. (2008) *International Political Economy. An Intellectual History*, Princeton, Princeton University Press.

Colorni E. (1928) "Roberto Ardigò", *Pietre*, III, 2, 10 February; E. Colorni *Art, Aesthetics* cit. 2022.

Colorni E. (1928a) "L'estetica di Roberto Ardigò e del positivismo italiano nella seconda metà dell'Ottocento", mimeo; E. Colorni *Art, Aesthetics* cit. 2022.

Colorni E. (1932) "Di alcune relazioni fra conoscenza e volontà", *Rivista di filosofia*, xxiii; E. Colorni, *The Leibniz Compromise* cit. ch. 2, 2023.

Colorni E, (1932a) *L'estetica di Benedetto Croce. Studio critico*, Milan, "La Cultura"; E. Colorni *Art, Aesthetics* cit. 2022.

Colorni E. (1935) "Prefazione", "Nota bio-bibliografica" ed "Esposizione antologica del sistema leibniziano", G. W. Leibniz *La Monadologia cit.*; E. Colorni, *The Leibniz Compromise* cit. ch. 4, 2023.

Colorni E. (1937) "La spontaneità è una forma di organizzazione", *Nuovo Avanti!*, June 12th; E. Colorni, *Critical Thinking* cit., I, ch. 2, 2019.

Colorni E. (1937a) "Le verità eterne di Descartes e Leibniz. Schema di un saggio", March, Congrès Descartes, Paris, 2–6 August; E. Colorni, *The Leibniz Compromise* cit. ch. 5, 2023.

Colorni E. (1937b) "La funzione del maestro nella scuola fascista", *Nuovo Avanti!*, July; E. Colorni, *Critical Thinking* cit., I, ch. 3, 2019.

Colorni E. (1938) "Leibniz e il misticismo", *Rivista di filosofia*, xxix; E. Colorni *The Leibniz Compromise* cit. ch. 6, 2023.

Colorni E. (1938a) "Libero arbitrio e grazia nel pensiero di Leibniz", *Rivista di filosofia*, xxxv; E. Colorni *The Leibniz Compromise* cit. ch. 9, 2023.

Colorni E. (1938b) "Programma" mimeo; E. Colorni, "*The Pilosophical Hillness*" cit. ch. 3, 2021a.

Colorni E. (1939) *Lettere*, E. Hirschmann Monteforte ed., vol. III, mimeo.

Colorni E. (1943) "Due lettere ad Altiero Spinelli" (May); E. Colorni *The Discovery of the Possible*, cit. III ch. 3 and 4, 1919.

Colorni E. (1943a) "Conoscenza e volontà in Leibniz", *Rivista di filosofia*, xxxiv; E. Colorni *The Leibniz Compromise* cit. ch. 8, 2023.

Colorni E. (1944) "Prefazione" to *Manifesto di Ventotene*, January 22nd; E. Colorni *Critical Thinking* cit. III ch. 3, 2019a.

Colorni E. (1975) *Scritti*, N. Bobbio ed., Florence, La Nuova Italia.

Colorni E. (1998) *Il coraggio dell'innocenza*, L. Meldolesi ed., Naples, La città del sole.

Colorni E. (2009) *La malattia della metafisica. Scritti filosofici e autobiografici*, G. Cerchiai ed., Turin, Einaudi.

Colorni E. (2019) *Critical Thinking in Action, Excerpts from Political Writings and Correspondence*, I, L. Meldolesi and Nicoletta Stame eds., New York, Bordighera.

Colorni E. (2019a) *The Discovery of the Possible. Excerpts from Political Writings and Correspondence*, II, L. Meldolesi and N. Stame eds., New York, Bordighera.

Colorni E. (2021) *The Final Year: 1943–44. Genesis of a Perspective*, L. Meldolesi ed., New York, Bordighera.

Colorni E. (2021a) *"The Pilosophical Hillness" and Other Writings*, L. Meldolesi ed., New York, Bordighera.

Colorni E. (2022) *Art, Aesthetics, Politics*, L. Meldolesi and M. Quaranta eds., New York, Bordighera.

Colorni E. (2023) *The Leibniz Compromise*, L. Meldolesi ed., New York, Bordighera.

Colorni E. and Spinelli A. (2020) *Dialogues*, L. Meldolesi ed., New York, Bordighera.

Comte A. (1830–42) *Cours de philosophie positive*, 6 vol., Paris; Turin, Utet, 1967.

Comte A. (1870) *Lettres d'Auguste Comte a M. Valat, Professeur de mathématique 1815–44*, Paris, Dunod.

Condliffe J. B. (1940) *The Reconstruction of World Trade, A Survey of International Economic Relations*, New York, Norton.

Coser L. (1971) *Masters of Sociological Thought*, New York, Harcourt.

Coser L. (1978) "A Superb Contribution to the History of Ideas", *Contemporary Sociology* n. 4.

Coser L. A. (1984) *Refugee Scholars in America: Their Impact and Their Experiences*, New Haven, Yale University Press.

de Cecco M. (2004) "Prefazione" to Albert O. Hirschman *Il Franco Poincaré* cit.

de Vergottini M. (1937) "Tavole di fecondità della donna italiana secondo l'età e il numero di figli avuti", *Giornale degli economisti*, February.

Degl'Innocenti M. (2010) "Introduzione" a M. Degl'Innocenti ed. (2010) *Eugenio Colorni* cit.

Degl'Innocenti M. ed. (2010) *Eugenio Colorni dall'antifascismo all'europeismo socialista e federalista* – Manduria-Bari-Roma, Lacaita.

Denis H. (1967) *Histoire de la pensée économique*, Paris, PUF; Milan. Mondadori, 1973.

Diaz Alejandro C. F. et al. (1976) *Politica econòmica en centro y periferia: Ensayos en homenaje a Felipe Pazos*, Mexico City, Fondo de Cultura Econòmica.

Dini V. (1974), Introduzione to A. Smith *Morale dei sentimenti e ricchezza delle nazioni*, Naples, Guida.

Dobb M. (1973) *Theories of value and Distribution since Adam Smith*, Cambridge, Cambridge University Press.

Dumez H. (1985) *L'économiste, la science et le pouvoir: le cas Walras*, Paris, PUF.

Dumont L. (1966) *Homo hierarchicus. Le système des castes et ses implications*, Paris, Gallimard.

Dumont L. (1977) *Homo aequalis. Genèse et épanouissement de l'idéologie économique*, vol. I, Paris, Gallimard; Milan, Adelphi, 1984.

Dumont L. (1983) *Essais sur l'individualisme. Une perspective anthropologique sur l'idéologie moderne*, Paris, Seuil.

Ferraresi F. (1987) "Laudatio", *Laurea Honoris Causa del prof. Albert O. Hirschman*, November 12th; A. O. Hirschman *Tre continenti* cit. 1990a.

Finzi R. (2004) "Postfazione. Uno studioso studente a Trieste: Otto Albert Hirschmann", in A. O. Hirschman *Il franco Poincaré* cit.

Fisher J. (2012) [Intervista], *Corriere della Sera*, May 26th.

Fleck C. (2020) "The Context of Otto Albert's politicization", in L. Meldolesi and N. Stame eds., *A Passion* cit.

Fry V. (1943) *Surrender on Demand*, New York, Random House.

Fry V. (1993) 2nd ed. *Assignment Rescue. An Autobiography*. New York, Scholastic.

Ginzburg A. (1983) "Introduzione" to Albert O. Hirschman, *Ascesa e declino* cit.

Ginzburg A. (2013) "Introduzione". "Crisi del debito o crisi dell'Europa?", *Economia e lavoro*, n. 1.

Gouhier H. (1933–41) *La jeunesse d'Auguste Comte et la formation du positivisme*, 3 vol., Paris, Vrin.

Gouhier H. (1965) *La Vie d'Auguste Comte*, II° ed., Paris, Vrin.

Gramsci A. (1953) *Note sul Machiavelli, sulla politica e sullo stato moderno*, Turin, Einaudi.

Hauser H. (1915) *Les méthodes allemande d'expansion* économique, Paris.

Heckscher E. F. (1935) *Mercantilism*, 2 vols., London, Allen & Unwin.

Heckscher E. F. (1936) "Mercantilism", *Economic History Review*, vol. VII.

Hegel G. W. F. (1807) *Phänomenologie des Geistes*, Hamburg, Heiner 1937; *Phenomenology of Spirit*, Oxford, Oxford University Press, 1976.

Hegel G. W. F. (1821) *Grundlinien der Philosophie des Rechts*, Berlin, Nicholaische Buchandung; Hamburg, Meinez, 1955.

Hirschman A. O. (1937) "La fecondità della donna italiana secondo l'età ed il numero dei figli avuti. Osservazioni critiche", mimeo; A. O. Hirschman *Early Writings*, L. Meldolesi, ed., Bern-New York, Peter Lang, 2025.

Hirschman A. O. (1938) "Note su due recenti tavole di nuzialità della popolazione italiana", *Giornale degli economisti*, January; A. O. Hirschman *Early Writings*, L. Meldolesi, ed., Bern-New York, Peter Lang, 2025.

Hirschman A. O. (1938a) "Les finances et l'économie italiennes. Situation actuelle et perspectives", *Supplément au bulletin quotidien*, 1 June, Paris, Société d'études et d'information économique; A. O. Hirschman *Early Writings*, L. Meldolesi, ed., Bern-New York, Peter Lang, 2025.

Hirschman A. O. (1938b) *Il franco Poincaré e la sua svalutazione*. Tesi di laurea; G. Gilibert ed, Rome, Edizioni di storia e letteratura, 2004; A. O. Hirschman *Early Writings*, L. Meldolesi, ed., Bern-New York, Peter Lang, 2025.

Hirschman A. O. (1938c) "Se e come l'elemento economico sia stato un fattore determinante dell'indipendenza delle Isole Filippine" – Tesina di laurea.

Hirschman A. O. (1938d) "Due metodi per la costruzione di tavole di nuzialità" – Tesina di laurea.

Hirschman A. O. (1938e) "Histoire de la lire de la revalorisation au contrôle des changes" – mimeo; A. O. Hirschman *Early Writings*, L. Meldolesi, ed., Bern-New York, Peter Lang, 2025.

Hirschman A. O. (1939) "Italie", *L'activité économique* n. 15, 16 and 17; A. O. Hirschman *Early Writings*, L. Meldolesi, ed., Bern-New York, Peter Lang, 2025.

Hirschman A. O. (1939a) "Mémoire sur le contrôle des changes en Italie", mimeo; "Conférence permanente des hautes études internationales", Institut International de Coopération Intellectuelle, xiième Session, Société des Nations, Paris, June; A. O. Hirschman *Early Writings*, L. Meldolesi, ed., Bern-New York, Peter Lang, 2025.

Hirschman A. O. (1939b) "Statistical Study of the Trend of Foreign Trade toward Equilibrium and Bilateralism", mimeo; *Political Economy*, 1988, January; A. O. Hirschman *Early Writings*, L. Meldolesi, ed., Bern-New York, Peter Lang, 2025.

Hirschman A. O. (1943) "The Commodity Structure of World Trade", *Quarterly Journal of Economics*, August.

Hirschman A. O. (1943a) "On Measures of Dispersion for a Finite Distribution", *Journal of the American Statistical Association*, September.

Hirschman A. O. (1945) *National Power and the Structure of Foreign Trade*, Berkeley, University of California Press. Reprint 1969. Paperback ed. with a new Introduction 1980.

Hirschman A. O. (1946) "Bilateralism and Proportionalism – Two Aspects of Trade Structure", *Review of Foreign Developments*, December.

Hirschman A. O. (1947) "Exchange Control in Italy" I and II, *Review of Foreign Developments*, March 11th and May 6th; A. O. Hirschman *The Postwar Economic Order*, cit. 2023.

Hirschman A. O. (1947a) "France and Italy: Patterns of Reconstruction", *Federal Reserve Bulletin*, n. 4. A. O. Hirschman *The Postwar Economic Order*, cit. 2023.

Hirschman A. O. (1947b) "Italian Exchange Rate Policy", *Review of Foreign Developments*, 16 December; A. O. Hirschman, *Potenza nazionale*, cit. 1987.

Hirschman A. O. (1948) "Inflation and Deflation in Italy", *American Economic Review*, September; A. O. Hirschman, *Potenza nazionale*, cit. 1987.

Hirschman A. O. (1948a) "Economic and Financial Conditions in Italy", *Review of Foreign Developments*, 14 December; A. O. Hirschman, *Potenza nazionale*, cit. 1987.

Hirschman A. O. (1951) "Industrial Nations and Industrialization of Underdeveloped Countries", *Economia Internazionale*, August.

Hirschman A. O. (1952) "Effect of Industrialization on the Markets of Industrial Countries"; B. F. Hoselitz ed. *The Progress of Underdeveloped Areas*, Chicago, University of Chicago Press.

Hirschman A. O. (1958) *The Strategy of Economic Development*, New Haven, Yale University Press.

Hirschman A. O. (1962) "Critical Comments on Foreign Aid Strategies"; R. E. Asher et al. eds. *Development in the Emerging Countries*, Washington D.C., Brookings.

Hirschman A. O. (1963) *Journeys toward Progress. Studies of Economic Policy-Making in Latin America*, New York, Twentieth Century Fund.

Hirschman A. O. (1964) "the Paternity of an Index", *American Economic Review*, September; A. O. Hirschman *National Power*, cit., 1980.

Hirschman A. O. (1967) *Development Projects Observed*, Washington D.C., Brookings.

Hirschman A. O. (1969) "How to Divest in Latin America, and Why", *Princeton Essays on International Finance*, November.

Hirschman A. O. (1970) *Exit, Voice, and Loyalty: Responses to Decline in Firms, Organizations and States*, Cambridge, Harvard University Press.

Hirschman A. O. (1971) *A Bias for Hope. Essays on Development and Latin America*, New Haven, Yale University Press.

Hirschman A. O. (1976) "On Hegel, Imperialism and Structural Stagnation", *Journal of Development Economics*, March.

Hirschman A. O. (1977) *The Passions and the Interests. Political Arguments for Capitalism before its Triumph*, Princeton, Princeton University Press.

Hirschman A. O. (1978) "Beyond Asymmetry: Critical Notes on Myself as a Young Man and Some Other Old Friends", *International Organization*, Winter.

Hirschman A. O. (1979) "Three Uses of Political Economy in Analyzing European Integration" mimeo; A. O. Hirschman, *Essays in Trespassing* cit. 1981, ch. 12.

Hirschman A. O. (1979a) "The Turn to Authoritarianism in Latin America and the Search for its Economic Determinants", D. Collier ed. *The New Authoritarianism in Latin America*, Princeton, Princeton University Press.

Hirschman A. O. (1980) *National Power and the Structure of Foreign Trade*, Paperback ed. with a new Introduction, Berkeley, University of California Press.

Hirschman A. O. (1981) *Essays in Trespassing: Economics to Politics and Beyond*, Cambridge, Cambridge University Press.

Hirschman A. O. (1982) *Shifting Involvements. Private Interest and Public Action*, Princeton, Princeton University Press.

Hirschman A. O. (1982a) "Rival Interpretation of Market Society: Civilizing, Destructive, or Feeble?", *Journal of Economic Literature*, n. 4.

Hirschman A. O. (1983) *"Ascesa e declino dell'economia dello sviluppo" e altri saggi*, eds. A. Ginzburg, Turin, Rosenberg.

Hirschman A. O. (1984) "Against Parsimony: Three Easy Ways of Complicating Some Categories of Economic Discourse", *Bulletin of the American Academy of Arts and Sciences*.

Hirschman A. O. (1984a) Erinnerungen an das Französische Gymnasium, mimeo.

Hirschman A. O. (1984b) "A Dissenter's Confession: Revisiting *The Strategy of Economic Development*", Meier G. M. and Seers D. eds., *Pioneers* cit.; A. O. Hirschman *Rival Views* cit. ch. 1, 1986.

Hirschman A. O. (1986) *Rival Views of Market Societies and Other Recent Essays*. New York, Viking.

Hirschman A. O. (1986a) "The Concept of Interest; from Euphemism to Tautology", *Rival Views* cit. ch. 2.

Hirschman A. O. (1986b) "On Democracy in Latin America", *New York Review of Books*, April.

Hirschman A. O. (1987) *Potenza nazionale e commercio estero. Gli anni Trenta, l'Italia e la ricostruzione*, P. F. Asso and M. de Cecco eds., Bologna, Il Mulino.

Hirschman A. O. (1987a) ["Io, detective dell'economia fascista"], Discorso di accettazione della Laurea Honoris Causa; A. O. Hirschman *Tre continenti* cit. 1990; A. O. Hirschman *A Propensity*, cit., 1995 ch. 9.

Hirschman A. O. (1987b) *L'economia politica come scienza morale e sociale*, L. Meldolesi ed., Naples, Liguori.

Hirschman A. O. (1988) Berlin Festvortag, mimeo; A. O. Hirschman, *A Propensity* cit. 1995, ch. 7.

Hirschman A. O. (1988a) *Come complicare l'economia*, L. Meldolesi ed., Bologna, Il Mulino.

Hirschman A. O. (1989) "Having Opinions: One of the Elements of Well-Being?", *American Economic Review. Papers and Proceedings*, 2.

Hirschman A. O. (1989a) "Opinionated Opinions and Democracy", *Dissent*, Summer; A. O. Hirschman, *A Propensity* cit. 1995, ch. 4.

Hirschman A. O. (1990) "Albert O. Hirschman", R. Swedberg ed. *Economics and Sociology*, Princeton, Princeton University Press.

Hirschman A. O. (1990a) *Tre continenti. Economia politica e sviluppo della democrazia in Europa, Stati Uniti e America Latina*, L. Meldolesi ed., Turin, Einaudi.

Hirschman A. O. (1991) *The Rhetoric of Reaction. Perversity, Futility, Jeopardy*, Cambridge, Harvard University Press.

Hirschman A. O. (1993) "Introduction" to Fry V. 2nd ed. *Assignment Rescue* cit.

Hirschman A. O. (1993a) "Petit discoure de Nanterre", mimeo.

Hirschman A. O. (1994) *Passaggi di frontiera. I luoghi e le idee di un percorso di vita*, Roma, Donzelli.

Hirschman A. O. (1995) *A Propensity to Self-Subversion*, Cambridge, Harvard University Press.

Hirschman A. O. (1995a) [Interview] *Évènement du jeudi*, May 25th.

Hirschman A. O. (1998) *Crossing Boundaries. Selected Writings*, New York, Zone.

Hirschman A. O. (1998a) "Melding the Public and Private Sphere: Taking Commensality Seriously", in A. O. Hirschman A. O. *Crossing Boundaries* cit. ch. 1.

Hirschman A. O. (1998b) "Places and Ideas in the Course of a Life", in A. O. Hirschman A. O. *Crossing Boundaries* cit. ch. 3.

Hirschman A. O. (2004) *Il franco Poincaré e la sua svalutazione*, G. Gilibert ed, Roma Edizioni di storia e letteratura; A. O. Hirschman *Early Writings*, L. Meldolesi, ed., Bern-New York, Peter Lang, 2025.

Hirschman A. O. (2020) *How Economics Should Be Complicated*, L. Meldolesi ed., Bern-New York, Peter Lang.

Hirschman A. O. (2021) *How Reforms Should Be Passed*, L. Meldolesi ed., Bern-New York, Peter Lang.

Hirschman A. O. (2022) *Three Continents. Political Economy and Development of Democracy in Europe, the United States and Latin America*, L. Meldolesi ed., Bern-New York, Peter Lang.

Hirschman A. O. (2023) *The Postwar Economic Order. National Reconstruction and International Cooperation*, A. Alacevich and P. F. Asso eds., New York, Columbia University Press.

Hirschman A. O. (2025) Early Writings, L. Meldolesi ed., Bern-New York, Peter Lang.

Hirschman A. O. and Bird R. M. (1968) "Foreign Aid: A Critique and a Proposal", *Princeton Essays in International Finance*, July.

Holmes S. (1988) "The Secret History of Self-Interest", mimeo.

Hultman C. W. (2001) Book Review: L. Meldolesi *Discovering the Possible*, *Growth and Change*, n. 3.

Jonescu G. ed. (1976) *The Political Thought of Saint-Simon*, Oxford.

Kant I. (1781) *Kritik der reine Vernunft*, Riga, J.F. Hartknoch; Anaconda 2009.

Kaiser T. (1979) Book Review: A. O. Hirschman *The Passions and the Interests*, *Eighteenth-Century Studies*.

Keynes J. M. (1919) *The Economic Consequences of the Peace*, London, Macmillan.

Keynes J. M. (1923) *A Tract on Monetary Reform*, London, Macmillan; tr. it. by Piero Sraffa, F.lli Treves, 1925.

Keynes J. M. (1930), *A Treatise on Money*, 2 vol. London, Macmillan; Milan, Feltrinelli 1979.

Keynes J. M. (1936) *General Theory of Employment, Interest, and Money*, London, Macmillan; *The Collected Work of John Maynard Keynes* vol. vii, London, Macmillan 1973.

Knibbs G. H. (1917) *A Mathematical Theory of Population*; HardPaper Publisher 2013.

La Malfa G. (2023) "La risposta di Keynes a Mussolini", *Corriere della Sera*, May 23rd.

Lacroix J. (1956) *La sociologie d'Auguste Comte* II° ed., Paris, PUF.

Lévy-Bruhl L. (1900) *La philosophie d'Auguste Comte*, Paris, Alcan.

Leibniz G. W. (1935) *La Monadologia preceduta da una esposizione antologica del sistema leibniziano*; E. Colorni ed., Florence, Sansoni.

Macfie A. L. (1967), *The Individual in Society*, London, Allen & Unwin.

Manuel F. E. (1956) *The New World of Henri Saint-Simon*, Cambridge, Harvard University Press.

Manuel F. E. (1962) *The Prophets of Paris*, Cambridge, Harvard University Press.

Marcenaro G., ed. (1973) *Pietre. Antologia di una rivista (1926–1928)*, Milan, Mursia.

Marshall A. (1890) *Principles of Economics*, London, Macmillan.

Marshall A. (1923) *Money Credit & Commerce*, London, Macmillan.

Marx K. (1867) *Das Kapital, Kritik der politischen Ökonomie*, Libro I, Hamburg, Meissner.

Marx K. (1905–10) *Theorien ilber den Mehrwert*, 3 vol., K. Kautsky ed., Stuttgart, Dietz; Turin, Einaudi, 1955.

Marx K. (1939–41) Grundrisse der Kritik der politischen Ökonomie, Moscow, Institute Marx-Engels-Lenin; Florence, La Nuova Italia, 1968.

Meek R. (1977) "Enlightened Self-Interest", *The Times Higher Education Supplement*, July 29th.

Meier G. M. and Seers D., eds., (1984) *Pioneers in Development*, Oxford, Oxford University Press.

Meldolesi L. (1967), "La derivazione ricardiana di Produzione di merci a mezzo di merci", *Economia internazionale*, n. 4.

Meldolesi L. (1982) *L'utopia realmente esistente. Marx e Saint-Simon*, Rome-Bari, Laterza.

Meldolesi L. (1984) "'Economia critica' e 'storia della lunga durata'. Un'introduzione". *Inchiesta* n. 63–4; English trans. *Review* 9, n. 1, 1985.

Meldolesi L. (1985) "Gli spiriti del capitalismo", *Stato e Mercato*, n. 15.

Meldolesi L. (1987) "Alle origini del possibilismo: Albert Hirschman 1932–52": in Albert O. Hirschman *L'economia politica* cit.

Meldolesi L. (1987a) "Per una nuova ipotesi interpretative della storia del pensiero economico moderno" *Rivista di storia del pensiero economico*, n. 1–2.

Meldolesi L. (1987b) "Su alcuni aspetti poco ortodossi dell'economia della scelta pubblica", XXVIII° Riunione scientifica annuale della Società degli economisti.

Meldolesi L. (1990) "Il futuro ha un cuore antico?", *Economia politica*, n. 2, August.

Meldolesi L. (1991) "Durkheim, Simiand e la riforma dell'economia": in F. Simiand *La moneta realtà sociale* cit.

Meldolesi L. (1991–92) "Gli spiriti del capitalismo", *Modernizzazione e sviluppo*, n. 3 e 1–2.

Meldolesi L. (1992) *Spendere meglio è possibile*, Bologna, Il Mulino.

Meldolesi L. (1993) "Aux origines du possibilisme d'Albert Hirschman", *Revue Française de Science Politique*, June.

Meldolesi L. (1994) *Alla scoperta del possibile. Il mondo sorprendente di Albert O. Hirschman*, Bologna, il Mulino.

Meldolesi L. (1995) *Discovering the Possible. The Surprising World of Albert O. Hirschman*, Notre Dame, University of Notre Dame Press.

Meldolesi L. (1996) "Su Colorni", in A. Forbice ed., *Matteotti Buozzi Colorni*, Milan, Franco Angeli.

Meldolesi L. (1998) "Introduzione. Colorni per tutti", in E. Colorni, *Il coraggio* cit.

Meldolesi L. (2004) [su Colorni], in M. P. Bumbaca. ed. *Eugenio Colorni* cit.

Meldolesi L. (2013) *Imparare ad imparare. Saggi di incontro e di passione all'origine di una possibile metamorfosi*, Soveria Mannelli, Rubbettino.

Meldolesi L. (2015) *Italici e città*, Rome, Ide.

Meldolesi, L. (2019–23) "Introduction" to Eugenio Colorni 2019–2023 cit.

Meldolesi L. (2017) "Infinitely Naïve? An Introductory Note on *National Power and the Structure of Foreign Trade* by Albert Hirschman-1945. *Long is the Journey…* n. 3.

Meldolesi L. (2020) Introduction: Is there a Methodological Break between Hirschman's Pre- and Post-War Work?, *Long is the Journey…* n. 4.

Meldolesi L. (2023) *Late Hirschman. Theoretical Exercises in Self-Subversion*. Bern-New York, Peter Lang.

Meldolesi L. and Stame N. eds. (2017) *For a Better World, First Conference on A. Hirschman's Legacy*, Boston, Oct. 6–7, Rome, IDE.

Meldolesi L. and Stame N. eds. (2018) *A Bias for Hope, Second Conference on A. Hirschman's Legacy*, World Bank, Washington D.C., Oct. 25–6, Rome, IDE.

Meldolesi L. and Stame N. eds. (2020) *A Passion for the Possible. Excerpts from the Third Conference on A. Hirschman's Legacy*, Berlin, Oct 24–5 Rome, IDE.

Mill J. (1820) *Essay on Government*, London.

Morrow G. (1923) *The Ethical and Economic Theories of Adam Smith*, A. M. Kelley, New York.

Morrow G. (1928) "Adam Smith Moralist and Philosopher", in *Adam Smith 1776–1926*, Chicago, University of Chicago Press.

Oncken A. (1898) "Das Adam Smith Problem", *Zeitschrift für Socialwissenschaft*.

Panofsky E. (1924) *Idea: A Concept of Art Theory*, New York, Harper.

Pantaleoni M. (1914) "Introduzione" to G. Preziosi *La Germania* cit.

Pareto V. (1916) *Trattato di sociologia generale*, 2 vol., Florence, Barbera; *A Treatise on General Sociology. The Mind and Society*, Dover, 1963.

Péreire A. (1912), *Autour de Saint-Simon*, Paris, Champion.

Piovene G. (1975) *Le furie*, Milan, Mondadori.

Preziosi G. (1914) *La Germania alla conquista dell'Italia*, Florence.

Raphael D. D. and Macfie A. L. (1976) "Introduction" A. Smith, *The Theory of Moral Sentiments*, Oxford, Clarendon Press.

Ricardo D. (1821) *On the Principles of Political Economy and Taxation*, London; Milan, Isedi, 1976.

Rosen G. (1978) Book Review: L. Dumont *Homo aequalis*, vol. I, in *Economic Development and Cultural Change*, n. 1.

Rosenberg N. (1968) "Adam Smith, Consumer Tastes, and Economic Growth", *Journal of Political Economy*, n. 7.

Rosenberg N. (1978) Book Review: A. O. Hirschman *The Passions and the Interests*, *Economic Development and Cultural Change*, n. 1.

Rousseau J. J. (1755) "Économie politique", *L'Encyclopédie*, vol. V, Paris.

Saint-Simon C. H. (1816–18) *L'industrie, ou Discussions politiques, morales et philosophiques, dans l'intérêt de tous les homes livrés à des travaux utiles et indépendant*, Paris, Cellot; Turin, Utet, 1975.

Samuelson P. (1948) "International Trade and Equalization of Factor Prices", *Economic Journal*, June.
Samuelson P. (1952) "International Equalization. Once Again", *Economic Journal*, June.
Say J. B. (1803) *Traité d'économie politique*, Paris.
Schumpeter J. (1954) *History of Economic Analysis*, 3 vol., London, Psychology Press.
Sereni C. (1993) *Il gioco dei Regni*, Florence, Giunti.
Simiand F. (1930–32) *Cours d'économie politique*, 3 vol., Paris, Domat-Monchiestien.
Simiand F. (1934) "La monnaie réalité sociale", *Annales Sociologiques*, D, 1.
Simiand F. (1991) *La moneta realtà sociale ed altri scritti*, L. Meldolesi ed., Naples, ESI.
Skinner A. S. (1979) Book Review: Hirschman A. O. *The Passions and the Interests*, *Economica*, n. 181.
Skinner A. S. and Wilson T. eds. (1975) *Essays on Adam Smith*, Oxford, Clarendon Press.
Smith A. (1759) *The Theory of Moral Sentiments*; new ed. D.D Raphael and A. L. Macfie eds., Oxford, Clarendon Press, 1976; Naples, Guida, 1974.
Smith A. (1776) *An Inquiry into the Nature and the Causes of the Wealth of Nations*; new ed. E. Cannan ed. 1904, 6th ed. London, Methuen, 1950.
Smith A. (1896) *Lectures on Justice, Police, Revenue and Arms*, E. Cannan ed., Oxford.
Solari L. (2004) "la lezione di Angelo", Bumbaca M. P. ed., *Eugenio Colorni*, cit.
Sraffa P. (1960) *Produzione di merci a mezzo di merci. Premesse a una critica della teoria economica*, Turin, Einaudi; Production *of Commodities by Means of Commodities. Prelude to a critique to economic theory*, Cambridge, Cambridge University Press, 1975.
Stigler G. (1975) "Smith Travels on the Ship of the State", Skinner A. and Wilson T. eds., *Essays on Adam Smith*, Oxford, Clarendon Press.
Tesnière L. (2020) "My Great-grandparents Forged Albert's Identity Card", L. Meldolesi and N. Stame eds. *A passion* cit.
Vianello F. (2013) "La moneta unica europea", *Economia e lavoro*, n. 1.
Viner J. (1935) "Mercantilism", *Economic History Review*, vol. IV.
Viner J. (1937) *Studies in the Theory of International Trade*, New York, Routledge.
Visco V. (2014) "Cosa vuole fare la Germania?", *Il Sole 34 Ore*, November 7th.
Walras L. (1896) Éléments *d'économie politique appliquée, ou Théorie de la production agricole, industrielle et commercial de la richesse*, Lausanne; new ed. Paris, Pichon, 1936.
Walras L. (1898) Éléments *d'économie sociale, ou Théorie de la répartition de la richesse par la propriété et l'impôt*. Lausanne; Reprint, Rome, Bizzarri, 1969.
Whale B. (1932) *International Trade*, The Home University Library of Modern Knowledge, New York, Holt.
Whale B. (1936) "International Trade in the Absence of an International Standard", *Economica*, February.
Whale B. (1937) "The Working of the Pre-War Gold Standard", *Economica*, February.
Whitehead A. N. (1930) *Process and Reality*, New York, Macmillan.

SUBJECT INDEX

INDEX OF NAMES

Albert Hirschman's Legacy

Works and Discussions

Editor
Luca Meldolesi

ISSN: 2576-9723

This series brings together select texts representative of the full range of intellectual output of one of the greatest and most eclectic economists of our time, Albert O. Hirschman. Covering a time span of over forty years, they recall his most prominent books and include many additional themes taken from essays of wide-ranging origin and content.

For additional information about this series or for the submission of manuscripts, please contact:

Luca Meldolesi, Editor
lucameldolesi@gmail.com

To order other books in this series, please contact our Customer Service Department:

peterlang@presswarehouse.com
(within the U.S.)

orders@peterlang.com
(outside the U.S.)

Or browse online by series:

https://www.peterlang.com/series/ahl

www.ingramcontent.com/pod-product-compliance
Ingram Content Group UK Ltd.
Pitfield, Milton Keynes, MK11 3LW, UK
UKHW021827100926
8556IPUK00003B/208

9 783034 356046